ABRACADABRA Rx

Remedies for Life

Malorie Barbaria

If everything is vibrational and I told you that you could change your energy to suit who you are, would you believe me?

In the midst of crazy, what if you understood that everything is just a creation of magnetic dynamics?

What if you did not have to be part of the overall structure of what is irrational and were just connected into your own natural law?

What if you could find magnanimous bliss from living in the moment?

Understand that nothing is normal or the same as it was. Even if things look the same, they don't function in the same way.

It's as if the old storyline was an alias that was standing in front of the real story and we are now tapping into the real story—the magical story!

Contents

Preface

1

The Caduceus

11

The Magic of Awakening

15

Part One—The Prescriptive Dynamics Of Awakening

20

Part Two—What To Do To Awaken

37

Steeped In Magical Possibility

69

A Magical Breakthrough

105

Magical Antidotes

131

Survive & Thrive

151

The Magic Of Integrity

171

Keep Dreaming

203

Align With Magic

223

Part One—Change Your Energy To Magical!

223

Part Two—Be The Magic!

240

Vibrate Higher

261

Our Alchemy

275

Remedies for Life

291

My Acknowledgements

313

Abracadabra Rx Disclaimer

315

Preface

"Imagination is the only weapon in the war against reality." —Lewis Carroll

This book is a survival guide based on literal information that slipped through a crack in the cosmic field right into my consciousness. This wisdom was all I could hold onto during a transition where my entire way of being was altered. At this time, I never felt more lost and had no idea of what to do. This illuminated knowledge came from many lifetimes of being a seeker and from my studies of mysticism, yoga, vibrational medicine and the inherited spark of magic that holds miracles. This book will remind you of whom you are behind the scenes, outside your limited mind, and beyond all your stories. Who you really are is an enlightened being who has been around the block a number of lifetimes and is now understanding that it's time to live this one awake and in your magic. Open this book anywhere to counsel yourself and to inspire your own remedies for life. The information that sparks for you is what you most need to know right now.

I imagine my story began with me arguing with God to please not make me come back here again. Surrounded by relentless spirit guides, I begged not to go, but they insisted. Every time I've come to Earth, I've forgotten my enlightened essence and have spent lifetimes lost in worldly measures. My spirit guides promised they would keep waking me up and not let that happen again. Little did I know that being awake was going to be painful and cause me to empathically feel harsh truths along with an abysmal excruciating unease while running on this obstacle course called life.

As a child, I felt prematurely torn out of my Wonderland when I was sent to school. Maybe this was akin to being torn out of an evolved divine dimension to come to Earth. While other children were learning to read, I was reading energy fields. I could feel the aching heart of the teacher from a loss of sorts and I saw the other children forming groups and beginning to play with power. I worried that the rules to keep us in line would kill my passion, so I went deeper into it. I also knew that at five years old, I was going to have to fend for myself. The first day of first grade, the teacher asked a question, I raised my hand and answered wrongly and she called me "Stupid!" That was it for me, I checked out and decided that I was not going along with their program and that even though my little body would show up daily on the school bus, they would never own my mind. This was also the time I realized I was never going to fit in.

Luckily my team of spirit guides had found me the perfect parents, they were unconsciously self-absorbed upper class New Yorkers who were too busy fitting in to care about what I was doing. My mother dressed me up as her baby doll, showed me off to her friends and then handed back all responsibility to the nanny of the moment. I daydreamed away my childhood, traveled on light beams and danced with dust particles that came through the classroom window. I escaped this reality by making up adventurous stories and was creatively alive in my own world. The school administers thought there was something seriously wrong with me as in the fifties there were not terms like: Attention Deficit or Dyslexia. If there were I am sure I would have been labeled as such. I was sent for IQ tests and was found to be in the 98-percentile intelligence rating of all children my age in the country. I did not end up getting expelled from first grade, I was just ignored, which was perfect.

I then decided that I was leaving school and educating myself as soon as I had any power, though putting up with their demands for the next eight years forced me to spend more time out of my body than in it. By the age of fourteen in 1969, I hung out at the fountain in Central Park, demonstrated against Vietnam, tripped on acid, and went to concerts at the Fillmore East. By fifteen years old I stopped showing up to school. Yes, there were truant officers called, that roamed around New York City looking for me, though they never found me. At this point my mother was spiraling into barbiturate drug addiction and my raging alcoholic father owned a restaurant and was out all night, slept all day, and was abusive whenever we crossed paths. I had gracefully escaped my parents by devouring books and from the age of six years old, I was never without one. At fifteen, I read Arthur Rimbaud's A Season in Hell, Sartre's ideas on existentialism, and Franz Kafka's The Metamorphosis. I became severely depressed, but didn't know it.

Hanging out at a famed downtown bar called Max's Kansas City, most characters I knew seemed as detached from reality as me. I roamed around the Chelsea Hotel, lived in the East Village with friends in a tenement apartment rented by an older girl who came home with piles of cash from God knows where. Dressed in bright velvet outfits with boa feathers, five-inch red glitter platform shoes and scads of make-up, no one knew how old I was. I was sixteen and changed my name to Sterling Silver. I slept all day and went out all night perusing the music world with Warhol types and met a glitter rock band called The New York Dolls and I fell in love. My boyfriend Billy Doll was the twenty-one year old drummer and within a few months he accidently died of an overdose of Quaaludes. I then decided that I was going to kill myself.

Based on the prior story, I had navigated around a psycho self-absorbed mother, paternal sexual abuse, rape, drugs, and now with this loss of love—I was done. I felt abandoned by a God that I thought was a jerk and didn't think it funny that my spirit guides might have thought I needed survival skills. I swallowed enough barbiturates stolen from my mother's medicine cabinet to kill an elephant and wrote a farewell letter, (that I still have) as I lay down on my childhood bed to die. My younger brother found me unconsciousness and saved me. Waking up days later in a children's intensive care unit, furious that I was still here, was an awakening. In my near death experience I traveled through a tunnel of white light, talked to my deceased boyfriend who told me to go back, while I looked at the world from the ethos. I was awakened by probably the same spirits who promised to keep waking me up. Damn them. At this point I planned to leave this world again as soon as possible. Meanwhile, in another argument with God, I realized I had strong negotiating skills. I said I was out of here if there was no equanimity I could count on, while collecting more pills. Six months after my seventeenth birthday, God sent me an angel in physical form to escort me through the rest of my life. Joe was then twenty-one and we've been together for many decades.

I went to Al-Anon meetings to cope with my drug-addicted mother, my abusive father, and started to do the inner-work of untying the knots of pain that poisoned my ability to function. In my early twenties, I became a hair and a makeup artist, who was quite successful and traveled the world on photo shoots. Joe had become a recording engineer to many of the famous rock bands of the Eighties and Nineties and we had a son. As an empath, I could still feel what people were not saying and what was going on behind the facades. My intuition was operative, my mind was scintillating, and my spark was activated. Suddenly my spiritual world rolled in and grabbed me when my son was three and we moved to an Ashram in upstate New York to study meditation and Hinduism.

Sitting at the feet of Gurumayi Chidvilasananda, it was a curious move, as we put everything we owned in storage and walked away from all our worldly professions, while family and friends believed we were in a cult. In the Ashram, Joe recorded all the chanting music, the Brahmin priests and spiritual scholar talks while I had a hair salon. Since there were many celebrities coming to perform, my salon was always busy. I can honestly say that I was not brainwashed or kidnapped by a cult, it was a period of retreat where I learned Sanskrit, explored devotion, and in my case I was seeking to find a God within. I certainly knew there was a devil within because I was doing constant battle with her.

We planned to stay for a summer and stayed for three years. *Tapas*, a Sanskrit word which means to heat, describes the difficulties of self-discipline and meditation. I felt like I was on fire struggling with myself to find peace. As described in the book, *Eat, Pray, Love*, living in an Ashram is not easy; it's actually torturous especially when there's a strict Guru roaming around. One day she sternly told me to: *Be Nice!* I argued and said I was nice. It was not correct protocol in the Ashram to argue with your Guru, but to me arguing is not really arguing, it's about taking things apart to explore every perspective. That *"Be Nice!"* command bothered me for years, as I struggled with the difference between nice and good. I did not get kicked out of the Ashram for arguing, but left soon after with my family.

We moved to Sag Harbor, Long Island, where I had a hair salon in my home and all was well until money became my new God. I went into real estate in the Hamptons and honed my great negotiating skills to propel myself to become the number one reigning sales agent of my company for over a decade. It was at that time that my Ego kidnapped me and changed my name to Satana. I was considered a pit bull in business and would bulldoze my black Range Rover over anyone in my way. Nevertheless I was still connected to my magic and wrote my first Abracadabra book when everyone who met me at the time was astonished at my overnight success and wanted to know my secret. You wouldn't know it from that book but I was now in the phase where power had hijacked me to teach me its dark side. This period was akin to being taken by Pluto to his underworld for ten years and yes my spirit guides did come and save me but the karmic repercussions of pain lasted another ten years. It was a very high and successful time, I was a real estate rock star in the Hamptons and it was also one of the darkest periods of my life in the sense that I had lost myself.

A healer that I worked with at that point told me that I was having an initiation and that she was not sure I would survive. I did survive. I started practicing yoga at Yoga Shanti with Rodney Yee, whom I considered to be the Yoda of Yogis. He would say things in class like: *"Any doorway that leads you to a deeper understanding of who you are is worthwhile."* Or, *"See it, recognize it, period."* And, *"Train yourself to be in awe of the subtle, and you will live in a world of beauty and ease."*

Yoga and meditation was the hand that reached in and brought me back to the light-filled being that I am. Through yoga, I began to understand the confines of my body and the expansion of my mind. My yoga practice held me up when I felt broken and carried me through all my most painful transformations. I arrived to class everyday and I put down my mat, sat there and recognized myself—period.

I then wrote *Abracadabra, A Book of Magical Wisdom*, as a guide to save my life. It did. This phase was the most emotionally violent part of my transformation where the ground was shaking so fiercely that working on that book was all I could hold onto. Writing it gave me the courage to deal with my fear, anxiety, hopelessness and depression. I learned to tune back into my enlightened spark and find my harmony. After finishing that book I no longer got away with anything that did not hold me to the highest level of integrity. I had to constantly do operative self-examination and then walk my talk. On top of that I no longer fit into my old way of life. Still not sure where I was going, the next lesson up was about holding contentment while in searing discomfort. This is akin to having a tea party in Hell. It's not easy, not fun, but ultimately liberating.

The smoke did not clear until I cleared myself. I was pulling remedies out of the ethers to get through, writing them out and then living them as if I had no choice. So this is how the book you are holding came to be. It's a guide to get through the turbulent times by doing the most poignant inner work to clear negative patterns. It teaches you how to jujitsu adverse energy, to connect to the highest frequencies possible and to vibrate upward. This book unearths the fact that in the process of losing and finding ourselves over and over, we discover our magic. The message I kept getting was that on this journey we are our Guru, our teacher, our inner healer and our own advisors, as we are the one we have been waiting for. It's time to step into a *Bodhi* moment of illumination, to receive messages, dream, imagine, and wake-up to find our solutions right alongside our difficulties.

The truth is that we no longer need to rely on the outer world to fix our inner issues or hand us our due. We also no longer need to rely on others for our measure of self worth or for the answers we seek. Everything we ultimately need already exists in our own inner sanctum as we now own the prize and must excavate it. The prize is our original spark that we've arrived with. So no matter what is going on, how hard, dark, and crazy it all becomes out there, on the inside our spark is still flashing and we are solid. So we show up, we recognize the illusions, what's important, and we focus on what's worth it. Once we know that we're worth it, even in our darkest times we hang in there because we are growing through it. There are no mistakes—only lessons. Our spark is our life force, our genius, our good spirit, and our alchemy. This book guides us to remember that the real us is already enlightened, our wondrous spark is active, and we are here to bloom. So use this magical book that instructs us on how to use all the aspects we are confronted with in the highest way—The Abracadabra Way!

The Caduceus

We All Have a Little Snake in Us

The image on the cover of this book is a *Caduceus*. It's a magical symbol that portrays two snakes traveling up a staff with wings to a sphere at the top. In Roman iconography, the caduceus is considered a protection tool that is used as an astrological symbol for Mercury, known as the planet of communication; it's associated with commerce, negotiations, balance, healing and alchemy. The staff going up the center of the caduceus bridges the duality of both sides of the brain, while the wings represent that the mind is most naturally inclined to reach towards Spirit. In many mystical traditions the intertwined serpent rising, exemplifies the *Kundalini* energy, which ascends up. It's elevating force is geared to reach and open the pineal gland, (represented as the sphere on top) in order for us to have perceptions beyond sight. Therefore, this powerful symbol denotes the sacred journey, which bypasses the lower realms and brings us to witness and be part of one-pointed beauty, healing, and divinity. Inevitably, all beings must take this journey in order to evolve into the highest dimensions.

The caduceus transformation begins as the snake sheds their old skin. As the outmoded is shed, the snake becomes very hypersensitive and is impregnated with an upgrade of bliss that pushes them into the new. Additionally being a symbol for fertility and new life, the snake portrays a combination of masculine and feminine energy that bears success. The caduceus is often represented as the emblem for the medical community because it portrays the symmetry of wellness that transforms what's connected to it back into its natural state of wholeness.

The Native American Snake Totem expresses that wisdom exists when one is in the core of one's medicine. The Native Americans also believe that if there is a problem then there's a solution right next to it. In the same sense that a venomous snakebite can kill, in small doses, the venom can be used to antidote poison. As the snake moves across the earth on its belly, following vibrations, which represents following our intuitive feelings, its perception of an obstacle denotes that when something is in the way they move around it. A snake can unlock their jaws to devour their prey whole, which represents taking in wisdom and digesting it slowly to assimilate every bit of its sustenance. Moreover, a snake unlike a caterpillar, does not transform into a totally new being but through sloughing off what it no longer needs, it becomes a new version of itself. In essence, we are doing the same.

The duel snakes on the staff represent the external and internal as a combined energy that completes itself. This relates to how we balance our emotions, our relationships, and our inner connection to Spirit. Duality is about bringing opposing harmonics into kinship by coming into accordance without disagreements. We do this by taking a situation as it exists and like a snake finding sunlight, we find the light in it and use it to step off from, or turn around on. Similarly, the Ouroboros symbol of the snake eating its tail represents creation out of destruction and rebirth that denotes survival and renewal. The Ouroboros exemplifies devouring pain as wisdom and since pain is part of life, the Ouroboros devours life whole. As human beings, we tend to back away from pain, though by going through the transmutations of pain, illness and imbalance, we come into our empowerment and transcend these things.

The Caduceus is the personification of an angelic essence in movement. It represents the fact that we too hold this angelic essence and are traveling with it to reach a heavenly state where all is well. In our reality, the dualities of all things exist in our garden and so we play with them to learn what moves us. Great serpent energy lies dormant at the seat of our spine, which is the staff of our life. This energy is alive, as it waits until we are ready to stop playing with only earthly things, so it can rise up to empower us to embrace our wings.

1) The Magic of Awakening . . .

"Experience is a hard teacher. She gives the test first, the lesson afterward."–Anonymous

What if this reality is a dream and when you die you wake up? Then again, what if you woke up now? Can you fathom this existence as another fall down the rabbit hole and understand that everything we think that's real is a small story in the blink of a bigger story? Blink, we were born. Another blink and moments of importance are forming our identity. Blink, now opposition is taking our identity apart. In-between all these blinks are waves of sadness and segments of love. Enlightenment is the understanding that every blink is a mode of transformation and we are now in the blink where we wake up. What does that mean? It means we realize we are dreaming and as such we don't stop dreaming we just dream more consciously while we are awake.

In this school of life we are starring in our own movie and the assignment is that we have to awaken from being lost in the movie to remember who we are. While in a world gone mad with rampant craziness, we're mostly freaking out and astonished by the goings on. We wonder how we signed up for this trip, is there a hopeful future, and why must we struggle so much? During the times that I feel lost, anxious, distressed, crazy and unsafe, it's just the story I'm evolving through. So when fear follows us down the road whispering innuendos that the worst is coming and we will suffer, that we don't deserve goodness, that everything is hopeless, then these are the lies we must dispel. The truth is that when our dark intonations get really loud, be on alert, for it's a signal that we're really close to the gold and at a turning point.

Awakening is like moving through a Hell zone where we have to put down our faith card to override fear. In the world of opposites and illusions, things will always fall apart before coming back together, it's part of the transformation process. The first survival tip is don't look further than your nose and keep the focus close to the heartland. When my world fell apart it was my passion for doing the things I loved that held me up when I was buckling. At the same time I saw this alteration as the universe demanding I switch channels and take the chance to do what I love because I had literally nothing to lose. If we don't have a passion then the imminent message is to find one. So when things go out of control it's time to remember this is a part of a story that is transforming us and nothing is more important than the script we're writing when we're in the process of falling back together.

In the midst of all our stories, we must bear witness to know what matters, as most of the story doesn't really matter only the underlying essence matters. Consider that when life gets turbulent, things are being rearranged based on our real story and if we meld with this concept, our transformations become magical experiences. In a magical reality, we do not get a memo when overnight everything is altered. One day I went to work and in a blink the real estate industry had turned corporate without warning. Suddenly there were new rules and I was gyrating because rules and I don't mix. Inside I heard the message: *Invest in dreams, as they will carry you beyond this mundane existence you are gyrating in.*

In a blink, we become aware that things are not normal because weird is now the new standard. The way to survive overactive weirdness is to immediately drop all burdens and go where you thrive. In the beginning where we thrive might be on a park bench with a cup of coffee, that's fine. It's right that we have some time to sit and dream because we're getting directions to our promised land. Our arrival calls for us to pass through the tunnel of our incompleteness, face our fears, explore situations with wonder rather than expectations, and trust the bigger picture. When things suddenly turned against me, (I was not imagining this) all I could do was pray. I had worked so hard for all I had acquired and was wondering if I would have to surrender these things. Really all that was going to be surrendered were my expectations and fears in order to be open to receiving what magic the great unknown had to offer. So yes when things get weird, step away and acclimate. Our spirit knows what to do and will advise us.

Awakening puts us smack into uncharted territory where situations present themselves as solid but nothing is really solid including our feelings of imperfection. Under scrutiny everything comes into focus for as we peel our emotions away from old stories, we arrive into the truth of the matter. When I woke up to realize that I had grown out of my reality my fear was shrieking, *"Don't listen to that crap, just fix this problem."* A problem is really an energetic push into a fresher agreement. Our awakenings demand attention and will not take NO for an answer, as they move things around to push us to the edge. So if you feel dislodged and have no idea what's going on: you are having an awakening. Subsequently our symptoms of despair are an actual healing crisis that is relieving us of all that is impaired and will no longer support us. Actually everything that is falling apart is in the process of making space for something new to fall into place.

The process of an awakening is about seeing alternate perspectives and knowing which perspective matters most. The Buddha sat under the *Bodhi* (awakening) tree and received spiritual enlightenment; though consider where he was prior to finding that tree. He was a seeker who was confronted with shocking hardships that were all rude awakenings. These awakenings popped the bubble on his cushioned reality. Still, he recognized the tree of life and thereupon his enlightenment came to the forefront as he surrendered into the unknown. So be the witness, don't let the ways of the world take you down—find your Bodhi tree.

Our awakening is ordained and messages are being sent, so something as straightforward as our car stalling is telling us to stop everything and deal with our issues. No answer is an answer and synchronicity is magic winking at us. I once escaped an entire winter functioning from my bed. I did real estate deals and wrote a book from there. Still, I would go to yoga class, food shopping and the gas station, but my bed was my office. I then traveled to Costa Rica where I woke up one morning in a bed that was shaking off the floor. It was an earthquake with the message that my bed existence in New York was over and do not go back to it. When we receive these kinds of messages, we understand that real language happens in situations and experiences.

During a time when many toxic relationships became blatantly disappointing, I dropped my iPhone loaded with contacts. A crack appeared down the middle of the screen and the lyrics by Leonard Cohen: *"The crack is where the light gets in"* kept playing in my mind. The message was that I needed to be open to new light-filled contacts. In reality many people had either turned out to be not who I thought they were or they changed, so we no longer resonated. Instead of being upset about it, the message to find more light-filled people was liberating and when I went looking for them they appeared. Another time, when I was in question of my next move, three people told me that they were going to follow their hearts, which was a directive to follow mine. Even our actual birth is a dispatch reminding us that we're not from here but have arrived with a gift to offer.

The dynamics of magic are abound; our saving grace is to engage these dynamics above all else. We might be juggling family needs with jobs and obligations to the hilt, but it's really an accomplishment to perform these daily tasks mindfully. Meanwhile enlightenment may happen as the water runs from the faucet onto the dirty dish and suddenly we've awakened into an altered consciousness. The point is to show up exactly where we are, to do what's in front of us, and forget about expectations. Dismiss from our intellect, likes and dislikes and just be completely where we are with a beginner's mind. By participating in the daily grind with full consciousness, our alternative seeing comes into focus and wakes us up to draw enlightenment.

Part One — The Prescriptive Dynamics Of Awakening

Abracadabra Rx: Awaken The Wakeup Call. In the first moments of waking up from a night's sleep if we remember our dream, we take what we need from it and let it go. Waking up in reality is the same; we remember the story, edit out the garbage and then zoom in on the treasures to separate them for safekeeping. Suddenly we see the world in a new way—a magical way. Our wakeup calls may be harsh, shocking and very scary, but on the other side they hold miracles. Upon awakening, the things we thought made sense quickly become nonsensical and we find that we now have to make our own.

I had a boss who was out to get me, he felt threatened by

my enthusiasm because he had none. It made no sense that he was a boss, but he taught me I am my own boss and this happily carried past his negativity. I was not afraid to ignore him and I did. It was not about changing anything on the exterior, it was being in the energy field of the magnanimous dynamic that delivers inner bliss. So we still show up at the job and they still do what they do, but it doesn't capture us. If you are not awake you know it, because you are living a life that you feel owns you. So take a seat, close your eyes, ring the doorbell to your soul and wake yourself up. Our spirit is high-minded and alive, our frequency is scintillating, our energy is active and from here we claim our magic and use it. So program your Wake-Up call to auto and stay fascinated.

Abracadabra Rx: Claim The Magic. In these precarious times we are the saviors at hand. We don't have time to test the waters by dipping our toe in because we are already in the water, so now we swim. Where are we going? We are swimming through realities and the one where we keep calling for the life preserver no longer cuts it. We are here to save ourselves and it's a radical shift to rely on ourselves to live the manifesto that pertains to how we spark our alchemy. My manifesto is: *I am a force to be reckoned with, as I am so immersed in the magic that supports me that I am the magic!* Now it's your turn to write your own manifesto and live it.

I imagined and intentionally finessed a story that I wished to happen around selling a house. It was not about the outcome, being successful, having my desire met or getting the gold. It was about feeling the essence of the magic itself. The first time I sold a multi-million dollar home, I framed the check. Still it was not about the check, it was about the energy and the magic that happened around the deal that I was framing. Real magic isn't about making things happen, but about being part of what is meaningful for us. When we ask for help from the Universe, it doesn't always give us what we want, but delivers what we need. In this process, trust is the activation for magic, especially when we have to look through the rubble for it.

At our turning points, magic likes to play hide and seek because it wants us to engage with it, to find it and believe in it. Magic is always scintillating somewhere even when it's hiding in the future. So instead of chasing the magic, we must claim it by remembering we have it. I was struggling with the fact that my way of being was crumbling. I kept trying to fix it, it wouldn't fix. I then gave up and focused on owning the essence of who I was now. I was the misfit in discomfort being asked to trust the process. Once I stepped outside of needing things to be a certain way, I was open, and my magic came back. The philosopher Friedrich Nietzsche who struggled greatly said: *"The individual has always had to struggle to keep from being overwhelmed by the tribe. If you try it, you will be lonely often, and sometimes frightened. But no price is too high to pay for the privilege of owning yourself."*

Abracadabra Rx: Instill Faith. At this point in our evolution, we can no longer go with what's on the menu and must forage for what feeds our cells, our minds, and our souls. I keep placing my order even when it means in the beginning that I have less than I wish for because at this stage of the game less is more. This might be hard to understand at first, but more of what we cannot thrive on makes us toxic.

Having less can be alarming, but what is actually happening is that we're clearing space for what is more useful to arrive. In a clearing process, it might feel like we are isolated, as if we've arrived to the party to find that everyone else has left. This means we are going to the next level where the only thing we can thrive on is faith and our spark of magic. When we are lit up, we believe we deserve to thrive and we create what we need to thrive on. I often repeat: *"I am thriving through this"* on those chaotic days when all Hell is breaking loose, Am I really thriving? Maybe not at that point, but this is the energetic I am invested in. By instilling this deliberation, within moments I am thriving on this uplifting contemplation.

Faith sparks magic and then delivers its manifestation to us. A sublingual implant of one dose of faith in magic is more potent than the mental distortion that our minds make up when we're not okay. Caught in turbulence, we must take a dose of sincerity that pierces through everything to show us what is holy. So as disappointments and life changes take us apart, at the same time our spark is still scintillating and we need to connect to it. My allegiance is aligned with the possibility that magic is always flourishing somewhere, even when I can't see it. Therefore I expect my harsh experiences will bear fruit because I sincerely believe there is fruit.

Abracadabra Rx: Stimulate A Flexible Mind. Our minds get stuck too often and we have to release them so they can fly out the window and divine other realities, dualities, and where the magic is. When our plans also fly out the window, it's a lesson in surrender and a catalyst for us to see beyond. When we cannot grasp an idea, forgiveness, or optimism, we must still stretch beyond where we are mentally. In a yoga stretch, on the days we go to bend and we can't touch the ground we must surrender our reaction and be where we are. It's our body saying this is as far as I am going for now, so we listen. By having a conversation with say, our calf muscle, we respect that it's tight and needs time. So we relax and suddenly this muscle relaxes and we find we can then go a tad farther. If at first we can't be flexible, we must stay with it and it will give way.

The mind constantly wants to go somewhere else. We want to be older, be younger, be sexier, and be richer, as it's always something. Still by honoring where we are, we yield into our true abundance. When we're stuck, the message is to loosen our concepts, which is a universal alert that wakes us up to show us the bigger picture. Driving down a dirt road in Costa Rica, I was obsessing about things that were not going well back in the states and I was not present. Suddenly I came head on with a massive bull charging down the narrow path. He stopped headlong on in front of my vehicle. I also had to stop since he was bigger than my car and there was nowhere else to go. We made eye contact and I was forced to honor the source of this powerful animal. I then realized that this bull arrived to tell me to let go of the bullshit running through my mind that was stopping me from moving forward. I got the message; the bull snorted and moved on.

We have to give into the fact that it's better to be open then right, better to listen more and speak less, and better to not grab but receive. When a mind-bender happens; it's a signal to stretch and adjust into another shift. So twist things around in your favor, think of rejection as a change of direction, trust that finding pennies means your abundance is coming, and lean into the point of view that's enchanting.

Abracadabra Rx: Animate a Sense of Humor. Humor will carry us across the abyss of crazy thinking and insane behaviors, especially when the seriousness of reality makes no sense. On a day I was feeling bad about myself, a known crazy person in my town cursed me out as I passed. I laughed because this is what I manifested in relation to what I was thinking about myself that morning, so the universe reflected it back. The universe can be a comedian, a terrorist, a lover, a magician and a zombie; it's everything. The writer William James nailed it when he said: "*Common sense and a sense of humor are the same thing, moving at different speeds. A sense of humor is just common sense, dancing.*"

The mean joke of nature is that if we mess with it, it will mess back with us. It's the same with the mind when we go down dark alleys and scream that the rope on the ground is a snake. So we must turn on the lights and laugh at the fact that we thought the monster was real. We can judge others, thinking we know or we can make light of the fact that we only know what we believe and be open to not knowing. I found an email on a site I rarely check from a woman who said that ten years ago I gave her a book that would help her. She said she would be in my town and wanted to return it. I didn't remember the woman, but asked what the book was. It turned out that I had replaced it, so I pulled it out and wasn't surprised to read the perfect solution for an issue I was working on. The universe has a funny way of delivering our goods, especially when we believe we're helping someone but in reality we're actually helping our future self.

In the deli by my apartment, the Iranian fellow bagging my items declared, *"Beautiful!"* on every item he rang up and put in my bag. He was blessing my food and there we were smiling at each other as if we were long lost friends, while in another country we might be enemies. Another time, I was on my way to a meeting in Manhattan and I put a yogurt and a plastic spoon in my bag in case I got hungry. Mind you I never carry food around. My cab driver tells me he has a stomachache so I give him my yogurt. I laugh inside because it's surely not a coincidence that I have his remedy.

I love the saying: *If you want to make God laugh tell him your plans.* We all have plans but when we offer them up to the Universe, a cat might pop out of our hat instead of the requested rabbit. Francis Bacon quoted: *"Imagination was given to man to compensate him for what he is not; a sense of humor to console him for what he is."*

Abracadabra Rx: Focus On The Magical Perspective. The absolute most potent magic exists in an alternate reality. Sometimes we can change our perspective to find the magic and other times, especially in transitions, we need to work on building a new foundation to find it. When times get dark we have to wonder if there can still be goodness in what is rotten? Consider that as an apple falls to the ground and decays that its seeds still grow new apples. During the times when we find ourselves in the trenches of imbalance with flaring anger, we're incensed. Our negative self-talk feels like Uzi bullets that slay us, while perspective is telling us to move around this fire-breathing dragon, as it's only illusion.

When I awakened in the transition of escaping my ego, I had to change the way I did business and come back to my magical self in a more integral way. I felt really bad about myself then and spent time beating myself up and feeling like a loser. In truth the only thing to lose was those feelings. How crazy it is that we must pass through our own lunacy on our way to heaven? It feels like a bad joke that when we're totally out of whack and have to focus on seeing what is best. Our consciousness is pushing us to live with integrity, to be authentic and impact our reality, while our lower mind is having mood swings and tortures us. The aspects that win are the ones we feed so don't feed the monster. We are living in a world of opposites; even our brains have opposite sides of reasoning. Likewise our hearts have a mind of their own, so no wonder we're gyrating, it's because our minds are having a shit-chat while magic is sparking down the road and we're missing it. The magic is real—believe it and so it is.

Abracadabra Rx: Evoke Evolved Consciousness. The Sanskrit word *Yoga* means to yoke together or unite. To balance and to restore harmony we knit opposites together. Consider sending love to an antagonistic person who does not wish us well. It's a crazy concept that we have to slam some love into our animosity. I sweeten it with the fact that I'm doing this for myself until I know better and can just do it for no other reason than it's right. We must keep in mind that we always have the choice to either enhance something or make it worse.

I constantly lose myself. It's as if the real me ran off and left me with a hysterical person who forgot everything good. My emotional counterpart is the bitch from Hell who creates repercussions that I have to clean up. Just by remembering that this happens, awakens me to call myself back from her. She can't be in charge anymore, but is kept around for when a good defense is really necessary and I can control her. At the same time when I recognize that I am in a story that is not my story, I know not to touch anything and keep going. Painful lessons teach us to grasp the perspective that moves with harmony and not the one that keeps us stuck in Hell.

The question I often ask myself is what can I find in the dung pile when I realize I am sitting on top of it. It's obvious not to go to the devil for healing or to listen to opinions that have nothing to do with us. On the high road, we don't follow the dark ramblings of the mind or take leave of our senses when lost in emotions. Common sense compiles and assimilates things into order, while our magic is in what's nonsensical and points out that there's a cherry in the snow. Therefore it makes sense to take what is common higher, so while perusing our options instead of focusing on what's wrong, turn your perception towards what's right. Once we stabilize our thinking, our repetitive stories get off the repeat mode and isn't it funny how there's a moment of what now?

Now we're stepping into a new reality with new challenges and the greatest dare is to reach contentment as a choice. How far outside of our ego, expectations and emotional madness would we go to master equanimity? Consider holding a stance of pure undoubted detachment when we literally have nothing. In this moment we own the fact that we're in the life preserver, we have a soul compass and everything we need for survival is on our radar. We are now in the blink of a new perspective and thinking with our higher mind.

Abracadabra Rx: Embrace Healing. Can we embrace healing when we are in crisis? Withdrawing into a dark night of the soul, I question if this is Ok. I question if I should I force myself back into a world I don't believe in or sit in the dark and cry it out. While I'm a hot mess, all my deities are on healing mode working on me and I notice that my imagination has come online. I'm beginning to see visions, maybe I still can't move but my mind has gone shopping in a new reality. I've been down in the underworld so often that I now know it's just a stopover on a necessary change of life tour, so I start dreaming my way higher.

We must go into a healing mode to process out a bunch of old crap and clear the energy fields so our visions can start sparking again. When it's time to heal, our energy will grab us and throw us across a room to dislodge and wake us up. It doesn't just dissipate after that, but undulates until we vibrate enough new energy to come back. Granted it doesn't feel good when we awaken through torment, which is why our inner healing is the priority. We all go through phases where we step in and out of the ring of life, as we get knocked around and have to go back to our corners to pull our life force back in. After a while we stop fighting and take the time to heal until we are strong enough to step out again. Our cracked open broken heart awakens us to know that love is all that's valid.

Awakening our magic is the conduit into the bigger picture, so we bypass the lowly, honor our beings and nurture them, and we take the time to embrace what is healing. We break open and our healing is the override where beauty, love, and serenity are the modalities that talk to our cells and conduct our heart-felt symphonies. As we pull in these harmonious themes to counteract our pain, we are reaching for the presence of our rhapsody. The fact is that our energy field will just as well thrive on our ability to act as if, because energy grabs energy so it will dance with the partner that shows up. Inevitably our final partner is love.

Abracadabra Rx: Arouse Self-Love. Suddenly our reality cracks apart and there we are standing among the broken pieces crying. Awakening to know that we are being called to create again, we sweep the damaged pieces into the trash and begin to visualize a new reality. In the midst of loss we will have breakdowns before breakthroughs. At these intense turning points anguish takes the form of an elephant in the room, which reminds me of *Ganesh,* the Hindi deity known as the remover of obstacles. Ganesh dances on one foot in total balance to teach us that form and matter are mindsets. In the midst of falling apart too many times, it came to me that the obstacles were instead messengers to change my mindset to meanwhile delve into self-love. I found that once my thinking embraced a higher perspective, the interference and the obstacles become smaller hurdles. Everything shifts as we balance by dancing on one foot while loving ourselves.

In the same way that an elephant can use its trunk to uproot a tree or pick up a needle, we too have the ability to create or destroy. So while scrutinizing for love, we must uproot all that does not come from or is in the way of it. The game is to notice that every time love doesn't exist, we must simply add it back into the mix. Really? Do I have to love what is hideous; the person who cheated me, the fact that someone broke my heart, liars and people I never want to see again? I hear loudly inside that the love I bring up will shine through the ugliness and when I immerse myself in it, it will heal my pain. So I surround these people in a wave of love and send them off. Is it many times make-believe? Hell yes! Though it works in the sense that by my not wishing evil on them I have not followed them to purgatory. What we hold out is what we are surrounded by energetically—so hold Love.

We often lose our self-worth when our lack of self-regard hits the fan. When relationships breakdown, when we have no passion for our work, when our writing stalls, money gets tight, we feel trapped and our health fails; it's a message that it's time for an expedition in pursuit of unconditional love. As we pack our gear, what we mostly need on this pilgrimage is a map quest for an open-heart. Of course we already own the love so the real journey is about finding it. The trick is that we must become the good witch who throws holy water on the wicked versions of ourselves in order to remember how our ruby slippers work.

A fellow whom I confronted over his lack of integrity called me crazy. He was totally right because I speak out when things are wrong. The consequences for this are that offensive people don't want to hang around me. So call me crazy but it's even crazier to lack integrity, which is a lack of love for oneself. Self-love lets go of barren relationships, crappy jobs, dark thoughts, and fears. Sometimes self-love is audacious; it spits out truths when we've set boundaries. Other times people do hideous things and it is way too hard to love a wrongdoer. Instead, as a radical act we must love ourselves on their behalf. It's radical to look past concepts of right or wrong, feel love over hate, and love ourselves through loss and pain. Correspondingly, self-love holds our hand, has our back, and overrides all else.

Abracadabra Rx: Accept Differences. The difference between right and wrong speaks for itself while our reactions are all that are worth pertaining to. How many times have we been completely wrong because we only could see things from a personal viewpoint? Our not being on the same wavelength with others doesn't mean that they're the enemy or wrong. It also doesn't mean that we have to dissect their behavior. It really means that we don't have to do anything other than to come back to peace within ourselves. The writer Umberto Eco said: *"It is sometimes hard to grasp the difference between identifying with one's own roots, understanding people with other roots, and judging what is good or bad."*

My yoga teacher Rodney Yee, once said in class, *"The only opponent is the Smurf within."* Therefore whatever is going on out there is really about how are around it. The question becomes are we affected or are we affecting? So when we turn the handle to open the wrong door, it's best to quietly shut that door and open another. Who are we ever arguing with anyway? The Smurf within loves to argue and needs to win and there is no winning. All we're doing is arguing with ourselves when we validate trying to be right, but our most valuable lessons are in being wrong.

Our failures have much to offer especially when we're waving our worthiness flag. The difference between judging and believing in something is that judging takes things apart and believing puts them back together. I have often gone crazy thinking that I have to find my place, only to realize that it's natural to gyrate when working things out. It's best to let our right place invite us to arrive into it and it does so when we calm down.

I was once addicted to thinking I had control and it wasn't until, as they say in Al-Anon: *Accept the things you cannot change and have the wisdom to know the difference that* things shifted. Instead of being constantly bothered we have to detach and alternately do something more proactive. An example is I can't change people, places and things to fit my format, but I can change my format to fit in with my higher reality. My reality tells me when I am uncomfortable, where to go and stand, sometimes I have to stand alone crying until I can come to terms with acceptance. The wisdom to know the difference is the wing on the shift of my awareness.

Abracadabra Rx: Envelope Worthiness. Every time I falter, I hear inside, *"This is a test, go to the highest state and begin again."* Beginning again is how we claim worthiness when we've lost it. When we don't esteem our worthiness, it will trip the circuit on our power source. So when we are in the boxing ring with ourselves, the knockout punch is to go back to our corner and love ourselves back to life. Our falling apart is actually a huge release where worthiness is right there in the operating room stitching us back together. Bossy and demanding, our worthiness will not stand for us to not stand with it. If we don't stand with it, it will swing us around until we do.

In finding reverence for ourselves we lose and find our way. We stumble, we rage, we cry, and when we're finally spent, we come to terms with ourselves. Our lowly thoughts of not being good enough, too old, too fat, too weak, powerless and hopeless, is the screech of discomfort pushing us beyond these inadequacies. These false feelings are ghosts of the past that come to open wounds so we can bleed them out. Self worth says: *I will not stand with these feelings; I don't believe or support them, so let's heal them.* Meanwhile our spiritual cohorts come forth and roll up their sleeves to help. We must meet our spirit on the path, open our arms to them and let them into our operating rooms to assist us. We are not alone, but surrounded by saintly advisors, angels and our past loved ones—they are all right here supporting us.

Once we come into worthiness with ourselves, we breakout of being bought, cajoled, or ruled. Worthiness has balls that come forth when we get up and leave a lousy restaurant, hang up the phone on rudeness, tell someone it's over, wear red lipstick when we're eighty, and have the courage to not be sorry when we are truly not. Worthiness is our true soul mate that walks us up the aisle to marry us to the best part of ourselves. Our good merit holds us through discomfort and vulnerability because we're our own partners in this dance, and our own lover looking back at us from the mirror. We are the one who picks us up over and over to get us through. Waking-up our worthiness is a matter of us holding our true essence of self for all the richness we're worth.

Abracadabra Rx Rouse The Magic. Our dreams are the breakthrough from this reality to the next. So first we dream, then we follow the dream, and then reality follows us. I constantly tumble around in a whirl of creativity where I bypass exterior social ambitions to delve into places where I'm nourished. Satiated, I no longer manifest from desperation or need to push or pull in order to receive. Instead, I imagine my way around and let my spark tell me what to do. You will know the magic is at work when you begin to feel inspired for no reason other than being alive. The poet, Langston Hughes said: *"Hold fast to dreams, for if dreams die, life is a broken-winged bird that cannot fly."*

In the world of magical things, since the unreal has the chance to become real, why invest in what has no magic? Historically we've been trained to only believe in what has been proven instead of the unbelievable, but magic breaks rules. Magic can make the impossible credible and will sprout possibilities even after the story is over. In the story of Alice in Wonderland, the Mad Hatter told Alice: *"You used to be much more Muchier. You've lost your Muchness."* He was referring to her need to keep going back to what was ordinary while in a world of wonder. The Mad Hatter also said: *"There is a place. Like no place on Earth. A land full of wonder, mystery, and danger! Some say to survive it: You need to be as mad as a hatter."* I took this to mean that when the craziness of this world peaks, it's telling us that it's calling for magic.

To rouse the magic we must let our reveries take us to the outer dimensions and know that during the times when our imagination leaves us wondering, it is giving us the space to fill in. It is truly a wakeup call to escape the ordinary and inspire the extraordinary and to find that we are living a dream. So here we are standing in the poppy field rubbing the sleep from our eyes and looking around. There's nothing ordinary here, because as we rub the sleep out of our eyes we're not the same. We've claimed ourselves by instilling faith, we've flexed our minds, animated humor, focused on magical perspectives, evoked higher-consciousness, embraced healing, aroused self-love, accepted differences, enveloped worthiness and roused the magic. We have remembered who we are!

Part Two – What To Do To Awaken

"Your own self-realization is the greatest service you can render the world." —Ramana Maharshi

Abracadabra Rx: Relax. One morning, my husband was overcome with anxiety while paying bills. In that state he went to wash some dishes, broke a glass, cut his hand, and was now in a worse state. Something then woke him up and it was the fact that he was sick of living this way. He told me he was moving full on into the moment and was going to enjoy tranquility no matter what he was doing. Recently, while taking a guitar lesson his teacher told him not to think while playing, just play. He was told to let his fingers holding the pick relax and let the pick fall into place on the string. He realized that he had to live by letting his energy lead and let things fall into place. He decided to prioritize on feeling serenity while doing the mundane things that are necessary. Once we relax, we do what needs to be done instead of being in a state of angst that does us harm.

On the transformative path of least resistance sometimes we must sit down like a gorilla in the jungle and eat a leaf while waiting for what's next. Our path might have thick detours and we will need to collect ourselves before we whip out our machetes to begin clearing. In the throes of active transformation, we do the opposite of gearing up, so instead we relax in order to clear our mental jungle. I was under great pressure to get a real estate deal done that I had worked hard on because I was about to lose it. Instead of pushing or manipulating it, I took a hands-off approach and went out to lunch. Driving back to the office it came to me to call a certain person whom I thought would love to purchase this property and they bought it. I had accessed this miracle by taking a timeout to unwind and get out of my mental way.

At certain times we must become so totally surrendered that even when we're not successful we still have total faith. We're relaxed because we know we did our best, which will attract what's best back to us so we may succeed elsewhere. My cat falls asleep in the backyard while birds are dive-bombing his head. He disappears into cat meditation and bliss and the birds finally give up on trying to attack him. My cat knows they're there but his relaxed attitude is a barrier with a message that says: *"I'm not a threat!"* I imitate my cat when I'm feeling attacked and go into an altered state where

I too am not there. People have often commented to me on the phone: *"Are you there?"* They sense that I've gone far away and I have. It's where I go when I have to process what is going on to decide how to handle it. In an argument, by relaxing into a non-threatening posture, we *Tai Chi* anger away so there's nothing left to argue about.

The modern world has an annoyance factor that's off the grid with rage: road rage, phone company rage, airport rage, political and terrorist rage, civil rights and feminist rage—we are enraged. Animosity is contagious and all this gyrating and posturing is exhausting and big a waste of energy. Try stepping aside to be the witness, as we can always do something about it later from a magical state. It's a radical move to do nothing, be nothing, want nothing—and relax. Being nothing is a holy state where we are not in desire but actually hooked into the best of everything. So relax and be nothing, as nothing leads to everything.

Abracadabra Rx: Clear Old Impressions. One night I dreamt that a very large woman had broken into my hotel room while I was on vacation and was laying on top of me, trying to smother me in my sleep. The vacation aspect in the dream represented the fact that I was leaving the reality I knew to travel elsewhere and the smothering presence was all the baggage I had brought with me. Since I was asleep, I was not in an awakened state and this attack represented how this happens mostly when we are not conscious. In reality I was in transition and the only way I could move forward would be to release my baggage. Though it seems that every time we go to let go of an old way of being, it grabs onto our ankles as we walk away because our minds want to retrieve what it knows. The devil we know is not better than the devil we don't when it's time to hang out with our angels. All devils need to go back to Hell and we expedite this by hanging out in a heavenly state.

A breakthrough is an agreement we make with ourselves that things don't have to remain the same and so we go out of our comfort zone to explore. By clearing our vision, we see the truth of things when our social network goes down and we have to rely on our real alliances. Consider the one ant that goes up to the top of the hill to see what's out there while his fellow ants, whose home under the log that just got washed away are busy rebuilding in the same spot. This one ant that went up the hill then comes back to tell his fellow ants that they are in a bad spot. Only a few listen and follow this smart ant up the hill. It's just like this for us when we wake up, as we can no longer spend time in the lowlands trying to arouse others, but must go up the hill to build a new life. Eventually others will see it and show up.

The directive to clear impressions is to not get entangled with them, just observe them. Impressions act like children who sneak into the cookie jar. Just by seeing that they're at it again, we've caught them. While the motive of an impression is to rule us, we must keep doing things in new ways to distract them and arouse our magic. Survival of the fittest is not about becoming the strongest in the same place but about the ability to go beyond. So we look at things from all perspectives, we trust the universe, but take responsibility to evolve. And when everyone is down the road fighting, we go into the woods to commune with nature and clear the air. Someone has to do it, someone has to step aside and be a channel for magic and miracles—and it's us.

I always thought the analogy of the word "No" meant to ignore obstacles, explore why it's "No" and then bulldoze it until it gives. I was wrong. The truth is that being stuck is a concept that holds an impression is only fastened by beliefs. There's no such thing as being stuck, it's the impression that's stuck. Impressions captivate us and when they become hard-nosed, we must remember that the opposite of what's set in stone is where the magic hangs out. So vision and travel with what you'd like to happen, step away from what's impressive, as false bravado is only enticing to the ones who can be impressed. The ones who tout their programs as being the only way or the best way, are programmers who are programmed. Don't be programmed! Instead of following impressions, use them to uncover the truth. The truth wakes us up; it moves the unmovable and goes the other way, so follow it. PS. No just means Yes is elsewhere.

Abracadabra Rx: Be Still And Know God. Stillness is a bypass journey that goes beyond the mental to awaken its allies in the heartland. From here our truth takes the stage while faith hangs out behind the curtain holding possibility. As we sit in Bodhi presence, the blur of everyday life slows down to bring us into a state of divine consciousness that empowers us. Meanwhile our ignorance is invited to take a cosmic carpet ride, offering us visions that we're encouraged to step into. And all we did was sit, shut our eyes, listen to our breath and turn off the outer world.

The proverb: *Be Still and Know God,* is a bridge into this cosmic field where we are awake within vast infinite wisdom. Here God is no longer conceived as an old man with a white beard fixing things. Alternatively we envision a supreme force that's passing us the joint on holy consciousness. In this awareness we wake up to realize that the almighty divine is in everything. There's no way around it, as love and light are the exit ramps out of darkness. So we have to go beyond where we are every time our world gets stuck. It's important to remember that we are magical conductors armed as vessels of light that can shift reality. So stay still and shine. We are here to live our Declaration of Independence in a United State of Consciousness.

Abracadabra Rx: Prepare For The Best. We came here to participate in this human experience and get our degree in Transformational Existence. All that happens, including all the ugliness we have to deal with is part of the course. Our reaction to all that goes on is also part of the course. In the midst of a bad story I hear inside: *Take what is best from this and shape-shift it into something else from the crème ingredients you find. Though if you can't find anything good then absolutely make something up if you have to.* As the sculptors of everything from reality to our actual bodies, which we created during our pre-existence and grew into, we give life to our ideas.

I am constantly inserting good tales into bad stories to empower better stories, as I believe the universe is conspiring in my favor. A friend was having a rash of stressful scenarios in the process of selling her home. She expected the worst and was busy diverting all the crises she imagined coming before they happened. As a result she created the exact energy field that attracted all the difficulties she believed were down the road. When our raving mind tells us we will be screwed, people will never come through, buyers won't pay our price and we will never get what we need, we're empowering these exact dilemmas.

The ticket out of this bad imaginary is to literally and completely believe otherwise. Beyond a doubt, we are going against the grain when we don't energize our mental distractions. Disbelief has its own parameters and does not invest in what it can't count on and nor should we. Then again when things don't go our way it's a safeguard on some level. So rejection is a message that our gold is elsewhere and the people who abandon us are not our tribe people and it's karmically correct to let them go. I believe that what does not come my way is what is getting out of the way for something better to arrive. So at times I have to put some good energetic weight on the scale to overlook what is useless and will not go anywhere good. Someone I know whom in the past did not have my best interest at heart invited me to participate in a partnership. I figured they had changed and I wanted to give them the benefit of my doubt. Right when we were about to shake on the deal they reneged. I was protected and blessed to not be engaged with them again.

Doing what's best is ammunition against insanity, so when crazy shows up, we don't accept it. I witnessed a woman on a tear, charge out of the subway screaming curses at her boyfriend. My friend grabbed my arm and said, *"Do not connect to that craziness."* Too late! It already bombarded into my field of vision. I quickly surrounded the shrieking woman with healing energy; as to offer help to another aligns all possibilities into harmony. Therefore when pulling the despair card, we must remember that somewhere inside us we have the antidote to move about in the midst of our difficulties. And when life throws a curve ball and we go down, we blame, we fall apart, there is drama, and then one day alone with ourselves, we call it out and realize we'd lost something important—our essence. In this moment we get it, that this is why all the anguish happened. So we sit and invite this spark of who we are in spirit home and our magic comes following along after it.

This Transformational 101 Class is about defining our priorities, so while we're not close to success, have no love for what we're doing or scared of what the future is bringing, nevertheless we still have to lay claim to the quality of life we can thrive on. Difficulty is a call for us to shift the energy of displeasure into acceptance and then empower what's best, which shifts reality. Isn't it provocative when our intention is having an affair with our intuition and in a blink we are live and direct, totally alert? Suddenly we can see clearly and once again the curtain rises, there is a story running and here we are conjuring up the outcome because it's our story.

Abracadabra Rx: Keep On Passing Through. While in the throes of awakening, as everything is morphing we're like the old dame that has seen it all and knows better. As we pass through the decades, we are constantly being thrust into unrecognizable places where nothing is customary. Blink, everything we knew counted on or believed in is displaced. Meanwhile our addictions come online and start yelling commands. The monkey on our back loves bad habits, but we know better because in an awakened state we jones for liberation over longing. So when the ride gets bumpy and the scenery becomes ugly, we just keep passing through.

It's best when passing through to not touch anything, don't put things in your cart, don't look at things too closely, don't look devilish people in the eye, or even pause too long in one place. Keep moving. If you find you've been caught up with something, immediately put it down. While you're in the dark and it feels like nothing is moving, note this as an illusion. Things are always moving, we are just not fathoming the results and that's fine because they're not important yet. Think of all the times you could not figure something out and months later the solution arrived and you knew you were blessed not to have known it sooner because it would have captured you. Whereas knowing the reason much later liberates us.

How many times have we stepped in it and then had to spend time cleaning our shoes? Watch where you're going and keep going! I consider it a supreme test to be in the whirlwind of change and not react to the turbulence. Instead I calm my nervous system down and stay awake to see where the next best stop to get off on is. I remember as a child being on the roller coaster as it was going up and knowing that I wanted to get off and couldn't. So I braced myself and went through it. In bracing ourselves we do not shut down, but call in all our forces to be strong enough to hold on and let go at the same time. Triumph aligns with courage to inspire all we've got to the frontlines. The situation may be literally awful, but by entrusting this interval as a sacred necessity we don't push back, instead we just pass through.

Abracadabra Rx: Be Ecstatic. Sitting around a dinner table with friends, everyone is sharing a story that defines them. It's mostly old pain stories that might be over but the pain is not. The pain comes from the illusion that we are not okay, which creates a pattern of repeating historic dynamics to try to fix them. The best story is to be hunky-dory now even if we're not. Just try it on for size to see how it would feel. In this one instance of feeling emancipated, we have pushed through a bad story. In the next moment, we get to decide if we're going back or not. Leaving our old stories behind, we may have a reaction of sadness when our pain is moving out. This pain is needling our heart meridian in the process of releasing itself.

A distraught friend and mother of two teenagers who was in the midst of a hideous divorce, made the decision to no longer fight with insanity. While there were many things in the divorce proceedings that were not fair and downright wrong, she chose to walk away and lose the battle in order to gain back her good spirit. She retreated into a serious belief in her own goodness to come and by letting go she cleared a way for it to arrive. She realized that there was no winning or losing, it was just about a return to love—for herself.

I once complained for a year about how awful the people in my real estate industry behaved and voilà it was the worst year I ever had. There were cheaters, back stabbers, liars and thieves all playing in my sandbox. My emotions were hanging out drunk at my own pity-me party. Amusing that these same backstabbing experiences had happened all the way through my real estate career and had never affected me prior because I was too ecstatic to care. The greatest turnaround is to be so in love with our quality of life that nothing beneath it sticks. Maybe in reality we are not in love; life is harsh, reality has gone nuts, people are doing hideous things and nothing is going our way, so we pretend. My bliss impersonations are a lifeline. I will act ecstatic over anything, even a cup of coffee and this feeling has cohorts of happiness that come with sidekicks of high-end spirited sparks, which grab us to dance and shake off the rest.

Abracadabra Rx: Observe Magic. The physiology in science called the observer effect, states that by looking at something changes it. Remember as children, knowing when we were being watched we put on grand performances and became show-offs. Being observed is exhilarating because being witnessed verifies our existence. To spotlight any objective animates it, so when we keep flashing on what's wrong, it becomes energized. Our scrutiny is like a snake charmer that arouses the spirit of the matter. So we must take control of the mind and the senses in order to manifest our true intentions by seeing clearly.

I experimented with the observation effect by spotlighting a certain dream and adding love to manifest it. The premise is that by looking at things with love or being looked at with love, sparks love. Can this be true? An experimental study was done where something that decays would no longer decay when in the process of being observed. It was attributed to a delayed quantum eraser that negated wave function to bring back an objects history. This led me to wonder that if we can observe our minds while thinking bad thoughts, then would our thinking eventually return to its natural wondrousness? It appears that with one-pointed consciousness, thought will always come back to its original intention so what once came from love would return to love.

In the case of spotlighting that certain dream, I constantly tuned into it. The trick is that even while the end result is not on the horizon, we should never focus on lack or think we've been victimized by disadvantage. Instead focus on the intention, observe the desire, and instead of going anywhere else with it just keep your eye on it until it begins flashing.

When it lights up smile, as this bolsters and amplifies it.

The weird theory of a delayed quantum eraser seemed farfetched, so I tried it on a day I was getting ill. I did not take remedies but simply observed the illness. I questioned what it was doing and if it had anything to say, which it did. It said it was a result of recent stress and that it was an emotional release and I needed rest. Usually this particular illness lasts a week, but it basically left in a day since I observed it. Yes, this is a pretty abstract notion but I am not giving up on playing with it. I want to get to the core of things and understand what sparks them in order to see where the magic exists. What we're observing when we look into the essence of something is what relays facts beyond reality. So instead of focusing on facts, we target the energy fields around situations to see what they're doing, where they are going and how they shift reality. An example of an awakened mind is one that goes beyond playing with things to play with creation.

The Buddhist teacher, Thich Nhat Hanh stated that an actual smile changes the energetic dynamic in one's body. If we smile for no reason, the inner smile boosts our cells and uplifts our energy field. To observe this dynamic activates the energy field of happiness and expands it. With this in mind, we must scrutinize our expectations to see where we make people, places, and things accountable for our quality of life. If we erase expectations we're left with the gift of being so in the moment that we don't have to strive for things, wait for something to happen, or fix things. Instead we can just observe what's going on with curiosity and send energy to what we want to empower. I am always taking a Buddha squat and observing magic—watching it sparks it to life!

Abracadabra Rx: Dance To The Beat Of Your Heart. Life is a wild dancer that likes to swing us around so we lose a shoe and have to dance in bare feet. Every time our feet touch the earth, we ground into being here, as our pure presence becomes the offering. Like whirling dervishes who dance with painful stories to let them go and reach ecstasy, the dance is always going. So we step in and out of our dance as we align our rhythm to a healing essence while dancing out our emotions. Anxiety is a badass dancer, jerking us all over the place until we collapse to once again get lifted by esteem that takes our hand and whisks us back to boogie on.

This dance of life is our teacher so even when we fall, we're now dancing with our humility, which brings us back to our natural rhythm. It's best to let loose and get down with what needs to be released in order to get back up. We must dance with what is to finally get to dance with joy. All that comes forward to take our hand wants to be experienced and when we consider for instance, that sadness or despair is escorting us to the next partner then each dance is not the *End All.* We are tripping the light with all the stories of creation and there is magic around being in the dance. Our chorography swings, spins, and rocks our world; it wakes us up to dance with our true lifeblood, which is the *Be All* part of us that does not back away, but transforms.

Abracadabra Rx: Remember What You Came Here For.
Sometimes I feel my spirit standing behind me, as my fear of failure is whispering lies that say I can't go where I am going. I hear my spirit whispering in my other ear, *"There's literally nowhere else to go but back to remembering the reason why you came here."* The reason we came here is because we were once evolved enough to make this journey—if we're questioning it, we've forgotten. Aligning with the valid fact that we are here for the magic takes the pressure off. Without the pressure, we go from doing to just being. Some days I have to make up a reason for why I'm here and by doing this, a new reason comes alive. We can always come up with a reason to be here, even in the times when we feel lost, as in I am here to find my way while being lost. When lost, I hear my spirit whispering, *"You are on the journey back to yourself because there is no journey that does not return home".*

A man I love keeps repeating a story that caused him severe pain. This old story instilled a belief that he was not good enough to be valued and it revolved around the fact that as a kid, his dad never took him took him to a baseball game. Once they came really close, they actually drove to the stadium, parked in the lot and his dad suddenly changed his mind saying that the game was already into the eighth inning and it was too late. They left. That game went twenty-seven innings. I asked this man to keep going farther back in time and he kept describing different versions of why his dad did not consider him, until I asked him who he was before he was born into that story. He looked at me and time stopped as he then remembered what it felt like to not be affected by this distortion. There was a shift as he felt the completeness of himself prior to the story. *"That's who you really are!"* I said.

Our reason for being here evolves as we evolve. When we think of a reason, even if the reason is to unfold in the mystery, then we're always in the process of coming back to the true essence of being. In union with ourselves, our spirit says: *"All that matters is to be one with me so what really matters can be with you."* A day where no answer is the answer is a good day to remember significant things, so peruse the archives and go back beyond reasoning to the spark of our matter and remember from there.

Abracadabra Rx: Go To Nirvana. Imagine if instead of being punished we were sent to Nirvana where we'd become so immersed in bliss that we would morph into saints. Good fantasy, but one I'm not giving up on. So ponder if you can find bliss in the mud, could Nirvana exist in the airport check in line, can we find happiness after another rejection letter? We could if we put our monster to bed, gave them a cup of chamomile tea, sang them a song and combed their crazy hair. Once the little monster inside calms down, we can overdose them with love so they may find their saintliness and end up in Nirvana.

The vibration of the universe exists inside all beings. It's known a spontaneous force of expression called *Spanda*. Spanda is the subtle creative pulse of the universe expressed in different forms as the primordial life force behind our mind. It's the pulsation beyond reasoning that exists as our natural cadence to live. I always wonder what the Universe has to say about some of the shenanigans going on around here and I'm reminded that the energetic pulse of the planet has its own divine consciousness. The universe never forgets that it exists on divine consciousness because pure energy always returns to its original pulse. It's the same with us, but we do forget and have to remember. Taking a hit of nirvana helps us to conjure up our original spark. So keep focusing on the pulsation of the greater vibration that is behind all things and vibrates life force. If we try to hear the heartbeat of this world, we will go to the source of our own creation because we came through it to get here.

Imagine if every time we lost it, started to keel over, felt beaten down and on the verge of anxiety; in lieu of going to the bar, the fridge or the phone, we preferably checked into the Nirvana-Sphere for a hit of enchantment and came back into this reality with stars in our eyes. Nirvana is a heavenly state that dissolves our Hell. It holds the most heavenly vital medicine that uplifts our dispositions, restores our energy, and brings our spirit back to life. Nirvana sends us messages to not place too much importance on failures, heartbreaks, and lost dreams. After a taste of bliss, we find the more potent dynamic is to look beyond into the sacred hub that holds our blessings. This divine existence is actually a blessed holy energy field and if we can hold this awareness for even a second—we're in Nirvana.

Abracadabra Rx: Follow Your North Star. Our North Star is the constant dependable light on our horizon. The placement of this star is used for setting our course, so like sailors we must look for our North Star when we are lost in the sea of reality. Identifying with this light field puts us in a star beam state where our inner constellation is connecting with its reflection. So when we're hanging out in a mud hole, under the guise of our North Star we don't mind, because we're part of a sacred lotus that is transforming this world back to love.

While connected, our North Star is a cosmic thread that reminds us what's important. Just thinking about our North Star sends forces through this envisioned telegraph wire and if we listen closely, we can hear its directive. I was in Mexico in a stormy cold front getting sick, which in a foreign country is Hell. My mind became fearful and I wanted to get the next flight home, but felt too ill. Sitting in a restaurant drinking tea, the song, *Do You Believe In Magic* came on the radio. It snapped me out of my fear of getting worse and led me to connect to my North Star. The directive that came through gave me antidotes that got me well enough to fly home where Nirvana was waiting for me in my bed. On the plane I saw the real North Star and knew it was always beaming on me, guiding my way, and shining on me because I was connected to it.

A young adult asked me why they are not like everyone else and my answer was, *"It is because you are following your own star and it's taking you down deep inside yourself instead of running you on the fast track."* All his friends were either successful or busy striving for success, whereas he was busy navigating his art. We spoke about the greater reasoning for why we're impelled to do what we do and my friend realized he was in the perfect place on timing. His greater reasoning was about discovering his inventiveness in artistry and so he was building a foundation that would eventually carry him far and wide. He was connected big time to his North Star. So chart your course based on your highest ideal, your priority, and most divine dreams. And don't worry about time because once we're following our natural force then time no longer matters. In truth we are traveling light beams crisscrossing the world. Our real navigation is not of this world anyway, for as James Kirk in Star Trek said, *"Second star to the right . . . and straight on 'till morning."*

Abracadabra Rx: Gather Yourself. Suddenly we no longer fit into our lives, as from one blink to the next we've grown too big for our shoes. Granted, it's a total shock when what was once so important suddenly has no meaning. It might feel like we've lost our spark but actually we've taken a leap in consciousness and the physical is still catching up. In the interim, we gather ourselves to be available for the magic of what's next. The craziest part is that we can't go back and hide in our old lives while we wait, because *Poof!* they no longer exist. What's also amazing is that now our authentic way has been pushed to the forefront of our existence.

Akin to a company takeover, our team arrived in the

middle of the night and rearranged our psyche, but what's so annoying is that they didn't leave a note telling us we're not the same, nor did they leave an instruction manual, so we're now living by experiment. Old thinking doesn't work, as those channels are now static and only new reflections work.

The best thing to do in times like this is to wake up our inner cohorts, gather them together and let them know it's time to play, dream, and source our way from the highest resonance around. Meanwhile our house has landed and we're stepping out, the first step is to observe what's different and the next radical step is to learn how to relate to ourselves in a brand new way. So we gather up all the aspects of who we ever were, we add in the wondrous new aspect of who we are now and walk out from there. We might not know where we're going, that's fine, but most importantly don't go looking for the wizard—just be the Wizard!

Abracadabra Rx: Act As If. There is a supreme state that most evolved beings live in. These beings have set the stage, erased the audience out of their minds and are roaming around the wild frontier for their own pure pleasure. What they know is that the magic exists in the sacred beliefs that we anchor into. So while craziness abounds, we can still sit in our holy-land and dream our way around it. Inside we are solid, we don't get pushed and pulled, because by living our advanced conjecture we've come to light. In this simulated mindset we hang out in the pregnant pause of a satiated moment and are tapped right into the magic of it. When we believe that we already have the goods and the love, then the ideas spark and there's no end to what comes alive.

Living in the act as if mode upgrades our quality of life, it awakens our cells, sparks the magic and invites miracles to happen. The Buddha stated: *"We get there by realizing we're already there."* So we are basically setting the stage for actuality to match up with our presence by taking our cause to the bridge. At this crossover we must drop our lowly feelings and shine a light on our truth, because when James Brown said: *"Take it to the bridge"* he was talking about totally grooving in this moment before jumping into the next riff. So vision your way and merge it with possibility to touch circumstance to magic by acting as if.

Abracadabra Rx: Take It To The Bridge. During times when bad things happen, our expectations are squashed, reality becomes mean, people around us act insane and lose it, we get cheated, knocked down, and love leaves us in the dust. It's a windswept storm that is pushing us across into a place of light filled wisdom. We can't let these things drag us down for too long, but only long enough for us to use these downer experiences to advance from. We are not hanging around to get down and dirty with what isn't good enough, we're rather on our way to the next continent where our enlightenment is bigger than life. We just need to get to the bridge and we don't even need to cross it, as just getting there in our mind instills us to put our bags down because we're not bringing them with us.

At a turning point in my career a deceitful man cheated me out of a large sum of money by not paying a commission on a huge sale I made happen for him. At first I was angry, then depressed and then I realized I had an old wound around being cheated that I needed to liberate. I communed with my spirit who asked if I would pay that huge amount of money to be liberated? The answer was yes. Immediately, my searing discomfort towards the cheating man shifted as I had taken myself to the bridge by trusting I deserved better. This experience changed me, it shook me up, showed me where my lack of worthiness was and set me straight in another direction, as the evil man and his thievery faded in the dust.

Even though I had expunged this thief and the entire bad experience from my psyche, my company still sued him. Five years later I got a call that the lawsuit was settled and I would receive the funds due to me, plus dividends. At this time I was thinking to run off my base and just work on my book. I kept hearing: *"Don't worry about it,"* every time I was fearful about how I would support myself. The truth is that I was not as cheated by that swindler as I thought prior. Instead, miraculously my funds were being held in a Universal bank account for when I really needed them. I had arrived to the bridge with nothing but faith.

A friend altered his entire consciousness in the process of preparing to pass on. We sat on his front stoop and focused on the trees. He said, *"The sound of theses leaves in the wind are like a boisterous symphony, do you hear it?"* We paused to listen to the leaves rustle in an operatic swell and then calm into angelic whisperings. My friend's presence was a bridge that took me with him into his state. He said that he heard birds singing their hearts out in a magical way and it brought tears to his eyes. Colors were so vivid, he felt like he could melt into them. The sun was a blaze of warmth and the night sky was a drapery of dreams into other worlds he was visiting. He said that at times the beauty he saw was so immense that all he felt was bliss. By touching upon evolved consciousness, we take everything to the bridge. We are just crossing over the trenches on our way back to heaven.

Abracadabra Rx: Be Secure. How farfetched is it that we are on a planet whirling through space in a solar system along with infinities of stars and in the midst of all this we want to be secure? The Earth never said to the cosmos: *I'm going to rotate around a bunch of other planets and be home to seven billion people in order to feel secure.* Security is an illusion beyond from which we are totally safe. So things didn't work out, how perfect. I am now miserable, how perfect. I now have to do something about it, how perfect. What's perfect is the fact that we are here, part and parcel in this world and as crazy as it all gets, we are still awakening through it.

Rodney Yee was sitting in meditation at the beginning of his yoga class while his students were talking loudly. The noise level was at volume ten, I even videoed it because I was amazed that this teacher was meditating in this chaos. After class I asked him why he did not silence the room to sit with him. He said, *"It's a great practice for me to transcend noise."* I pertained this teaching to holding a sense of being secure while things are falling apart.

Can we step so far out of ourselves that we could touch upon the eternal and come back into wholeness? May we deeply embrace ourselves with so much self-love that we are embedded with such good spirit that it holds us through our dark nights? The fact is that we've all arrived here with an inner guarantee and it's time to re-read the small print on your lifetime warranty. It states that for every breakdown on this human model there will also be a breakthrough when this being assures itself. The small print also certifies that this being has arrived with all it needs to function and does not need to be fixed, but has every ability to fix itself. Therefore on the grounds of being firmly planted in the self, we are coded to be secure while in transient settings. And like birds that sing not just to be heard, but because they have to burst into song, in our true nature we are complete.

Abracadabra Rx: Be Genius. The definition of genius in humans is that of beings having an exceptional capacity to naturally go beyond themselves. This Universe is based on inventiveness that shows us that a state of genius does not need to be acquired it already exists. We too have the capacity of genius, so we might spend a few moons sitting around and looking at the sky or whiling away time by daydreaming on a bench as we're calling our Einstein essence forth. The philosopher Immanuel Kant said, "*Genius is a talent for producing something for which no determinate rule can be* *given, not a predisposition consisting of a skill for something that can be learned by following some rule or other."*

Our genius is the inventive chef in our consciousness that has the ability to concoct masterful meals out of leftovers. This sprite of artfulness will find the one missing ingredient needed to spice up our fare because their goal is to create masterpieces. When things get tough, when we're getting pushed around, when we're doing mind battle over what's not working, our genius is out there stalking a solution. This mastermind will illuminate the philosophers stone in a night dream showing us that our mistakes and breakdowns are really stepping-stones to breakthroughs. In the periods where we feel stuck and it appears that nothing good is happening, our inner Einstein is fully functioning in other dimensions, divining the cosmos and tracking our magic.

In Roman mythology a genius is known as the divine nature that is present in individuals, places, and things. Dr. Clarissa Pinkola Estés, the author of *Women Who Run With the Wolves,* has related the word genius with angels, she says: *"Humans are being called to rise up into their most angelic bloodline."* With this in mind, consider that these times are calling for human consciousness to rise up so that we can live with self-empowered virtuousness no matter what. It's a time to connect with and empower our inner genius to be our virtuoso and be masterly while ignorance is rampant.

The World English Dictionary outlines a Roman myth that states a genius as being the guiding spirit who attends a person from their birth to death. This conjures up our wunderkind that takes apart reasoning and goes right to the source of brilliance. So while we've been trained to go to others for counsel, preferably go into your cosmic conference room alone with your genius squad and just hangout. We are actually our own healers, psychics and business advisors, and being that our answers don't always come from this Earthly dimension, neither do we. So it's time to rub our genie lamp, call out the fairies and hang out in Lotus Land. We don't need to know where we're actually going because our inner genius is creating the road as we go.

Abracadabra Rx: Be In The Miracle Zone. We all arrived here with nothing except for the spark of us. Surrounded by unfamiliar people, the only language we had to communicate with was love. It was one courageous act to leap out of one dimension into another and if you don't believe in miracles, then think about how you got here. You came through a miracle zone and you will be returning there in the end, but in the interim we are still in one. A friend was walking with down a country road with her tiny dog, Yogi Bob, when he seemed to disappear into thin air. Our community came forth, posted signs everywhere and went on searches. He was not found and many feared a hawk or an eagle had gotten him, as he was so tiny. A year and a half later, a woman from our area who had moved at least fifty miles away and worked in an animal shelter, noticed a dog had arrived that looked like Yogi Bob. She called my friend and not wanting to get her hopes up, said, *"I'm not sure this is your dog, but it might* *be."* It was! Our entire community celebrated this miracle.

Miracle consciousness is that gut instinct that always believes otherwise no matter what goes on. It's real that bad things happen, that we get smacked in the face and have to deal with it. I want to go down with it, but I'd rather believe that there is still goodness somewhere. It's like taking a trip where we roll up everything that's a drag and sit back and smoke it until it delivers satisfaction. So while on this planet during such a dark period, I know the light exists alongside and is more powerful than ever. At times we feel abandoned, like the universe has not heard our prayers, or our dreams are not being delivered. Maybe God got the wrong order? What really matters is that we are part of this order in a way that is magic, so there is no wrong order in a miracle zone.

Living by the ocean, I often say prayers and commune by the sea. On a day I was distraught over letting go of my entire way of being to do something new, I said my prayers and for some odd reason I requested to see a whale breech as a confirmation that my prayers where heard. Mind you, I have never seen a whale breech, as it's just not common here. Nevertheless I sat and waited to see the whale—no whale arrived. Leaving to go to my car I took one last look and said I'm counting to ten. I counted and still no whale showed up. I then laughed at myself while driving home for having such big expectations and threw them to the wind.

I don't normally ask for such huge confirmations on my prayers so I apologized to the Universe for being demanding and not trusting that I was heard. Once home, I got the urge to connect with an old friend I had not spoken to in many years. I went to her Facebook page to see how she was and the first thing that appeared was a video of a humpback whale breeching. The Universe delivered!

Miracles are the seismic shift of supreme magic that comes alive in our child-like nature. Even as we wash the dishes, it could be in that odd thought that the water is magic. An unabridged being is neither lodged in the here or there and will shrink or grow to get through the keyhole. So while all the craziness is going on, always ask for an overnight delivery of what's best. Ask for directions to your Promised Land and always offer gratitude for what is received. Imagine often that you've wandered onto the path of never-ending miracles—you have. We don't need keys for this keyhole, as the magic begins with the acknowledgement that we are the actual miracle.

Abracadabra Rx: Live In Your Promised Land. We keep stepping in an out of this game of life until we realize that we are actually playing the game. Who is it that sees this? What mind behind the mind is watching the show and reporting back? Our witness is the spirit essence of us, the seer and sparked visionary with keys to our kingdom. Our detour into a land of plenty stops the world to show us that it no longer owns us. Here we find we're in the world but not of it. We identify ourselves as not this or that, but simply as *I Am*. Our *I Am-ness* is the part of our consciousness that is conscious. It knows where the light is and becomes one with it. It's like when we think about the light at the end of the tunnel, then suddenly *poof* the tunnel is gone and we're in the light.

We have a sacred temple inside us; its altar is our mirror of creation. Its hearth is our heart center, its skylight is our consciousness and this is where we go to change the world. As excavators on behalf of everything holy, we've already dredged up the whole shebang and offered it into the fire of grace. Surrounded by our spiritual cohorts, we ask for the power to transform all that is diverse into what sanctions us to be pure vessels of grace. Knowing we are here for a greater reason, we have no agenda other than to be in sync with it. We trust that whatever presents itself; either has a teaching instilled in it or has directions to get us to our sacred party

Living in our Promised Land changes everything, as once we experience it, it hands us the Crayons to color outside the lines with. In essence, all we are doing is rising up from the poppy field of one dream to be part of many more elevated dreams. So we awaken and rub the sleep out of our eyes to find that our field of dreams is a gift that keeps on giving, as long as we see it this way. This awakening is the turn around into our empowerment, where we know we must wave our wands to make magic happen. One blink into our Promised Land delivers us there. It's a feeling not a fact, so on the ethereal plane check into this sacred homeland and roam around. It's from here that everything is bestowed. Our Spark is alive, we're instilled with magic and empowered to use it in the highest ways. The light at the end of the tunnel is inside our hearts and knowing this is the awakening.

Abracadabra Rx For A Magical Awakening . . .

Rx: *Awaken this wake-up call.*

Rx: *Awaken into your enlightenment.*

Rx: *Awaken your sense of adventure and embrace the absurd.*

Rx: *Awaken the story you love and live in it.*

Rx: *Awaken love and add it to all your stories.*

Rx: *Awaken to know the perfection in all things.*

Rx: *Awaken to believing in your dreams.*

Rx: *Awaken beyond the stories that don't serve you.*

Rx: *Awaken to what really matters and go from there.*

Rx: *Awaken your inner wizard.*

Rx: *Awaken magical concepts and perceptions.*

Rx: *Awaken wonderment.*

Rx: *Awaken to the messages from the universe and use them.*

Rx: *Awaken to knowing stuck is another story.*

Rx: *Awaken visions and dreams of new options.*

Rx: *Awaken what you thrive on and keep it close.*

Rx: *Awaken to stretching into new possibilities.*

Rx: *Awaken your sense of humor; it's your ally.*

Rx: *Awaken your strength to not retaliate.*

Rx: *Awaken your ability to affect all circumstances supremely.*

Rx: *Awaken your contentment.*

Rx: *Awaken goodness and follow it.*

Rx: *Awaken the seeker within—explore for treasure.*

Rx: *Awaken acceptance as opposed to judgment.*

Rx: *Awaken your sensitivity.*

Rx: *Awaken your gratitude.*

Rx: *Awaken your ability to change the channel—many times.*

Rx: *Awaken to being in sync with your passion.*

Rx: *Awaken to remembering who you are.*

Rx: *Awaken the concept of zero limitations.*

Rx: *Awaken the gathering of yourself into harmony.*

Rx: *Awaken your trust.*

Rx: *Awaken your joy—allow it to satiate you.*

Rx: *Awaken compassion to carry you when you are hurting.*

Rx: *Awaken your courage.*

Rx: *Awaken to accept differences and find love anyway,*

Rx: *Awaken letting go—over and over.*

Rx: *Awaken your consciousness.*

Rx: *Awaken your ability to just be.*

Rx: *Awaken your presence in the miracle zone.*

Rx: *Awaken a shift.*

Rx: *Awaken through your broken heart back to love.*

Rx: *Awaken your genius.*

Rx: *Awaken your ability to transform.*

Rx: *Awaken your skills to get through difficulties.*

Rx: *Awaken your communication with your divine source.*

Rx: *Awaken into your Promised Land.*

Rx: *Awaken to believe there are no mistakes—only lessons.*

Rx: *Awaken to the truths that are being revealed.*

Rx: *Awaken your "I AM" consciousness.*

Rx: *Awaken to no longer being in pursuit of magic—instead be immersed in Living It!*

2) Steeped In Magical Possibility . . .

"Imagination is more important than knowledge. For knowledge is limited to all we now know and understand, while imagination embraces the entire world, and all there ever will be to know and understand." —Albert Einstein

So we've awakened, now what? We delve into possibilities, we distinguish higher perspectives from our heartbreaks, we take the write offs and we don't get lost in any of it. A friend complained how difficult her husband was. So I asked her if he was worth it and without hesitation she said yes. Is it worth it? This is the big question, because like a surgeon with a scalpel, it cuts away what is not magic. So when I'm getting up at daybreak to write a book, it's worth it. An even bigger question is am I worth it? When we're worth it, we don't indulge in all that is beneath us, but go after what has possibility. The days of hanging out in closed concepts are over, so step out from under the influence of your dark-talk and come up with grand ideas, cool abstractions and even a bevy of fool's notions. We are now taking a grand leap off our conceptual edge to land on the pillow of our own behalf.

On a day where obligations overloaded my happiness, my mind and my heart were disputing personal politics. While my mind wanted to go into a safety zone, my heart wanted to leap into magical possibilities. We had a Powwow and passed the stick. I asked my mind where we'd end up if we went their way and if there was magic there. I was told we would be safe and could find our magic later. My heart said it was surrounded by magic, pumped magic and only followed its magic. I threw the stick in the fire and followed my heart into possibility.

Possibility has no boundaries; every aspect of its likeliness leads into a new expression that says, *"Play with this and see if it entices you."* You might think who has time to be playing with a theory that might not deliver—though we must. So twirl with the poignant moments that grab you to show you where your real prospects are. In an exquisite interval where we get lost in a song, a vision, a smile, a book, works of great art or new ideas, we're being carried by these affinities. As riders on the storm, the great winds of change are pushing us through the eye of the needle where possibility is triggered. As we feel our way beyond form to touch upon what else exists, we ride the magical mystery tour where our prospects percolate. Just blinking in this direction coerces us to turn things around and choose what's best, as it tempts the magic into our story.

Historically, it's a time for the books, as we are nowadays

evolutionists who exist in the paradox where nothing makes sense and we can't count on what was. This is not a time to play follow the leader, but to make something out of what exists in our enlightened minds. It's also a time to pass go on being stuck in any of what's going on and put our iron in the fire of the outside chance where our real prospects are.

I posed a question to an astrologer friend about how nothing appeared to be working. She sent me a very charged email about how the patriarch was being disassembled and how I had to let go of what no longer worked, even if I had no idea where I was going. There was one line in her email that said, *"We have discussed this ad nauseum."* I got stuck on this line and had a whiteout where I could no longer hear her. Things kept coming up over the next few months that pertained to letting go of what doesn't work. It seemed to be the message of the moment and it pulled me to regularly go back and read that email until the energy of her message poured in and shifted me. Another message was: Don't get stuck in sharp words when there is love behind them.

Possibility is about not throwing the baby out with the dirty bathwater or getting stuck on scenarios, but honoring the truth because that's where the magic is. It's best not to let ambiguity abduct us, but to focus on incentive, which is the brainchild of what is genius. We are now going full-force into our empowered inventiveness, for as we reach through the darkness to feel for the light, in the next blink we're in it. Our creative spirit does not live in reality—it lives in a State of Possibility. Call for your carriage—off we go!

The Abracadabra Prescriptions for Magical Possibility:

Abracadabra Rx: Delve Into Possibility. Quite frequently we have to take our foot off base and make a run for our magical life in order to align with a vision. While possibility is the space between the bases, instead of running to the next base, we must run out to left field and lay down in a meadow of flowers to dream of what impassions us. Passion wants to be impregnated and really we have no idea what it will give birth to, we just know we have to mesh with it to see what sparks. When our faith is aligned with a sparked idea it's like we have a sacred secret that we carry like a talisman and our love activates it. So as we run for our magical life, it's our magical life that inspires us to want to run.

Daydreams are journeys into dimensions that have gifts to deliver. I had one where a feeling came over me stimulated by something I saw. The next thing I knew was that my arm had grown a mile long and was grabbing for what was on the horizon of this feeling. My psyche then quickly downloaded the essence of this new awareness into my consciousness and something shifted. I was drinking in an experience from beyond my mind, a triggered fantasy with ingredients that satiated me. As I came back into reality, on a subliminal level I felt the shift of something wonderful coming into being. It was as if I already owned this experience even though it was a total mystery. When an understanding sparks us, puzzlement must take a backseat and in the height of this paradox we

72

must focus on what will be celebrated, not grieved.

Engaging with possibility is not about going out there and grabbing at things, forcing an outcome, or thinking we know what we need. It's about the ways in which we're open to the overture of the next move even when we have no idea how its debut will pan out because we're too enamored to care. All that's ever possible hides out in an undisclosed location messaging sparks of truths to trigger the synchronicity that implores us to find it. Possibility does not take no for an answer, as the word possibility itself is a mantra that says: "I believe in believing."

Abracadabra Rx: Invest In Wonder. We are being called to believe in what may be and then insert this new concept into what is for it to unfold. In reality this may look like we are stuck in a boring job, or we are in a position where we have to give too much. We show up for our commitments while our hearts are not in it and at the same time, we're kindling a spark that hangs out in our dreams. Wonder is not stationary and loves to explore the terrain. While we're stuck in a crappy job, wonder snatches us away from misery by distracting us to enjoy the things we take for granted. Wonder will then ask, *"Maybe this is not where you'd like to be, but can we make something out of this?"*

Consider how wonder collides into new experiences and recognize how in the mind of a child whose senses are exploring the world something like mud can become a cosmic trip. When we understand that things are not exactly what they appear, it makes sense that what exists is magically expansive. Consider the person on the mesa who played with mud to find it hardened when dried and then decided to build an adobe home out of it. Thereafter they considered the effects of rain and then made a roof out of branches and straw to protect their creation. This is how creation comes to be; at first we play with what has no concept and then an impression comes into play to tell us what it needs to complete itself.

Matter is an observable physical manifestation with literal mass and volume. It's a completed thought form that has manifested itself. On the other hand all situations are not solid or set in stone, so what exists today in the now can flip into something else or even dissolve into nothing. There are endless possibilities to all things, so when we consider that a situation is in fact a certain way we are closing the book on its story. Certainly there are times to definitely close the book on an old story because there is more possibility in a new one. Stories are explorations and when there's nothing left to conceive of the story is over. Though when wonder shows up, it will take an old story and transforms it.

I remember climbing the monkey bars in the park as a child. Every day, it was a new experience. It was not about just getting to the top, it was the feel of the cold metal against my skin, how my body fit amongst the bars of steel, and the smell of iron on my hands. It was about the coolness of how the bars felt on a winter day and how I learned to respect intimate space by easily moving around others. It was the air blowing on my face, my vision of the world while hanging upside down and finally looking across the park from the top of those monkey bars to feel very high. So it was not just about the outcome of being at the top of the monkey bars, it was the fascination of the journey.

Going out of bounds helps us to encapsulate experiences from ordinary patterns or forms to feel its mass and volume. Nowadays, we have the ability to see ordinary things anew in order to fit our energy in with an interesting prospect when called to do so. Being aware of movement is about knowing what moves us, so consider the unwavering possibility in the things that don't work, the job that doesn't come through, the friend who betrays us, the apartment that becomes excruciatingly small, our discomfort, the diagnosis or the misdiagnosis, politics we don't agree with, and the fear that our future is in danger. All these things are leveraging us to balance ourselves out and while a zillion possibilities exist at all times, the ones that exist for us now are the ones we spontaneously say yes to.

The energy field of "Yes!" is a power place with legs that run around collecting what we need. In the event of too many negatives, there's a message telling us that we must get lost in wonderment and wander out of bounds because inevitably we will come back bearing gifts. So wherever you are right now, sit down, explore the paradigms, think outside the box, don't pay attention to the false wizard and always wonder about the conversation you would have with your ruby slippers—then start that dialogue.

Abracadabra Rx: Override Low Level Thinking. A dark-side simultaneously hangs around our light side, though this haunted-ness is only our business if we make it so. And while the darkness feeds on light and tries to devour it, it becomes quite minimal when we blast even more light into it. Our minds like to rotate around what's wrong. They love to describe what's not fair, not our fault, and question if we're in trouble. These annoying mental intonations need to be controlled. When our minds go on a rampage into the bowels of low-level thinking, we have ammunition. I always recite mantras: *Om Namah Shivaya* is mine, but *Sat Nam* is good, or any of the mantras. We have to shift the energy of bad thinking so it does not infiltrate our psyche and mantras do this. Next, I pick one of the annoying thoughts and twist it around to use as an affirmation. So, I don't deserve this becomes: I Deserve Only The Best!

We cannot get to what's better until we invest, believe in, and hang out with what we can cultivate. In the event that life becomes unfulfilling, we still have choices. As Morpheus in the Matrix Trilogy said: *"You take the blue pill—the story ends, you wake up in your bed and believe whatever you want to believe. You take the red pill—you stay in Wonderland and I show you how deep the rabbit-hole goes."* Personally, I would have taken both pills, because honestly this life for me is about the combined experience of being here now and being out there exploring my dreams at the same time. Our consciousness likes to travel, it loves food for thought and cultivates it into dessert.

I have walked away from people, places and things, many times. I often step into new realities and succeed in receiving what I believe I deserve, as I have this underlying supreme faith that believes I do deserve. So when things go to Hell, conceptualize taking the red pill and believe what you want. And in the times that you need to create a new reality, then energetically pop the blue pill, travel into your Wonderland to find what inspires you and go from there.

The truth is that nothing is ever in a fixed state because we're always experiencing and empowering possibilities. So when false mental intonations have gotten under our skin, it's time to decide which way we're going. Years ago, when I first went into real estate my first purchase was a used black Range Rover. Co-workers argued that you do not buy a car prior to buying a house. Too late, it wasn't the car I bought into, it was the dream and it delivered. How I got to the top of my game in real estate was in the fact that I imagined my way, I built a castle in the air and moved into it.

Steve Jobs said, "*Everything that is around you, which you call LIFE, was made up by other people. Once you understand that, you can change it—that's the most important thing.*" People make up the story that everything around them is fixed and then they call it a fact. What we believe stands guard at the door of our minds. By believing in what serves us, we will be served well. Our mental emotional disruptions are like traffic jams that need to detour, so welcome them and say: "Oh you're here again, thank you for reminding me to focus on other possibilities."

Abracadabra Rx: Create Space. Movement is the key to transformation and it only stalls when it's in the process of breaking something down to create more space. Since energy moves in a certain way the trick is not to get stuck in what appears to be, but align with what the energy needs. A good businessperson invests in a concept and then creates space for its existence by holding emptiness for its arrival. If we don't create space there's nowhere for anything to go and we wonder why nothing is happening. The problem is that we can't see what's occurring when we're too obsessed with what's not. When a new reality is called for and is on its way, we have to honor what we've originally asked for and be there with open arms to receive it. Creating space also pertains to headspace, which means to clear our thoughts and be open to the magic. Even just mentally saying: *"I'm open to the magic"* does it.

Sometimes we're pulled along by enthusiasm and other times we've set the stage and must wait for the actors to show up. This is when we're challenged to stay in our inspiration with the belief that our creation is in process while we're sitting there with nothing. To me success is not about the money or the award for being the best. Instead, it's about being aligned with the magic. So if I create space inside the space of something I'm dreaming of and I hang out in there, then I am making that space sacred and empowering it. And maybe it's empty for a while, but I would rather live empty believing in magic than full of you know what.

Relationships even call for space, the poet Kahlil Gibran said, *"The oak tree and the cypress grow not in each other's shadow."* A friend was having a painful relationship with his lover, they were both locked into a pattern of projections on each other. In order for change to occur, one of them needed to alter the pattern. A disagreement is really a state of consciousness that needs to work itself out, while judgment stops a conversation dead. In order for better considerations to come into play there must be enough space for us to clear our perceptions and see how we contributed to creating the disturbing dynamic. My friend understood this and decided to envision the most amicable outcome, which he held onto instead of the argument. When the argument lost its charge then his lover had nothing to argue with and showed up for the outcome he envisioned.

The nature of all things is to evolve, so in essence things will wobble when absorbing a shock and then process it out to find the right balance. When insanity exists or violence occurs, the entire planet wobbles. We feel like we're going to fall down and maybe we do. At this time, we must create the space to pull in the opposite of violence, which is love and we must sit with this love until we can get up again. So when things are going hellishly wrong, we create space for things to go magically right. We hold certainty that everything going on is either in the process of clearing something out or inviting something new to come to be. All we are doing is creating space for magical possibilities that love empty space and are drawn to it.

the road. Within moments, an emergency medical intern just happened by and went into action. My unconsciousness son was airlifted to a trauma center where miraculously he survived. He was bruised, stitched up and in shock, while contemplating his life. There was no rational reason why he and his friends should all be alive after an accident like this, as the car was flattened like a stepped on can. My son didn't want to go on this trip in the first place, but went because he'd committed to his friend. He thought the accident happened was because he wasn't listening, but greater than any reasoning he could come up with was the wisdom that he now understood his existence was a total miracle.

At times when we don't know what's going on or why, it's because we're on a journey to retrieve a part of ourselves we sincerely needed to continue on with. I'm sure that before we were born, when we were out in the ethers, we weren't in self-help therapy trying to figure things out, we were just *being!* The trick is that we now have to stop trying to figure things out and instead allow our primordial intelligence to surface. The enlightened sage within knows they are one with everything. They know there is no reason to define the why of things, as wisdom will break down reasoning to reveal the things reasoning could never fathom. Wise sagacity is the adroit wizard who leaps into the beyond to grab a flower from another dimension and deliver it to us with a new story of love. We might not see the actual flower, but the fragrance somehow permeates our reality and on some level we know that we've been blessed by possibility.

Abracadabra Rx: Retrieve Yourself. Suddenly we're not complete, we feel out of sorts, something's not right, we're lost. What's going on is that a part of us has jumped ship and we must retrieve ourselves. It's time to track our missing essence so we sit in parks, browse bookstores, walk through forests, and lay on beaches communing for our spirit to come back. When we realize that we've been holding up a cracking façade, we get that our falling apart is necessary for our full recovery. In the process of our rehab, we come into our Holy Land where our Great Spirit hangs out and tells us that our spark was never lost, we just misplaced the state where it existed. So we return to our native soil and take care of our inner lotus. We become the shaman who coerces our lost spirit back home.

Shamans believe that when a piece of soul energy has gone, an animal spirit accompanies it. So they contact the animal to retrieve its spirit medicine first, this is then translated to the soul of the being that's lost, so their animal can bring them home. When our passion is gone we become chronically tired or depressed because we're incomplete. It happens when we have not honored ourselves, maybe sold out, not been in our truth, or have an issue that we've ignored for too long. At these times, our spirit will go to hang out with our ancestors or guardian angels to retrieve the energy, the wisdom, and the sacred medicine what we need to carry on with.

Other times it might feel like we've been affected by dark

energy that was not ours. You notice this when people do awful things and it seems as if they're possessed. Our journey out into the wilderness to retrieve ourselves is the most powerful endeavor we ever take and the one where we battle dark forces that drag us down or capture us in addictions. Sometimes these dark forces tear openings in our auric fields and alter our frequency. In the case of getting drunk, its the perfect time for a dark force to arrive and coerce us to do things we will be sorry for later, as we're left thinking I can't believe I did that! Our guard came down while we were under a chemical influence, which altered our brainwaves enough for us to be influenced.

It's poison when we're doggedly swayed by opinions, failures, jealousy, pressure and downright deceptions; these aspects throw us off our center. People are always warning us to be careful, while our fears are screeching, *"Watch out!"* Our unprocessed grief and depressions alter us and in a weakened state we can't see clearly, but we're blindly called into our temple to feel our way back around to our true self. We must call out what's missing, what's too distraught to function, and target love where there's no love. Our call for amnesty is how we show up for ourselves. The love and the goodness is sometimes forgotten but never lost, it will always rise up once again when truth clears the horizon. So during our hard times, we might go down but it's only to retrieve ourselves, as we only leave to come back.

The soul retrieval topic is a book in itself. I suggest reading Soul Retrieval by Sandra Ingerman. Our souls are the holders of our remedies and one moment of true harmony with ourselves, pulls us back together, it shifts the distorted paradigm and clears our vision. On the days we have to be shamans, we will go into our wilderness and ask the advice of our spirit. I always ask for instructions on how to captivate my psyche back to paradise. All we are doing is dropping what does not belong to us, maybe standing for a while with nothing, as we toss ideas around with the counsel of who we are behind the scenes.

Abracadabra Rx: Dive Into Love. Love is our legacy, as an essence of love once felt may change form but will never expire. A friend who lost her husband of thirty years told me that after he passed she felt him in the air, in her breath, in her cells, in the trees, just all around her. She said she felt so close to him that the loss of his physical being pushed her so deeply into her heart that she found him again. Could this be enough? My friend sincerely grieved this loss, but the residue of this love carried her. In the sacred place where all realities merge, there is a light-filled dimension where we are not stuck thinking we're just a physical being with a name and a story attached to it. It's a place where the parameters of our minds bypass everything to get to the source where we're not separate from the heart and still love across dimensions.

As a child I was always lost in daydreams; one moment I was sitting on a kitchen stool and then like liquid I would melt into a daydream and be gone. There was a feeling of supreme satisfaction and bliss as reality dissolved. Nothing recognizable was left. I was so gone that not even the version of me that I knew still existed. The bizarre part was that I felt a sublime level of comfort that felt totally familiar. I didn't know where I was because there was no was. It was just an experience of presence that expanded to the point where the concept of who I was did not matter. Upon returning to the kitchen I knew I'd gone somewhere magical. It was a journey where my personal identity surrendered itself into my spirit and there was a self-realization that substance doesn't need to exist to be felt, it just is. These encounters are where one is able to disconnect from where they are in the earthy realm and tap into the spirit of beauty, passion and creativeness. As the mind steps aside, suddenly there's an opening for admittance into a state of divinity and blink there we are right in the center of our universe. We come away from these experiences knowing that we've touched upon what is sacred and embedded with love.

A lack of love is love calling out to itself to come home. We are surrounded by loveless-ness when people act insane, when we lose ourselves, and in the times that anger overrides understanding. When we pull love into our experience all reasoning shifts, as love is the only reason. I practice shifting into love in the most forlorn moments to obliterate what feels awful. Love is an escape hatch that grabs back more love. So even when people are hurtful, maybe I do wish I could push them off a cliff and then I bite the bullet and pull up love. I do it because I love myself too much to be toxic and love leaves no room for anything else.

Abracadabra Rx: Adjust The Medium. In the same way that a data processor opens numerous windows, we too have access into infinite mediums. If we send our consciousness towards an idea, when the resonation is a match it captures the idea. And so by juggling the dichotomies of reality, we toss around the ideas that serve us and toss out the ones that don't. We must adjust the medium around us instead of adjusting to whatever is running and letting it control us. So when I'm sitting in an airport waiting area surrounded by edgy people, I'm blessing them. In the fact that I'm about to get into a metal tube with wings and fly across the land together with these strangers, I want the energy to be positive and so I have to adjust my frequency to adjust the medium around me.

A friend with issues around believing in himself always validates his actions. I always tell him it does not make a stick of difference who believes in us as we face the last mirror before the exit door. In the same way that we adjust into a yoga posture, we must adjust all the disagreements in our minds and come to the place where we agree to even just disagree. Therefore we don't empower anger over differences of opinion, we stop defending things and heal our psychic splits by adjusting our medium. We can't keep fighting the ways of the world, instead be like the moving crew and move the furniture around for a better view of the possibility vista.

I was working to sell the house of a person who was paranoid and twisted every interaction around into insanity.

I decided to use dealing with him as a practice to let him be crazy and adjust my medium. Relationships like this are like kids playing in the sandbox, one makes up a game and the other agrees to play it. I quit his crazy game and in order to reach me, he had to tune into my channel. The big secret on clearing bad energy is to insert a better story into it. And after you un-believe whatever clogged your wheel, then send some love in to lubricate the axis and you're done. It could be this simple if we have the mastery to change channels often, tune into higher aspects and make-up better stories.

Abracadabra Rx: Use Fear As An Ally. A friend, who is a Stephen King fan, reads the scariest books she can find. She loves fear because she has a lot of it. When these stories scare her to the bones she finds herself overcoming fear in a reality that's not hers, which helps her overcome her own. We can use fear like my friend who used it to overcome it. Fear can be an ally that arrives to tell us where a weakness is, where trust needs to be and where faith is not. So we must speak up and show up for ourselves and if this means get real, get honest and strip-search ourselves, we must.

In the greater picture when bad things happen and fear arrives, we must see what it's saying. By using fear as an ally, we align with the possibility that everything is not the enemy only the illusion. Sometimes I feel the fear and then wonder if its real, the wonder shifts the fear to possibility. It becomes an ally when we align ourselves more towards the power of the good possibility hiding in fear, than the fear itself.

Abracadabra Rx: Lift Off. My cat sits by the window purring and staring into space. Mesmerized by raindrops running down the pane, she's in bliss. I see the rain and go into what to do about it and how it will affect my day. My kitty reminds me that bliss always exists and I need to see more of it or simply design it into existence. Seeing this is a reminder that it's lift off time. Where am I going? To the most magical place of not sure and from here I'm just letting my mind wander into a poignant resource where possibility has its own ideas that grab me.

Our minds travel and lift off without notice, we might be in a conversation when something catches our attention and suddenly we're gone. It may happen when a person walks by that reminds us of someone and we dissolve into a memory. We hear a song and travel into another time or look at a menu and think of our grandmother. We see a flower and drift into a story, we let go of where we are in the back of a taxicab to dream, or we pick up a musical instrument to play and are whisked away. What's going on is that we are in one place physically, but our spirit has traveled elsewhere taking us along with it.

Remember how as children, we constantly explored other realms and played in dreamlands? We were connected into the ethers while singing and moving blocks around to build a castle because it was natural for us to play with the invisible and invite it over for a tea party. Our discomfort tells us when we're in a homogenous reality that has no depth, so of course we migrate out of our physical realms to meet the conductor who reminds us what orchestra we're playing in. These wordless meetings inspire us and when we return into physical time we're instilled back into our childlike nature that knows magic. Therefore if when I'm laid out with a back spasm and my inner child tells me that a lightning bolt from another dimension has hit my spine and altered me, what's not to say that in some way all the things that happen, alter us. We look for treasures to find that the actual treasure only exists in the way we see it. So when stuck and nothing feels worth it, we have to take every story we're involved in and slam some possibility into it to lift off.

Abracadabra Rx: Spark Ingenuity. I went to pitch for a real estate listing at the last minute when I did not have the information or time to do the research. Noticing the seller had an award for a play he'd produced on Broadway back in the day, I found my ammunition. I had seen this play as a child with my mother and remembered the hit song as my mother often sang it to me. I belted out the song and the homeowner started singing along with me, we harmonized and he gave me the listing. Ingenuity has the talent to brighten up what is dull. It fills in the spaces of lack with what's creative because it stands out and entertains.

Our savoir-faire jazzes up the ordinary, charms up the atmosphere and attracts magic. It's inventiveness that gifts us the insight to turn things around. So when life gets dull go out on a date with yourself, get all dressed up for no reason, plan a dinner party and invite people you don't know, travel alone, take time off and do something radical. Tell people how you really feel or don't tell anyone anything and just profoundly transform. You can then tell them after the fact when they don't recognize you. Ingenuity is an action packed walk on the wild side that says: *"Hello, Possibility, Come In."*

Abracadabra Rx: Untether. Our great spirit will not stand around when we've lost our way. This sprite will set up scenarios that send bullhorn messages to dislodge us. They set off alarms that exclaim: False Path, False Path! The message is to untether, which means: Drop everything and walk away. Another ding-dong awareness is that most of our dysfunction is created by us when we agree to what is un-agreeable. The first rule is to untether from all the lies that we tell ourselves, because in believing things should be a certain way, we're not open to seeing what other ways exist.

At one time, a psychologist I was seeing insisted that I sever my relationship with my mother who was subliminally trying to pass her toxic lunacy down onto me. I untethered from her to realize that behind all the craziness my mom was offering there was still love. So I re-tethered to just the love. It's like sorting the rocks from the beans, we have to decide where the value is in things and throw out the rest. We all know the person who complains over and over about the same old thing and does nothing about it. Another friend can't stop decorating their apartment because they're not comfortable. Comfort likes to play hide and seek with us because it always needs something else to be Ok. How about untethering from even being Ok? And just be.

Possibility reins when we take matters into our own hands, like maybe we did not get the literary agent we hoped for so instead we self-publish our books. It's radical to be creative, to have mental agility around our inabilities and walk the freedom road anyway. I consider the lessons of untethering from dysfunction as a reminder that I am here in the name of magic and my struggles have avenues that lead me there. Did I make that up? Hell Yes!

Abracadabra Rx: Deprogram. The statement: *Be in the world but not of it,* is speaking about not conforming to the patterns that exist. By honoring the sacred order of our natural un-manipulated mind, we're so solidly our own color that we're pulled into the rainbow. When we hold our own, we no longer believe what we're told. Instead we believe in possibility and two options are: A) If it doesn't spark don't touch it or: B) Play with it and spark it yourself.

In a child's mind dirt is exquisite, a rock is to throw or climb, a wave is to dive into, and the edge is to leap off of. And then someone with fake power comes along and says, *"Don't play with dirt, don't throw rocks, and stay away from the edge."* If we're smart, we continue exploring these things because we know it's way more dangerous not to.

The group consensus as a whole believes many things that are not proven as fact, but are agreed upon by the masses because it's convenient. We once believed the world was flat until someone had the courage to sail out to the edge and proved it to be round. Un-believing whatever is constricting doesn't mean there won't be discomfort. There is hellish discomfort when we are breaking down lies and pulling our energy out of them. This kind of discomfort is the messenger of growing pains that tells us to stop fixing what's broken and focus on what works. Though when anxiety and fear are trying to squeeze our feet into shoes we've grown out of, this is the valid discomfort that tells us to order the next size up. I have walked out of meetings, hung up the phone, and knew that when things were not going anywhere good—that I had to.

In a winter dark night of the soul that lasted for months on end, I was snowed in often so I delved into the quiet and wrote everyday. I read books, cleaned, danced to loud music and faced things in myself that needed to blossom. I then began to feel like a recluse; restaurants were too noisy, my favorite pastime of shopping was overwhelming and traveling was too exhausting. I went on a vegan cleanse and stayed put in my peaceful abode. This was not my normal pattern whatsoever, as every Winter I traveled, I went out often and enjoyed dinners with friends and now I was having none of that. And then the crazy thoughts arrived to tell me I was not Ok. I argued that monks go into caves, holy men took forty days in the desert and I am just taking a winter in my house on Long Island. I then asked my son if I had lost it and he said: "Mom, I wish I could do what you're doing."

In that moment I knew that I was in the place to see lit

stars in my dark night sky and deprogram my crazy thoughts. Deprogramming is about doing what we feel is right, what's needed and having no regrets, as regret is a lesson unlearned. So instead of continuing to focus on what's wrong, look to see what you can take from it. Make sure to take at least one good insight away and then reprogram your thinking from: This is not right to . . . I Now Attract What Is Right!

Abracadabra Rx: Make An Offering. Every thought is an offering to our being, every breath is an offering to our body, and every action is an offering to our life. Things resonate in a magnetic way to each other, so as the craziness in the world is out there trying to find its magnetic counterpart, the goal is: Do not be part of the craziness! On a day I was stuck in a shopping center traffic jam, the reactions were insane. One woman with a child in the car was spewing curse words out her window and alternatively yelling: *"I can't take this!"* Our eyes met and I told her she could take it if she thought of it as a game. She smiled and continued cursing. Another fellow whose car was blocked, angrily yelled for her to move up a few inches, she gave him the finger.

I interrupted and asked her politely, *"Excuse me but can you please move so I can go?"* She looked at me and said, *"If it helps you, sure."* Off I went to realize the reason she moved for me was because I was offering to help her to calm down, so I got released. Our peace offering around chaos is the gift that says: *"I understand you are not in balance, but I am, so walk with me."* As we practice the art of not reacting, we consider our every mood as an offering. We've all heard the statement, "You have to give to get." When we feel other people and situations are taking too much, then our giving quota is off kilter. We have to put the oxygen mask on first before we can help the person next to us.

A certain person was acting like a vampire and I wondered what I could ever give them that would make a difference. I then realized I could give them the space to just be that way and in doing so, it was no longer any of my business and I could be free of their dynamic. Sometimes the offering is to let things be and just move on to let the universe handle it. The question then becomes what will we offer to be in peace, what will we offer for love and what would we offer to be free? Even though we have no control over the world, our offerings are the divine work we do on ourselves. And on behalf of this planet, no matter what the story is or what looms, our pure vibration is the highest offering.

Abracadabra Rx: Vote Yes On Unlimited Concepts. We never really know what's going on, we only know what we think is going on and it's mostly an analogy we have created in order to be comfortable or make sense out of things. When we let go of defining things, the limitless field of possibility becomes activated. During the times that we think nothing is moving and energy is at a standstill, it's because we aren't focusing on possibility and therefore we miss what's actually happening. An unlimited concept is one body of consciousness that expands into a higher consciousness.

So consider the thought that a drop of water from the ocean is another ocean in itself and then consider that this exact moment in life holds everything.

Imagine if one night we went off in a spaceship to hang out with our real family of light beings. They did energetic surgery on us, cleared the toxicity from our beings, then surrounded us with love and sent us back here. We might become so miserable and heartsick with yearning for this other family that we could no longer function here. So our memory bank got swiped accordingly in order for us to continue to hang around Earth in her times of need and shine our light here, which is basically vital. Could this be true? A concept is an abstraction that once we agree with it, it becomes a reality.

Abracadabra Rx: Remember We're Visitors. As guests in this holy land, we all came bearing gifts, though some of us lost ours along the way. We don't ever actually lose our gifts; we just forget we have them. We've also forgotten that we're visitors here. Our host, the lady of the house is our Earth mother who is our source of life even though she did not birth us. Once we remember that we are in a sacred interval, we find that we have total access to all the energy, healing and love that we were immersed in before we came here. All we need to do is to remind ourselves to use it. Then we are visitors bearing gifts, who are not blinded by any one specific reality, because we alternatively see the absolute scintillating magical reality right inside all of them.

Abracadabra Rx: Hang Out In The Unknown. There is a verse in the *Sanskrit* sacred text of the Guru Gita that says: He who thinks he knows, knows not, and he who knows not knows. When we think we know, we only know what we think. When we're empty we don't need to know, as there is no ego involved. There's no manipulator, no needy one and we are just open. When we create a magical space that is open to wisdom, it will trigger what needs to happen next.

I don't know is a most magical aspect where nothing is defined and everything is open to exploration. My friends had no water on and off in their apartment for weeks. The plumber came everyday, but spoke no English, except for one word: Water. They were experiencing scarcity on many levels at the time and dealing with issues of lack. One day my friend turned the faucet on, there was still no water and he forgot to turn it off and came home to a flood. Life is like the waves that roll in and roll out and when they roll out, we must wait and see what rolls back in. My friend realized the plumber was like Yoda, telling him that water is life and the flood was a message that surplus exists.

Nothing stays the same and the good news is that we're adaptable. We might not feel adaptable because our human nature wants to cling to what it knows. So we freak out, thinking things are falling apart and while we're in a pity puddle on the floor, our spirit is out stalking possibility. The unknown is a gift that drags us off base to disarm what we cling to, because we're going to the next base. A good commandment around this is: *Thou shall not be afraid to travel around in uncharted territory.* So we let the unidentified swirl and ponder what's enticing about it. Once the dust settles, we see that nothing was ever disguised it just wasn't formulated by our minds yet. Most magic is not obvious, so we have to play with it to begin to see it. Possibility springs forth when we let it do its thing.

Abracadabra Rx: Follow Certainty. We are in uncharted territory being asked to have certainty without assurance. Unquestionable certainty goes against the grain; it arrives out of left field and says this is what I believe now. Suddenly we own concepts that were way too farfetched to fathom prior. This kind of certainty comes with a boost validated by the heart, informing us that this is the way we must live now. Our credence shows up when we're no longer resonating passion where we are, so it quickly escorts us out the door. We are then slammed into our own absoluteness, which takes us beyond where we are to the next magical place.

Being in certainty might be shocking, as we find that what might be considered havoc is actually a message that we got what we need and are moving on. A woman I knew had a big blowout wedding. Six months later her dog died and her new husband made a flippant dismissive comment that she should just get a new one. In that distinct moment, she knew her marriage was over. Painful or not, our certainty is an Honest-to-God knowing where we literally come from beyond a doubt, smack into Matter-of-Fact-Ness. What's happened is that what is unquestionable is now a stunning phenomenon that slams into circumstance and literally demolishes it when things have played themselves out. This recent bride saw something in her new husband that she couldn't erase if she wanted to, so she left him. Even though it was painful, her certainty had set the stage for her future quality of life.

Another friend shares she feels lonely and incomplete. Utter loneliness teaches us where our sureness is. How crazy that we might feel broken and incomplete in order to find our certainty. The late spiritual philosopher Krishnamurti said, *"You are fully awake only when you are not trying to escape from the inevitable, which is to be alone. And through the ecstasy of that solitude you will realize the truth."* I think about this often, as I know that my spark was created in my aloneness and this exact bliss is what will be holding me as I transcend this existence. We are always in the process of holding on and letting go at the same time. Sometimes the ground beneath us shakes, so we lose our footing and question faith. When nothing definitive is on our radar, possibility demands that we step out of our own way and hone into what we believe exists beyond what appears. It's a magical moment to put the faith card down, swat away false illusions and be powerful enough to stand in question without questioning and wait for certainty. One thing to know for sure is that we divine our worthiness, we decree our benedictions—our blessings do not come from this reality anyway and nor do we. We come from a place of unlimited possibility that has a profit margin of manna from heaven. Abracadabra That!

Abracadabra Rx Magical Possibility . . .

Rx: *Believe in possibility.*

Rx: *Always Look for where the exception is.*

Rx: *Keep an open perspective.*

Rx: *Get out of the crazy way.*

Rx: *Don't push but feel for your course of action.*

Rx: *Invite what's for your highest good into your sacred space.*

Rx: *Be in the mystery.*

Rx: *Focus beyond to see what else is going on.*

Rx: *Everything is multi-faceted, so look in all directions.*

Rx: *Align into higher consciousness.*

Rx: *Choose to be comfortable in what is unknown.*

Rx: *Remember how to play and be in the folly of things.*

Rx: *Make up your own rules.*

Rx: *Connect to the essence of bliss no matter what is going on.*

Rx: *Allow yourself to not know and hold faith.*

Rx: *Maintain a state of wonder and welcome what creates it.*

Rx: *Divine your reality.*

Rx: *Forget about time—you are not in a tick-tock reality.*

Rx: *Send love to the distorted aspects you see.*

Rx: *Move into effortlessness.*

Rx: *Understand the essence of things beyond the things.*

Rx: *All our old ways no longer work because we advanced.*

Rx: *It things are unfamiliar; there's magic and possibility.*

Rx: *When things are spinning out of control, connect with your inner child. Children love spinning new possibilities.*

Rx: *Deprogram from disbelief.*

Rx: *Always be partly lost in love.*

Rx: *Be the offering you wish to receive energetically.*

Rx: *Spark ingenuity into possibility.*

Rx: *Prosperity is your belief in possibility.*

Rx; *Rearrange things to attract new energy.*

Rx: *Have a conversation with possibility—this energizes it.*

Rx: *Don't get lost in what is.*

Rx: *Don't get lost in what isn't.*

Rx: *Do get lost in moments of bliss, wonder and divinity.*

Rx: *Be open to accepting what you don't understand and look for what brings harmony to it.*

Rx: *When one door closes the universe embraces us—let it.*

Rx: *Delve into the possibility of now—don't question it—delve.*

Rx: *Engage the unexpected, talk to the invisible, reach for the stars and ask for help from other dimensions.*

Rx: *Turn your why not into how and go from there.*

Rx: *Insert a bad story into a bigger better story.*

Rx: *When one thing is not possible another is.*

Rx: *Surrender your set ways to be part of new options.*

Rx: *Imagine what you need and download it into your being.*

Rx: *Unlimited possibility must be called for.*

Rx: *Certainty is truth in action targeting new possibility.*

Rx: *Hold onto possibility like there's no tomorrow, so all that's not possible can't thrive today.*

Rx: *Recognize the road to freedom is not paved with opinions, routines or ego, and is everywhere these things are not.*

Rx: *You are responsible for your experience—make it special!*

3) A Magical Breakthrough . . .

"The only thing worse than being blind is having sight but no vision." —Helen Keller

"You can't make me, you can't make me," screamed the child and her mother thought, "Oh yes I can!" Though when her mother made this statement she knew she could never really make her daughter do things her way for the long haul. While the struggle with her four year old was exhausting, this mother decided to reach beyond ultimatums to ponder how it would be possible to empower her daughter to do what was best for herself. She came up with giving her daughter choices, as our best learning experiences come from our mistakes. The thought alone of wanting to empower her child instead of ruling her neutralized a lifetime's worth of power struggles between mother and daughter. A real teacher shows us where to look and doesn't tell us what to see.

Sitting in meditation in my sacred space, before I even begin to watch my breath, emotions arrive to mess up my entire inner house. Now the doorman, aka my witness, is standing guard at my gate checking cerebral identification tags and scrutinizing all thoughts for their pass to get in. I am so tired of mental *Ashtanga* and wish to have a peaceful *Satsang,* meaning being in the company of the truth with my higher thoughts. Having a calm mind accesses higher thought as it breaks through impatience. Sitting in stillness is a battle that we must breathe peace into until it surrenders.

A friend says she cannot meditate because she's way too agitated. What she is really saying is that she is not prepared to sit with fierce patience. My husband always says patience is power when I get too jittery. He is always looking at the results upfront and knows crazy thinking brings on a crazy outcome. Focusing on prospects brings us to turn a corner towards inevitability. So I sit in meditation with my crazy mind and think about how I will feel when peace descends in twenty minutes and I wait for it.

Since we are persuaded by thoughts and words, scientists have discovered that our DNA, besides being responsible for constructing our body is also used for storing data. It's thought provoking that our DNA is holding our mental reflections in storage and this is why repetitive patterns of self-talk and mood swings are triggered from vague instances that shadow old wounds. Think of it as there is some dank storage bank of old what they did to me crap from way back and someone now says one key thing and the vault from hell opens to blast them. It's time to empty the vaults, as this old programmed DNA is toxic sludge. The witness opens the vault and turns the lights on, as what is seen comes to light.

Another friend said she was processing her emotions and that she felt she should not stuff them away. I personally don't feel a need to entertain all mine, as I know them pretty well by now. When there is something mandatory to deal with, there's no choice, as it's breakthrough time. One moment we're fine and the next minute we can be heard shouting with a bullhorn out the car window. There comes a point after eons of going crazy that we must now know better. On the days when there's no way around a negative attitude, I know a breakthrough is upon me. On wobbly ground I find myself falling apart in the act of coming back together. I then remind myself how sometimes my legs shake uncontrollably in yoga when I'm using muscles I didn't know existed. Once these muscles are strengthened they no longer shake and hold me easily in the new posture. So when I'm unsteady I remind myself that even though I've no idea what's going on or where I'm going, that I'm in a strengthening process because I am preparing to leap.

A quantum leap will many times come as a crisis in the sense that it arrives in order to empower us to pass through the eye of its needle. Meanwhile all day long there are mini crises and we're either breaking through them or having a breakdown with them. The issue is that when we get lost in things, these things become interference. I went to sew on a button but in the search for the sewing kit I ended up cleaning out the entire cupboard. I then noticed the floor was dirty so I started vacuuming it and the button I was going to sew, fell off the counter and got vacuumed up. Now I'd have to go through the dirt bag in the vacuum to find the button—this is getting lost in interference.

Each time we come to the precipice of a major transition, it's always about a magical breakthrough and not so much about the exterior experience. For instance I've come to the end of one way of being and suddenly there's fear. I'm not sure what to do next. The breakthrough is really not about the dilemma, but about once again facing fear. It's as if we're rolling along when fear pops its ugly in head to say: *"Hello Dearie, I'm still here."* Once we can dredge it all up and deal with it, we're done, for now. Then as things blow out of proportion once again, we're back in practice to deal with it again. When we get that fear is never going away and that we have what it takes to work with it, it loses its unnerving power. By seeing our difficulties as an escort into a magical breakthrough rather than crisis, we are aligned with the prospect of magic itself. And as far as the breakthrough goes, our level of comfort resides around how easily we can stretch into the next blink.

Oliver Wendell Holmes, Jr. said: *"A mind that is stretched by a new experience can never go back to its old dimension."* Consider that a human being can mentally change their entire biological system by instilling a positive force into it. So when we're lost in a chaotic world, trying to figure out a way through, our high-minded equitable fortitude is our escort. In the act of breaking through paradigms and coming into enlightenment, we must instill light in and around ourselves. Meanwhile when chaos is having a free-for-all and challenges are banging on the door, it's best to step off to the side and focus on possibility. We decide if we're having a magical breakthrough or not and what aspects have an opening into one. Actually our magical perspective is the avenue to turn right on . . .

The Abracadabra Prescriptions for Magical Breakthroughs:

Abracadabra Rx: Come Around. A tempest rises to disrupt the atmosphere when our emotions explode, while anger acts like a storm, but patience is the eye of the storm. In a heated discussion with my son, every time I raised my voice or got defensive he would say, *"This is not going to get you what you want."* After about the fifth time that he said it, it penetrated. I paused to think about what I wanted and he was right, I just wanted understanding and love. Yelling at him was not bringing it. My ego, acting like a child, stole my control pad and was hitting all the buttons. I grabbed back my self-control and responded from there, the turbulence stopped and he thanked me for coming around.

It's crazy when our mind gets on a high horse and parades down the avenue of I know better. We blare injunctions: like how dare they, I am the mother and you have no right. Next comes the wave of threats: Don't you ever, if you don't do blank I will never do blank for you again, don't ask me for anything, I will cut you off and I'm leaving. Next are the blaring trumpets declaring that we've won this false victory and finally our inner child is walking behind this spectacle crying and waving a white flag. And there we are, the witness in the bleachers deciding what parts of ourselves to embrace. All this to come around to the fact that we created the storm, fanned its flames and now must stand in the rain until it all cools down.

It's called drama with a capital D, which is all about being involved in lunacy and then trying to become the hero that fixes it. Come around from there, is the message. In the ways that a lover will say strong things for our benefit, the higher option does the same and will not act dormant once awakened. It's the voice that's directing our bad traffic and says: "Stop it!" A friend was stuck and rambling in all directions about her back-stories. I couldn't get a direct answer to any question, so I stopped the conversation by asking her if any one of these stories was the one she was living for. This question unglued her and in that moment she saw that those stories were not very important. Our coming around is the blessing we bestow upon ourselves when we stop the games, get our bearings and breakthrough the lies in our minds.

Abracadabra Rx: Change Your Mind—Change The Story. The word crisis drawn out is composed of two Chinese characters being Danger and Opportunity. Though another meaning could be conceived of as coming to a critical point. So we must consider that when everything is falling apart, we're not actually in crisis, but at the crucial juncture of change. How we build on this story will define if there is an opportunity or if we're in danger. Our higher self knows that *kismet* is our back-story even as we go through danger, so the crisis story is mostly opportunity in disguise.

In the way a movie film has millions of images, we also progress through thousands of stills to experience their stories. When you stop the film, the story becomes a still life and it's in this stillness where we can change the story. It's the same with the mind, it goes all over the place trying to discover its own nature and when we meditate the mind will dissolve into the divine self and we are free from stories.

John Henley, a neurologist, says that we only use ten percent of our entire brain. He argues this analogy by stating that one hundred percent of our brain is active over a twenty-four hour period. He describes that in sleep, the frontal cortex is online controlling our higher-level thinking and self-awareness. So while we're sleeping we're actually still specifically awake, because our divine consciousness that's always active in a dream state is chaperoning our mental capacities. Now consider that when we're in the process of transformation there's a part of our consciousness holding court in the part our awareness that is sending messages back. Consider that our normal way of thinking when hooked into abstract conceptualizations moves us to evolve. So when our minds go on tangents, give it a directive that empowers positive thinking, it will naturally latch on.

My mind is a trickster that needs discipline; it hates change and loves to play with crazy stories. At the same time, change wakes us up and pulls our consciousness to the frontlines. Meanwhile depression comes along to shut us down in the name of the protection, which is a total lie and a pitfall. We are depressed when we're not comfortable and since we are mostly not comfortable, then it's the day-to-day living that's wearing us out. So change is as necessary as breath, as it instills a continuation of life. It also holds a huge bank of available energy that we can tap into if we don't shut down. As we stand at the fork in the road without a road map, we can go either way and shift up the story as we go. And it's really not the outer story we're changing—it's our inner story in relation to whatever that outer story is. George Bernard Shaw, the playwright quoted: *"Progress is impossible without change, and those who cannot change their minds cannot change anything."*

Abracadabra Rx: Shift Your Attitude. Consider that when looking for a friend in a crowd, we're scanning the crowd and bypassing everyone who is not them. Shifting our attitude is equivalent to scanning crowds, in the sense that we're scanning our moods to tap into an up-zone, which lights up our DNA and reconditions our brainwaves towards happiness. So in the midst of say an argument, a small voice behind our arguing says: I don't want this! Then there is a pause and right in that pause is a moment of choice, take it.

A woman in my office came over to me at a company party as I was talking to my manager and pushed me. Yes, that is nuts, welcome to real estate behavior that is not even behind the scenes anymore. I had gotten a listing she lost and she was mad. After she pushed me, I tried to talk to her but she was too far-gone. I wanted to push her back but walked away bothered. The weird thing was she kept popping into my mind, like a ghost representing a wave of all things wrong in my life. Bingo! The smoke cleared and I saw that it was not about the angry woman, but was about if I was getting the message. The message was to move away from things that do not serve me in the highest way and if this is not totally possible, then I must serve myself well even in the midst of lowly things. It was as if the universe came and pushed me to shift my attitude. What had to move was my stupidity, which was bothered by her stupidity.

Our human-ness is based on sensitivity, so we must decide which sensation to reside in. In a conversation with my son when he was feeling stuck by exterior circumstances, as he described them every which way from Sunday, there truly did not seem to be an exit door in any of it. Finally when no solution was on the horizon, I asked how he was going to get out of it. He replied, *"I am waiting for the magic to shift it."* Where most mothers would think their child was lazy, I loved that my son believed in magic. He was waiting for the energy to change so he could catch a new frequency. At the end of the conversation he said, *"When you want to see how insignificant problems are, look at the sky at night and you will see the expanse of real magic."*

As an *empath,* being a person who feels everything and is tuned into what is not obvious. On days that I feel a very deep sadness for no known reasons, I vision myself as a processing station where I am clearing energy by feeling it deeply and processing it out. Maybe this is just a good story that my deep feelings are a filter that clear out pathways and atmospheric pressure, but really if this story makes me feel better and validates me to feel uplifted, then good for me. Many of us are called out to feel more than we can handle, it's called giving a damn. So as we slip into dark mindsets and are swirling around in our underworlds, consider that you just came down to do the laundry. I have a friend who sings as she irons, I remember this and use it as an analogy for when I have to iron things out. I consider it as smoothing out the wrinkles in my mind so I can be in peace. The upside of reaching for happiness when all Hell is breaking loose is that at the end of the day it will not be about what happened to us—it will be about what we did with it.

Abracadabra Rx: Be In The Truth Of Your Matter. The mind of an enlightened being bypasses rules for logistics time and reality don't own them. Reality is a form of created substantiality that we believe in and therefore the world is in the mind of the believer, so the beyond only exists when it's explored. In the way that a scientist studies a hypothesis, a scientist and an enlightened being both grapple with the unknown, but the enlightened being is witnessing it and not attached. The scientist will try to prove logistics while the enlightened being explores beyond the realities, as the truth of the matter is not a matter of fact—it's an exploration.

Louise Hay, when she published her first book, *You Can Heal Your Life*, printed five thousand copies. Her mentor said that she would never sell that many books. She has now sold over forty million copies of that exact book. This book was her calling and it shared a new level of healing needed at the time and was well received because people were ready for it. That book changed my life and I still pick it up often for the deeper meanings to healing because it cuts to the truth.

Our turning points are scary as Hell, but they call us into the truth of the matter, which we have to follow instead of the fear. George Bernard Shaw also said: *"You cannot be a hero without being a coward."* This means our cowardice is authentically sincere, but brings our hero out. In the truth of our matter we strip down all that doesn't have the substance of our genuine nitty-gritty. The message is: Don't enmesh with the darkness, just witness it to find the truth of the matter and even while in our underworld, the more alarming the truth is the more ability it has to set us free.

Abracadabra Rx: Be In A Magical Frame Of Reference. While considering what's real or illusion, we can argue that a chair is real and can't fall down the rabbit hole. But how far out there can we go? When things get ugly and I get upset my husband follows me around saying, *"Be like water my friend!"* It's a Bruce Lee quote that goes: *"Empty your mind. Be formless. Shapeless. Like water. You put water in a cup it becomes the cup. You put water in a bottle it becomes the bottle. You put water in a teapot it becomes the teapot. Water can flow or it can crash. Be* *water my friend."* My husband and I play with this concept. We repeat it often and then do a Tai Chi dance in the living room to become happiness. We take the frame of reference that has legs that dance and just dance with it.

I always go to a beach by my house at sunset, as certain places magnetically attract magical moments. One evening, two women trotted by on black and white horses, which was very unusual. The horses reminded me of the Chariot Card in the Tarot deck. The image on the card imparts a driver sitting on a throne as black and white (darkness and light) sphinxes are pulling him. The charioteer is armored with integrity that he uses to rein in the sphinxes. Motivated by faith, the charioteer is in control of his inner battle while traveling through the mysteries of the universe. Across the top of the card in some decks, reads the word **Abracadabra,** which means, hurl your words like a thunderbolt or create as you speak. So with the combination of self-effort and grace the charioteer's journey is ordained for success.

At the time success had evaded me since I was seeing it from a polluted aspect. Our frame of reference goes beyond what's on the table; it gets under the table to be part of its own reality. In my angst over the fact that I could no longer walk with what was not in my heart, I felt like my shoes were too tight. The message was to walk the other way alone and barefoot to call back my empowered self. It's so crazy when we realize that our discomfort also holds the keys to our paradise. My frame of reference came online to tell me to stop giving a damn about how my alternative ways go against the grain, because our magical discoveries always go into wild frontiers. The directive is to take our most magical stand and implement our considerations into the frame of reference where our goods are and claim them from there.

I was purchasing a nail polish in the makeup department of my favorite store. The sales woman saw that my credit card was titled in the Abracadabra name of my LLC. She looked at me and asked, *"Abracadabra! Well how do you motivate when things are horrible and you feel awful?"* I was thinking of my answer when she went on to discuss how Einstein found the eleventh dimension, a field theory of symmetry and relativity and how this pertains to creating magic. It's about layers of dimensions that we can't see, but that we are vibrating with at the speed of light and can affect. She then said, *"You did not answer my question!"* I replied, *"Since you are in the Make-Up department—make it up as you go!"* She laughed, as we agreed we had entered a magical frame of reference in an ordinary dimension that was parallel to the eleventh dimension because we created it.

Abracadabra Rx: Release The Struggle. Struggle is the constant battle for comfort over necessity. We desire instant relief, instant fulfillment and instant enlightenment. No wonder we're tired. Our struggles may be righteous, but the skirmish actually depletes our energy field and wrangles us into victim consciousness. We're working against ourselves when our ego drives us, while our higher consciousness constantly hits the brakes. And in the throes of struggle, our inner child is throwing a tantrum while fear blows shadows into monsters. At this point, the monster captures us and in order to be released, we must call a truce within ourselves to see from a higher perspective where we have guts.

Take my analogy of Fear and Guts; it's a story about two potent dichotomies that have never jived but finally merge. Fear and Guts were walking down the road while Fear kept trying to strangle Guts. Finally Guts turned to Fear and asked why Fear would not just let them be? Fear responded that it was their life's work to stop Guts from being what they were. Guts stopped and thought about it and also believed that it was their life's work to release Fear. They looked clearly at each other and weighed out the options. Should they part ways, ignore each other, talk each other out of it, give in or continue to try to annihilate each other? Finally Guts came to the conclusion that without Fear they would not be Guts so they continued down the road.

Things don't move until we get what we need from them and we can't get anything good if we're busy fighting. At the times I feel stuck by imagining things will never change—they don't. I was in an argument with a business associate over money; he would not budge and was now furious that I asked him to do the right thing. I lost in that combat but when I then apologized to him for even asking and told him he was right that I should not of even asked, the energy shifted and I walked away winning. Being in an amicable energy field of good vibrations is worth more than the loss of money and eventually attracts greater abundant interactions.

Our struggles exist until we let go of them, as when we come through the millstone, we win back our magic.

Abracadabra Rx: Grow Out Of It. What's happening is that we are constantly being brought close to crisis because energy surges are instigating us as if we were in labor to push ourselves into other actualities. These energy surges empower us to grow out of what we struggle with. Physical growing pains happen when new bone is adding onto bone in order to make us taller. As a child, I remember how much it hurt to grow but I grew anyway. Mental growing pains happen when the concepts we expect to support us, don't. This is another painful shock that we must grow through in order to break into the fact that we are responsible to grow out of what we no longer want..

We all have dark stories and have the resilience to grow out of them. Remember that you are as powerful as that one flower that can grow out of a crack in the sidewalk and will push through anything. In fact, we pushed ourselves through a birth canal to get here, so we're certainly not wimps. Many of us were welcomed with a slap on the ass, others swaddled and led to believe that all would always be well, both were wake up calls. The message to rightfully consider is that once we honor that we're always growing, we use what exists to grow through it. Someone I love is stuck and we argue about it. Once I realized his stuck-ness is my gift, as to unstick him I must unstick myself from messing with him. We can't fix another persons story, we can only make it better by being the best version of our own story in their presence.

As a lotus grows out of the mud, it becomes a thing of beauty. We are doing the same by blossoming through the Hell we must go through. An open lotus flower that has blossomed represents enlightenment, so when we're dragged through the mud, we still sprout our magical potential. The point is that we must pull nourishment from all things to renew ourselves. The muddier the water around the lotus, the more beautiful the flower is. Therefore like the lotus growing in mud, our difficulties pull us to the surface of our experiences to unfold into our enlightenment. John Keats, the English romantic poet said, *"What the imagination seizes as beauty must be truth."*

Abracadabra Rx: Deliver Yourself. Difficult times demand that we reinvent ourselves once again, because every stage of our life holds different levels of magic. When there is violence, we hold peace. If we want to be the opposition against darkness then our most important act is to imbibe light. Witnessing the extreme greed and violence at Standing Rock, made me confront where in myself I was ever greedy. Even neediness for love is greed, as we must first deliver what we need for it to come around. So as we become the change we wish to see in the world, we accept that we're living in a world of change and must deliver ourselves well.

In the event that things are now happening that have not happened before, we too must go where we've not been. This means mentally, as we decide we're not having another dose of misery. So we take the time to step away and then deliver ourselves into the magnanimous existence we dream of. The other option is that when we can't change our exact reality, instead we change our outlook. It's annoying when people say, "You chose this or you wouldn't be here." It's annoying because it's true. The antidote to all the ugliness is to birth our own beauty and light in the midst of the conspiracy against it. We must deliver ourselves into our dream. This means don't react and yes we do resist, but only in the way that we are firmly planted in an integral state. And on the days that we're scared as Hell, we still walk out on the stage of our life and play with our creations, our magic and what goodness there is to offer. Reality is our partner and we often have to labor with it to get it to deliver.

Abracadabra Rx: Heal. All things have energy fields that are alive and at this stage we are constantly doing our own healing. Every time we take a leap, like an athlete we have to strengthen ourselves first, which means to heal what is weak. We are surrounded by healing energy and need to go into its frequency and align with it. The first step to healing is to be in the consciousness that it's time to heal. I was exhausted for too long and knew something was off. So I went to my bookshelf, closed my eyes and pulled a book. It happened to be a book on the Bach Flower Remedies. I flipped it open to the remedy of Hornbeam, the flower essence for exhaustion. When we network with our healing consciousness, we tap into the magic of healing and annex our remedies.

I believe that our dogs, cats, and all pets, are healing agents that radiate assistance. All the animals on this planet are doing the same and so are we when we're conscious and remember. Unusual animals always appear at my house. An owl telling me I'm wise, a coyote in a dream showing me where the tricksters are, a crow who is constantly hawking outside my window to tell me about sacred law and what in myself is out of whack. Native Americans honor the crow as the guardian of magic and healing. My magic tells me that to become my healthy self now, I must embrace my healing. The act of loving ourselves and following our passion is a powerful form of medicine.

A woman my husband worked with was diagnosed with stage four lymphatic cancer. Chemotherapy was prescribed and since she still had some energy to be functional, she first wanted to do some things that she had always put off. Her thinking was that when she had less energy she would then succumb to treatment. The one special thing she always wanted to do, but never had time for was to sing. So she signed up for singing lessons and went everyday. As she sang, she had no idea what was going on except that she was feeling more energy after each lesson. So she sang all day long, while in the shower, in the kitchen doing dishes, doing laundry, driving and shopping. She was often seen walking down the street with headphones on belting out songs. Miraculously, her tests showed the cancer diminishing. There was no message to sing to heal cancer; she didn't go into it with any hope of that, as she was just exploring what her heart wanted. She was miraculously diagnosed cancer free without going on any special diet or following any prescription other than her own passion, her cancer healed itself. This is a true story, as my husband was her sound engineer and recorded her album.

In the past, most tribes had a Wise One, a Medicine Man, Jesus, Buddha, or even a grandmother who knew more. In the modern world we have Google to research what is wrong with us. Still, the underlying fact of whom we listen to and what we do around our healing is guided by our intuition, which is connected to who we are in spirit. We must initiate our own healings and magical breakthroughs, as they are ordained to advocate success. We all have a medicine being inside us, known as our Wise One. Sometimes its the brain in our gut that speaks. I am constantly hearing gut instinct directives like don't listen to this advice, look this up, ask this person, or open a random book.

I have walked out of doctor's offices and once a hospital with my two-year-old child when his hip was sore, probably from bouncing off the bed. I was told that he had an infection in his bone and needed a hip replacement. Mind you, a few days later my son was fine and grew up to be a strong fellow with his original hip intact. Another time, when I asked about and said I was worried about what kind of reactions a prescribed medicine had, the doctor fired me. Then there are lifesaving doctors who are so on target they are miracle workers and angels in human form. A medical evaluation can be priceless though we must do what feels right, which means we must heal ourselves in tandem with it. It's mastery to understand the magic of healing and like the Chariot driver ordaining success; we must be part of the healing to heal. Everything that takes us down has access to what can bring us back up. Our problems have solutions and our humanness has a soul that knows how to heal us, even as we take its hand to let go of this life.

Abracadabra Rx: Claim Mastery. Where are we going on our Chariots? Some of us are traveling to the core of our beings and others are playing out the eternal tale of the great never-ending battle. Are you busy slaying the nine-headed demon that just keeps growing new heads? This story is so old it's gothic and running out of wind, which leaves room for the new story. The new story is about how we're way more powerful than any darkness, but to own this new story, we must pull our sword (fear) from the stone (reality) and claim mastery. Mastery is not about perfection or being the best at what we do, or even winning. It's about coming into a state of being at peace with what is and handling it well.

The *Pantanjali Yoga Sutras* describe mastery as it pertains to meditation in the way that you keep bringing the mind back into one-pointed focus. After a while (magnetically) and though no effort of our own, the mind is drawn to its own highest inclination by its own accord and this is considered grace. Being in control of our emotions allows our actions to naturally revolve around ethics and integral considerations. This means not being involved in inferior posturing, arguing, revenge, ill wishes, and the continuance of negative gestures in any way. This tall and powerful order is totally beneficent and has the ability to override all that is beneath it. As my own mind puts me down, I question what team my mind is on and how an ailment can be inside me that isn't for my highest good. I then realize that it's active fear that got in and is jerking me around. I believe everything that shows up has something for us to unfold with. Mindfully, I consider my failures as sacred lessons and that it's between my spirit and myself to master the truth in them.

There is a person in my job who is always opposing my goodness, he twists things around and is immersed in power struggles. If he ever has the opportunity to put me down, he grabs it. It used to bother me and I would argue and try to show him what he was doing. It never worked and I realized it's the nature of money-oriented businesses to have some devils around. I figured I had to master my feelings around this man since everything going on is happening for us to achieve mastery. The lesson was to not be affected by him and it took years since he was such a great devil, but I did it. I taught myself how to dissociate, so every time he pulled a maneuver I dodged it by loving my life and myself so much that anything he did was meaningless and even comical.

We must take our difficult situations and do some fancy footwork around them. A few of the questions I ask in these instances are: Is this person more powerful than I am? Where in this situation does the real power exist? Is the power I'm seeing real? Am I powerless here? If so where does my power exist? I remember that my challenges bring on my magical breakthroughs and I always have a wand.

Our mastery lies in what we try for, how we treat others, what we offer, and how we hold our own in the face of all these challenges. Byron Katie, a teacher who uses perception to pierce through bad stories, said that her most amazing spiritual teacher was depression. She had an enlightened awakening while laid out in a puddle of pain on the floor. True mastery is the art of facing disturbances as we take things apart and use everything we can to get the better of them. So consider pain as the journey not the destiny and know that we are moving through it. Mahatma Gandhi said, *"It's the action, not the fruit of the action, that's important. You have to do the right thing. It may not be in your power, may not be in your time, that there will be any fruit. But that doesn't mean you stop doing the right thing. You may never know what results come from your action. But if you do nothing, there will be no result."*

Abracadabra Rx: Bliss-A-Tate. Bliss is coded into our original DNA and because we are not used to accessing its natural form, we've settled for artificial drabs of it through eating, sexing, drugs, drinking, and escaping into illusions of grandeur. If we can just stop right where we are, we can look around and target bliss, even in the sunlight alone. We did not come here to be Ok in someone else's world or to be good at things we don't care about. We've done that before, so now we get to be the ones to decide how we're going to be, no matter what exists. Since we have the bliss gene, the only reason it's not naturally running rampant is because we haven't allowed it to rightfully do so. Consider this as the time to activate bliss naturally and start recognizing where it exists so we can be in it as often as possible.

We know we can exercise to blow off steam and do yoga to get into harmony, though some of us have exercised our way into pleasure and are bouncing along on endomorphs that are so potent bulls could run on them. We have gotten used to using whatever we can to pump ourselves up while our joy cells are starving. A big spit in the wind moment is to sit and feel bliss for no exterior reason. This pure bliss is medicine that travels our circuitry and flips the switch to on. It's not the reason for bliss, but the bliss itself that is the transformer. So do what brings bliss, like dancing, art, music, creating magic and being in love. Since the joy factor exists in these kinds of things, we have to do more of them to instill it, as once we're infused, bliss sparks bliss into things that don't hold bliss and then there's more bliss.

I am constantly flipping the bliss switch on in the most forlorn moments. Try holding bliss in a traffic jam, in an argument, or in our scariest transition. Bliss is like a helium balloon that lifts us off the downturn. In the same way that we take our vitamins, to take a hit of bliss on the hour is our weight-o-f-the-world reduction plan. This negativity cutback regimen alleviates the heaviness of personal and world events so they don't take us down because we've harmonized higher. Bliss is the end result of everything we will ever strive for anyway and the secret is that we can have it now without striving for it. Just take it!

Abracadabra Rx: Become A Secret Magical Agent. I used to believe that I had to fight for everything because it was me alone, who like Atlas, was carrying my world. So I lived as my own mercenary. I protected myself, went out to hunt for pots of gold and came home exhausted every night. One day I decided that this is not the way I wanted to live, so I defined my new story around: Screw this and don't do it! The garbage in our minds is an active live and direct comedy show, so when we've lost our minds and a rude Queen is shouting: *"Off With Her Head!"* we agree. Yes, off with that crazy head that cares about such crap because it's the perfect time to go sit on a mushroom and grow a new one.

Lets take the ugly realities and color outside the lines to transform them. Lets leave a trail of light behind us as our offerings. As secret magical agents we wave our wands, spark our own goodness and revamp our world with the beauty we uncover in all things. So imagine popping your head out of the rabbit hole and laughing at the absurdity of what bothered you, because you now see what really matters. This is a time to spark our inner flame and define it. This is the perfect time to gather up all that we've gone through, shake out the goodness in it and use it to lift off on. If you believe the universe is conspiring in your favor, this is the moment to launch your dream. So step out of the throes of worry and fear, shake yourself off and start sparking! This is the magical breakthrough we came here for! PS. If you don't believe you are a Secret Magical Agent—Start Believing!

Abracadabra Rx For A Magical Breakthrough . . .

Rx: *Shift inside first and then see what shifts outside.*

Rx: *Leap into the state you wish to empower.*

Rx: *Do not resonate with what doesn't bring inner peace.*

Rx: *Listen to your heart and beat out a dream.*

Rx: *Hold your intention to match the reality you wish for.*

Rx: *Act well when you have to act at all.*

Rx: *Always look for where every rule bends before it breaks.*

Rx: *Look to the future to see if it's worth investing in.*

Rx: *Be aware not wary.*

Rx: *Look for an alternative route–always believe there is one.*

Rx: *Excuse yourself from all that is not sustainable.*

Rx: *Validate your visions.*

Rx: *Don't believe what you hear, believe your heart.*

Rx: *When things seem impossible, check your beliefs.*

Rx: *Target your own happiness.*

Rx: *Pray, meditate, and divine on all that you do.*

Rx: *Don't let your ego define success–let your heart define it.*

Rx: *Be in service to the greater good.*

Rx: *You are not falling apart but back together.*

Rx: *Use your failures as lessons.*

Rx: *Understand everything is a learning experience.*

Rx: *Rely on your imagination to expand all possibilities.*

Rx: *Never go along with anything you don't agree with.*

Rx: *Time is an illusion; we have all the time in the world.*

Rx: *Rewrite your story, add magic and then act as if.*

Rx: *Engage being neutral when things are going crazy.*

Rx: *Implement bliss.*

Rx: *Hold mastery over intolerance.*

Rx: *See everything as teachings and grow through them.*

Rx: *Surrender what is not of the highest good.*

Rx: *If it's not working let it be, something else will come.*

Rx: *Align with what creates peace.*

Rx: *When things don't work out, work something new in.*

Rx: *Believe in yourself and take the magical high road.*

Rx: *Don't get stuck in the struggle.*

Rx: *The only struggle worth it is to strive against struggling.*

Rx: *If it's not magical, make it so.*

Rx: *When life is going wrong, go right through it.*

Rx: *Deliver yourself well.*

Rx: *It might feel like a breakdown—it's still a breakthrough.*

Rx: *If you are lost, meditate your way around.*

Rx: *Surrender often, forgive repeatedly, and love much.*

Rx: *Honor the magic that exists and use it to carry on with.*

Rx: *Realize there are no walls only ideas—crush the bad ones.*

Rx: *Be in the magic you wish to have in the world.*

Rx: *Magic is its own consciousness—imbibe it.*

Rx: *Difficulty is a sign that a breakthrough is upon us.*

Rx: *Every transition has a door to a magical breakthrough.*

Rx: *As a Secret Magical Agents, we revolutionize our world.*

Rx: *The ingredients you throw into your world are offerings to the greater world—so use the best ingredients.*

Rx: *Our only exit is at the entrance of our next breakthrough!*

4) Magical Antidotes . . .

"...when the present stung her, she sought her antidote in the future, which was as sure to hold achievement as the dying flower to hold the fruit when its petals wither." —Elspeth Huxley, *The Flame Trees of Thika: Memories of an African Childhood*

The term antidote is derived from the Greek word, *antididonai,* which means given against. If we impinge one thing into another then the original thing cannot exist as it was. In the same sense in order to access our antidotes we must leave our burden bags at the doorstep to tap into the concept that all is well. All is well is the passcode into the circuitry where the universe matches what is needed. Maybe everything's not really going well, but in order to change the possibility of the immediate reality we must firstly believe that wellness exists. This way the frequency connected to wellness will embrace us. When our state of mind attracts a belief, a higher state of consciousness attracts the benefits.

It's time to drop into seeing things as sacred and honor

what exists, so our giving and receiving quota expands. Consider sending love to people who don't wish us well, like people who are competitive, unconscious, mean and morally selfish. It's a practice to do this as the antidote to not get lost in these lowly aspects. Yes, it's not easy to send love to the enemies we perceive of, but we are doing it for us, not them. The more love we can pull up and send, the more removed we become from any reality other than the one we divine. It's mastery to feel peace in the chaos and to have complete faith in our venerable all-powerful state. Implementing love into our consciousness is the antidote for anxiety, fear, and sadness. So when anger or fear arise, consider it a wave of energy and transpose a light-filled antidote into it.

Consider opening the fortune cookie that says, "*You are now the counter-agent for all the dreck you perceive.*" Once we understand that we are agents of change, we are downloaded with an inherited superpower that holds light for the planet. The days of complaining are over, as we have to look the other way, not in the sense of ignoring reality, but only to pull in a higher frequency in order to elevate ourselves. In this mindset, whatever chaos we encounter has a calling for it to be balanced by its opposite. The universe is a guide and will tell us when to push or to let go. In the same sense, a lack of love tells us where more love is needed.

We become one with the solution when we surrender the problem. It works in the ways that we tap into our gifts and use them as tools to balance energy, to restore harmony, and to heal. I was gyrating to move and change my life because it felt as if I needed a clean slate though there was no other destination calling me. I was told inside that if I continued not being at peace where I was, I would never find it. It was worth it to master my feelings over my despair as it stopped me from moving, the antidote was mastery.

On the days I am caught up and confused, I consider the possibility that this lifetime is the antidote to something that happened before I even arrived here and I came to be part of it. I vision that I've been reincarnated into a continuation of a story I was once a part of that was not finished and it still needs my help. I like to believe in bigger pictures and that when darkness arrives, its not to slam us into oblivion bur to invite the light to come around. Like with homoeopathy, when an energetic dose of poison is given against the miasma that is affecting us, we strengthen and heal. So the hellish, painful and disturbing aspects all hold antidotes to spark us to do something that balances them out.

I consider stars as antidotes, the hurricanes are antidotes, and our ability to shift our perspective to heal is an antidote. Equality, justice and natural goodness within humanity is embedded in and behind the craziness as antidotes. So when life becomes overbearing, step back and observe nature, the stars and converse with spirit. We must do what it takes to heal and find our way back to our power, even when the medicine is harsh. In the fact that we are here, we came for this exact experience. All we need exists, as our antidotes appear when we match their energy field—so be the Antidote!

The Abracadabra Prescriptions For Magical Antidotes:

Abracadabra Rx: Imagine The Antidote. What if you happened to come upon a wall with an opening and a sign on it that said: Enter Vortex? Would you step into it if you knew it was a zone where you could walk into a magical life? Though what if the caveat to enter was that you'd have to leave everything behind? This is what happened when we arrived here to planet earth. We arrived with nothing and then acquired everything we now have. This includes our identity, our personality traits, and our beliefs. Now imagine that you've done it again, dropped everything, arrived naked and are stepping once again into that same vortex at this stage of your life to recreate yourself because this is indeed what's happening.

The web of magic is an ally for us to spin our reality and capture the goodness we thrive on. In the act of creating uplifting realities, we get everywhere we're going by firstly imagining our way. So we spin our webs to connect to the things we love, to find magic in the mystery, and to be part of the solutions needed. In our mastery, when it gets hard, we get softer and instead of fighting, we envision. Can you conceptualize the antidotes? The trick is to first believe that the antidote exists. If we believe that what is most needed exists, then it begins to come into focus and in the next blink, it's here. So believe that antidotes are available and within reach. Most importantly: Act in an antidote state of mind to draw them out.

Abracadabra Rx: Break Restraints. During a time of transition where was I confronted by restrictions, it seemed as if everything was against me. The antidote was to take my foot off base and advance past self-doubt into certainty. This antidote is a leap of faith as we tiptoe past the gatekeeper of what's expected. The same old thing is an addiction where there's a psychological pattern in the place that the broken record gets stuck. When you notice the pattern, then dare to surrender the way it has always been. I told someone the truth about a way I felt about our relationship and they thanked me for ruining their day because they were not available to go to the edge with me. When others won't leap into an understanding with us, we must surrender the way things have always been so we may be with what is new.

It's uncomfortable at first especially for the meek when they need to find their voice, or the bully when there is no one left to push around. And as we step out of these personas of the victim, the rejected one, the lost soul or the unloved then we're dropping character references and getting real. An unfeigned way of being gives us elbowroom away from dispositions, attitudes, and ego. It's like dropping a bathrobe to the floor and stepping into the shower to wash off. The things we release are the things that release us, so as we step out without inferences, we know that comfort is not the priority; freedom is. And as we look back, we find that comfort was the restraint we broke in the name of being liberated from restrictions.

Abracadabra Rx: Subscribe To What Upholds You. A problem is nothing more than a puzzle where we keep playing with the pieces until something fits. If you were one of those children who flung puzzles across the room, or ate the pieces, then we can assume problems might be an issue. I myself just wanted to escape what was puzzling. I was more into Crayons anyway; so I could draw my way out of reality. The reality I was slipping past were all the lies that didn't uphold me. The reality that has always upheld me is my sense of self that is constantly pulling me into its embrace. Once upheld, it's as if I am lost in the magic that makes my problems less important.

Swami Muktananda taught that whatever the mind dwells on, it becomes identified with and takes on its very nature. So when we are down in the pit slithering around with the snakes we become one of the snakes. When we are entangled with the liars, even just by arguing with them, we are caught in the lie. When we argue with the unconscious mind, we merge with it energetically. Whatever revolves around us is like the carnival man teasing us that one throw of the ball will get us the prize. A switch-a-roo back into the true ideology we subscribe to is the antidote that upholds us.

Abracadabra Rx: Shake It Up. Consider that inside our beings, we have gridlines with avenues that run along our nervous systems processing things in and releasing what we no longer need. The same thing is happening around the world, as huge scenarios are in flux and are now being refined. Handling the conversion pertains to what we can bring into play during the shake up. It takes a sage mind to process the truth and then attract the magic to shift it when necessary. So when the world is shaking, it's a message for us to shake up what's inside us in order to cleanse. What's shaking is our emotions are being stirred up, so our reactions and anger are quaking for us to dislodge them. The things that falter and fall away are unstable anyway.

Our relationships are often rattled to take us deeper into ourselves or to even let them go. An argument ensued with a close friend and we both demanded an understanding from each other. It quickly became apparent that in order to receive an understanding, we had to offer it. An offering of kindness and compromise is our walk down the freedom road out of pain. So we hand money to a homeless person, listen to an elder tell us the same old story and validate that we hear them. We rescue an animal, or let someone off the hook because we want them to feel good. And in the bigger picture we protest, we hold peace in the name of love, we don't let our fear boss us around and we don't compromise as a concession. Instead we focus on the happy medium and we shake things loose to get there.

Abracadabra Rx: Adjust The Pattern. A pattern ruining one of my most important relationships put me on alert. I thought I had broken this pattern by acting a different way. It was about turbulence going on in a sacred relationship. I had to give up trying to be right and invest in not reacting to get to the deeper crux of the matter. I began to observe the situation and it revealed the revolutionary truth that love needs respect. As soon as I got this, it was as if the disruption was created by some other entity that just packed up and left. I even looked for them because it was hard to believe this feud was over. It was.

Beyond arguments and patterns is the calling to create a new conversation. The truth is that while arguing, we are fighting with ourselves and acting out by getting lost in plain sight of our objective. The antidote to craziness, to heartbreak, to being stuck, and being close-minded is to observe the mind behind our mind, so we can be with who we are beyond the beyond. Once we step far enough away from who we think we are, we get a clear view of the bigger picture and see the patterns as lassos that are holding our wildness in check. Our wildness should not be detained, only the patterns that sabotage it should be impounded.

I love to curse, the rush of the expletive, the powerful damnation of swear words, but when my son was born I put it in check, as I was being the good mother. One day driving with my two-year son in his car seat, I screamed, "Asshole" out the car window at someone. For twenty minutes my two-year old son parroted this word because it wasn't the word, but the energy behind it that was interesting. As time passed I realized that I could express myself poignantly without cursing but once in a while my vulgarity comes out to play and there I am cursing like a truck driver. In this day and age curse words have way less power and are just expressions, but when every other word is a four letter variation it gets boring and is a pattern of cursing and not conversing that's Fk'd!

Patterns have directives and destinations, so if the pattern isn't going our way, we must adjust the patterns. Consider our digestive system, it functions like clockwork though when we mess with its natural setup it goes berserk. So as the planet spins one way, we too are geared to spin in our highest way aligned with our centrifugal force. When this is not happening, we are in the wrong template. For instance, we are stressed and what causes it is a pattern that is going the wrong way. We are magnetically reversed and many times we keep trying to fix things when we need to reset. Adjusting our pattern is the counteragent to finding the antidote that accelerates our motives. Every arrangement has a pattern, a quantum field and a magnetic draw that fuels it. The trick is to match up our true essence with the reality we seek; this implants an impression into the desired characteristic. We are then matched and adjusted to a new pattern.

Abracadabra Rx: Be Still. In the midst of turbulence, standing still is the hardest practice. My Yoga teacher, Rodney Yee, describes *Tadasana*, also known as Mountain Pose, as the activity of always coming back into balance. Rodney says that ever since we first stood up, we have always been in the process of falling and catching ourselves. Mountain pose is mostly a state of mind because beyond the physical strength of standing up, it takes mental strength to be still. When one stands in relaxed power everything aligns because alignment is not stiff, but is like a tree that moves in the wind. Stillness really isn't still but has an ability to flow. It's a weird concept, but the sense of stillness opens into an infinite expansive phenomenon that holds marvels. So on the one hand we're still and on the other we're able to travel the cosmos.

Interestingly, the eye of the storm holds stillness while everything around it is affected. Now consider that as the earth is spinning on its axis, a mountain that is solidly still is at the same time in motion. So while the earth is spinning, we can sit in stillness and feel the vibration of its spinning. It's also a most crazy concept that we're hanging out on a oscillating planet and because of gravity we are not physically flying off into outer space, though we can mentally traverse it while sitting still. If we can pull into the center of our storms then they're no longer our storms, they're vortexes that hold treasures. So since this existence is a wild ride, our retreat into stillness is where we are free to hang out in our magic.

In stillness, holding one-pointedness is the antidote as the universe rotates around us. Maybe being the center of our universe is an illusion, which others declare as a self-centered derogatory way of being. Screw that. We're bringing illusions into focus and dispelling them. Never the less, we can still personally offer our state of peace towards wars, pollution, other people's hatred, political insanity and heartbreak. By being centered in the self we can change how we personally move with these idioms and root into what matters most. In the face of all the craziness we're confronted with there may be times that we will stand in the warrior pose and call to the Gods for strength. At other times we will stand strong to let the winds of change do what's needed.

Abracadabra Rx: Be A Light-Filled Source. A feeling of gloom encapsulated me in a fog of hopelessness that I was having trouble shaking off. I had a dream around this time in which I received a bulletin in a dream email stating Exclusive Report: *Mirror The Sky.* This was nuts and a hard one to figure out. I contemplated on how the sky is moody and shifts from clear to cloudy often like me. The clouds also block the light and reflect the water, but the true essence of the sky is that it is neutral and only changes based on the weather it's reflecting. Also beyond the sky is the unlimited field of the cosmos. While trying to analyze this dream, I realized that since I was feeling gloom I was reflecting mood-clouds, which were blocking goodness. The message was stop clouding the light.

Our spirit of undomesticated truth will always come forth swinging its magical lasso to pull us into a hub of ideas that show us which way to go when the going gets rough. This resonant guide speaks to us in pictures, in stories, in dreams, feelings and through others. The advisory in my strange sky dream was to invite a light filled source in and let it roam free. We don't need to know exactly what this illuminated mystery is doing, its reasoning or what's down the line, as the bulletin is enough. When we can get beyond the mind, one word is enough to shift us—mine is trust.

Another message I received around trust was that it was time to pull the chance card on acting as if the goodness I desired was mine to be had. At the same time, one morning I read about a woman who shared with her therapist about her fear of becoming homeless. The therapist went silent for a few minutes and finally said, "Oh, what a great adventure that could be." The woman then imagined the scenario she was terrified of and saw where there could be an adventure in it and burst out laughing at the madness of that. In that moment her fear of becoming homeless was dispelled.

Reading about it and having a touch of that kind of fear myself, I too imagined myself as a homeless woman. I saw myself in front of a department store on Fifth Avenue in an outrageous outfit with a band of pets, giving a speech on my deepest truths. Then the vision flipped and I saw myself with Oprah, it flipped again to seeing myself living in a penthouse overlooking Central Park. I too laughed over this fear that had legs, which ran into an elevator that went straight up to the penthouse. How we shift our reality is by delving into it head-on to perceive all its possibilities and then envision it another way. Like Dr. Seuss says, *"I like nonsense, it wakes up the brain cells. Fantasy is a necessary ingredient in living; it's a way of looking at life through the wrong end of a telescope. Which is what I do, and that enables you to laugh at life's realities."* And as far as being a light-filled source, it's a concept of say-so, so when we are being rejected, to alternatively see it as being protected takes our misgiving off the table.

Abracadabra Rx: Shield. I had a client, who the minute I saw his name on my phone, I wanted to hide. He would just talk incessantly and energetically suck on my life force. I then would have to repeat myself over and over as he pretended he did not understand what I was saying. All the while he was talking away to keep me on the phone so he could drain my energy—he was an energetic vampire.

The Vampire theme is about the archetype of thievery, the living dead who walk around like zombies, the needy types who are never okay, the parent who thinks their child was born to worship them for life, the friends who always take and never give back. It's an energetic disease that feeds on other people's life force and is a viral dynamic that exists because some people are so weak-minded that they have zero vitality in their energetic bank account. If you feel totally drained after a conversation with someone, you were since they fed on your joie de vivre.

Vampire types are always pilfering because they are never satiated. I once found myself in a sneaky dynamic with a certain psychic who was always telling me incredible news. She was like a drug dealer, first telling me about all the good that was arriving and then when I reached for more, the information got darkly opinionated and poisonous. What this psychic was offering was a total trap, a set up to make her clients believe they needed her in order to be Ok. This psychic was a total manipulator who beguiled people to be indebted to her so she could live off them. By getting down to the truth of this bogusness, we realize we have our own in-house consults, so why talk to a stranger when we can go into a light-field where our spirit tribe of wise ones, our ancestors and the Universe is holding all the wisdom needed with no payback necessary.

Vampires are prevalent these days; I bumped into one walking through the health food store. She said she could see that I was not in my body and that I needed an immediate session with her to restore myself. I felt perfectly in my body and recognizing vampire activity, I let her know that I was fine and I quickly turned down another aisle. These types of users don't want us to be fine so they can fix us. A real healer knows that in order to heal, their patient must believe and also participate in their own healing. The patient must not believe there's something wrong with them and that they need this healer to fix it. Real healers have healed themselves and assist their patients to also heal themselves.

In the process of shielding ourselves, we step aside from vampires and clear the energy around us and then like the snake, we quietly move around the obstacle. In the way that a tattoo is permanent, we can install an everlasting shield around us. Granted, the shield is made out of beliefs but isn't everything? So when a storm is raging, we have a psychic umbrella and we start whistling as we walk through it. The antidote is to go to our real source of energy and bathe in it. I take salt baths to cleanse my energy fields, I mentally stand under waterfalls of light to remove negativities and also surround myself, my house, people I love, and my pets, with an etheric shield. It's a silver wall or bubble that like a mirror reflects back dark energy but allows in light.

So throw up a shield in the midst of an antagonistic conversation, place a pyramid around yourself, especially in crowds. I always put a silver pyramid around my house and over my bed before I go to sleep. I shield myself on my yoga mat, as others process out their stuff while doing yoga. The intention is everything; therefore state that only good motives may pass your shield so you are not be totally closed off. At times we have to cleanse toxic encounters, thoughts and beliefs, and then block them by re-shielding. Ultimately, holding a light filled state is the most potent natural shield. When we can get ourselves into a hub of goodness, we're on auto-shield. Shielding is not about a lack of trust, it's about taking care of ourselves, like in the saying: *Trust God but tie your camel to a tree.*

Abracadabra Rx: Attract Goodness. Sometimes we don't always get the good seat in the movie or the best table at the restaurant and we have to decide if we are leaving or staying. When we get handed less than we expect, then our mastery is about graciously letting it go and walking away. We no longer make scenes, but make it our responsibility to handle things well. So we don't take revenge or spew animosity but sidestep in a most charming way to be on the wavelength where we are immersed in our goodness to attract more of it.

A client whose house I had an offer on lied to me. He said he needed to speak with his father who was traveling and would be back in a week, so he could not respond till then. I saw his father that night at a restaurant. Instead of confronting my seller, I decided that I would no longer do business with him. I saw his lie as my liberating walk away from his reality. Dishonesty attracts craziness and it's better to move onto something better—my buyers agreed.

Our new energetic Jujitsu is to not get involved with the erratic flotsam that hangs around or floats by. At the same time we also don't support the things we don't believe in and so we stop getting entangled with what we cannot thrive on. Granted, we can't change the past, but we can play with the present and this changes our future. If our past has been turbulent and the now is uncomfortable, then life is telling us it's time to attract the goodness we need to move into our future with. We attract what we resonate with and in the fact that everything is energy, we vibrate best in the energy field that shines for us.

In the words of Ralph Waldo Emerson, *"Once you make a decision the universe conspires to make it happen."* It's time to have faith that we deserve to attract goodness. Marianne Williamson says, *"Faith is not blind, it's visionary."* As visionaries we must invest in the bigger greater good and constantly must ask for guidance on it. *"Dear God, Universe, Higher Self: Let me become your vessel for goodness. Please give me the knowledge for healing; give me the perception to receive divine antidotes. Let me be an antidote of goodness and grace in this world."* The consciousness of this, *"Let Me"* request is the dynamic of the word Abracadabra. The word is a command to open the door so we may gain access to grace. Let me live in service to the highest cause of magic is the key to the door.

Rx: Be The Antidote. Aside from looking at things analytically, every situation will blatantly tell us what it needs and we need to be awake to see it. If something is not working for us it's because it's working itself out, as in out of our lives. Once we are detached we will find the necessary amenity, it's always obvious, but we need to let go of the attachment to see it. Our antidote could be as simple as taking a nap when exhausted or as complex as packing up and leaving. In a moment of anxiousness, I asked for an antidote. A minute later, on Facebook, I saw a post about how our fingers are energy fields and the thumb represents anxiety. It said grab your thumb with your fist and hold it tight for two minutes. This worked. We have to ask for the wisdom to receive the antidote that makes a difference.

We are all gifted and need to own it. Think about your true purpose and if you're honoring it. A fashion model in her late twenties was not being treated well in the industry. Ridiculous that at twenty-eight she was considered old and this is the role model for beauty? She felt berated and said she would feel more self worth being a waitress. The antidote for her was to not rely on her beauty alone because she had so much more to offer. I quit being a hair and makeup artist was because the message the beauty industry was selling did not honor woman of all ages. I see beauty in all beings and more so in elders who have ripened. Sometimes all we have to offer is what lights us up to be the change we wish to see. I constantly say, *"I am love, I am light, I am a Godsend, my energy is the antidote."* and it becomes so—therefore I Am.

Abracadabra Rx to Magically Antidote . . .

Rx: *Look for what is right as opposed to what is wrong.*

Rx: *Do not get entangled in what depletes your life force.*

Rx: *Be clear of aggressive interactions—hold your own peace.*

Rx: *Instill good expectations into unnecessary suffering.*

Rx: *Surrender what is not important and do what is.*

Rx: *Clear your channels every day—send light through them.*

Rx: *See yourself in the best story no matter what appears to be.*

Rx: *When you don't know what to do—do nothing.*

Rx: *Work with your imagination to balance discomfort.*

Rx: *Shield yourself.*

Rx: *Be still and wild at the same time.*

Rx: *Look for where there is an option for freedom.*

Rx: *Don't travel into your future unless you are bringing gifts.*

Rx: *Look for the best and when you can't find it make it up.*

Rx: *Maintain a constant conversation with your highest self.*

Rx: *Neutralize.*

Rx: *Release negative reactions and be positive.*

Rx: *Never tell a poor-me story.*

Rx: *Counter fear with courage and anxiety with trust.*

Rx: *Counter hate with love and animosity with peace.*

Rx: *Empower your truth and drop the rest.*

Rx: *Imagine the antidote and use it.*

Rx: *Be still and then move the energy.*

Rx: *Understand that nothing is as real as it appears.*

Rx: *Poison is a concept we agree to—don't agree to it.*

Rx: *Don't get caught in the web, instead create your own web.*

Rx: *Attract goodness and then empower your story with it.*

Rx: *Be responsible to create and find magical antidotes.*

Rx: *Enjoy what is good and don't get caught up in otherwise.*

Rx: *When asking for help, always make an offering.*

Rx: *Bring kindness to what is angry and turn it around.*

Rx: *Be in service to healing.*

Rx: *Maintain serenity.*

Rx: *When the mind is having a fit—meditate.*

Rx: *Be the good you wish to see in the world.*

Rx: *Go into your inner sanctum and ask for wisdom.*

Rx: *Request for the antidote to show itself.*

Rx: *Imagination is a pharmacy that delivers.*

Rx: *You can make a difference by being different.*

Rx: *Antidotes do grow on trees, even imaginary ones.*

Rx: *Ponder; dream, and divine remedies, and they will come.*

Rx: *Don't give up or give up or give in. Just give yourself what you need. You know what it is.*

Rx: *Breathe out anxiety and breathe in faith.*

Rx: *The directions and answers do not always come from this physical dimension—reach for the stars.*

Rx: *Find the gift in yourself.*

Rx: *Be in the state you hold as blessed—so you're blessed.*

Rx: *Experiment with your ideas; good energy antidotes bad.*

Rx: *There will be many days where you will be called to be the antidote most needed—so be the antidote.*

5) Survive & Thrive . . .

"Life is thickly sown with thorns, and I know no other remedy than to pass quickly through them. The longer we dwell on our misfortunes, the greater is their power to harm us." —Voltaire

Hitting the bottom guides us to know that we have reached the bitter end of all we can endure. When we can't bear to carry on and life seems hopeless, we feel we're beyond recall. Our grief is too much to handle and we believe we will never recover, but the truth is we are still passing through. Bottoms are tricky; they bring us to suppose that there is nothing left to hold onto, that there is no return, our happiness is forever over and so we give up. It's a state of confusion not certainty, because we can still turn on the lights in the underworld. I did it by internally screaming non-stop and demanding that if there ever there was a God or a God force, it better show up to come help me—and it did.

Down in the underworld, way in the background, we hear an odd voice that urges endurance. Hope takes the role of a trickster that says *"Don't you want to see what is at the end of this dark tunnel?"* Curiosity will always buy us some time, for if we detach from our pain for even a minute, just to see where our curiosity is going, we get distracted. What's happening now is that the universe is banging on the door of our minds to grab us out of the dark. Our struggles in the dark are the natural flailing of our actuality coming back to life.

Meanwhile our bottoms are searing experiences that never leave us, they scar us, branding us as survivors. In the process of enduring these eclipses into hell, we come face to face with our own demons that are exceedingly more abusive and deceitful than any exterior madness. These demons are liars who tell us at our lowest times, that we are worthless and have nothing left to live for. It happened to me. As a suicide survivor, I triumphed in this battle when I gave it up. It was a miracle I was found alive after overdosing myself, but it was not my time to exit this world. Out bottoms demand we stop arguing and start letting go to let miracles happen.

On the day that I went to the other side and saw with a totally intact consciousness that our existence is not a be-all-end-all, the message I received was to hang on. I saw that the greater picture is so magnanimous that it's incomprehensive to a human mind and takes the soul's psyche to comprehend it. My passing over taught me that pain would eventually transcend itself. I didn't realize it at the time, but this opening of the exit door bestowed me with a powerful essence of survivorship when I faced Hell and lived through it. My passion had transcended pain to leave me curious.

The knowledge that we're here for a reason brings the desire to explore it. Still while going through our hardships, it's hard to understand the why of our pain and we might never grasp a meaning we can ever agree with. Nevertheless, we are most awake when in a crisis. Does this mean everyone on this planet will hit bottom and face his or her maker? No, it means we have a karmic path that unfolds our destiny. As we know, some of us don't make it. We've all lost friends and loved ones to their hardships and we must also survive this heartbreak. It's so crazy that we could ever be grateful for our difficult times, but when we get on the other side of them, they become our legacy. Consider Malala Yousafzai, the Pakistani activist for female education who was shot in the face on her way to school. She went on to win a Noble Prize for being a human rights advocate and yet she still speaks of forgiveness while she powerfully justifies her cause.

It's a dark time on planet Earth. In Sanskrit, this time is known as *Kali Yuga*, being the darkest period before the next season of a golden dawn. Kali Yuga is an occasion of low moral virtues and an age of confusion. The way to survive it is to remember who you are behind all realities and lock into this essence. By doing this we are nearest to spirit and in this beneficent virtuality we accept this magnificent adventure in consciousness even through darkness. In the next blink, we will come into a blessed golden age, though when we first find it inside ourselves and experience it in sacred moments, we bring it forth. So yes, at times we will be called to speak out for the safety of the environment, to oppose political upheaval and corporate greed, and at the same time we will keep blinking in the most magnanimous direction, as we are actually the bringers of the new dawn.

Psyche is the Greek word for soul, though in Greek mythology the word *Psyche* also means butterfly as it depicts the *Goddess Psyche* with wings. In Latin, Psyche is depicted as an animating spirit and in the Greek myth, the *Goddess Psyche* did not obey the advice of her beloved and almost perished under the weight of suffering. She did survive and in the end she represented a divine embodiment that was purified by her misfortune, enough so, to become worthy of pure happiness. This tale imparts that we are strengthened by our misfortunes and as such are empowered to fly above them like butterflies. So when we feel torment, we don't back away, but go more deftly into the part of our psyche that soars above oppression and liberates us from our stories.

Supreme messages come through on the spirit network to talk us through our Hell zones; they hold our hand and walk us back to hope. Endurance and expectation is embedded in our psyche as a survival force that makes us fight for our life. Underneath our fragility, we are strong and have what it takes. My family lost my niece to an accidental overdose and you never know how strong you are until you have to be. Our survival strength will hone into what's important when slammed to our knees, as we kneel in prayer to ever rise again. Surviving is not always sweet and light filled, as it will take us where we need to go to get exactly what we need to carry on with, if it's our destiny.

Hope is a most powerful force that's out there waving our wand; it demands consideration and says: *"We are now going this way."* I recently saw a homeless person with a sign that said. "Homeless not Hopeless!" It reminded me of a saying I love by the long passed Chinese writer, Lin Yutang, *"Hope is like a road in the country; there never was a road, but when many people walk on it, the road comes into existence."*

The Abracadabra Prescriptions to Survive & Thrive:

Abracadabra Rx: Recognize This Is A Hero's Journey. Many times the degree of pain we feel makes no sense as it seems insane and unfair. We gyrate to try to escape and it's inescapable. We can drug ourselves, numb ourselves out and do everything possible to escape, but the pain will still be there under the haze waiting to transform us. There is no one who hasn't experienced loss and grief many times. When we pull the grief card it's not because we're being punished, it's that we're going into the depths of pain where we will be shattered. Here we'll feel great anguish and amid our struggle to survive, we will heal what needs healing.

Our hero within goes down, but keeps getting up over and over. The strategy isn't about doing battle, but about instilling the endurance needed to be into the bigger picture during difficult times. This does not mean we will not suffer, it means we will thrive anyway. So in the times that we look to the future, it's our survivor aspect that's looking for an opportunity in the rubble and not getting lost the downfall.

A real estate client jerked me around, which made me think about walking away. I interrogated an old belief I had, which reckoned I deserved to suffer in order to make money. After hearing a huge NO on this, I immediately quit. Empty for a period with no clients, I was wondering if I was crazy to walk away from the money I needed. I then realized that the Universe was recalibrating its energy field to match my decision and it was taking a minute. Within a month the phone began ringing again and I was back in business. It took balls to not allow myself to be accosted, as my courage drew a more faultless prosperity plan to me.

As heroes, we sometimes learn the hard way to not touch what has thorns. We also learn that when a dark story grabs us, there is still a light-filled storyline running alongside it that goes to grab us back. We have to learn to use the crap thrown at us, as fertilizer for what we wish to germinate. So empower yourself to withstand dark times and still hold light. When we've lost everything, it's a time to sit with nothing and exist on consciousness alone. Our task is to free ourselves from all limiting beliefs that clip our wings, for on this hero's journey—we came here to fly.

Abracadabra Rx: Hang With Your Inner Child. Children always see things in other realms because they are open and are not locked into one dimension. In innocence they enter the Kingdom of Heaven when they talk to imaginary beings and believe in the otherwise. As we accept that things are not always what they appear, things become amusing. Our childlike essence is always on call to get in on a game, to make up great stories, to believe in angels and even speak to them. In our times of darkness when the bad guys are fighting and we can't find the good guys or when greediness grabs all of the pie, a child's mind will still enjoy the tiny piece of pie that's left, even when it's purple and blue and made out of Play Doh.

A mother shared that during 9/11, she ran through the streets with her three-year-old daughter in her arms, as the Twin Towers were collapsing right behind them. Trying to shield her child's eyes from devastation and horrific visions, she told her daughter to keep her eyes closed. When they finally got far enough away, she put her child down and with tears streaming down her face she looked to her child and was amazed to see a look of ecstasy on her little one's face. This child looked up at her crying mother and said, "*Mommy don't cry, didn't you see all those angels flying around in the sky, there were so many.*" This child was not traumatized because she didn't see the buildings falling down, as she was just watching the angels. Her mother said she never believed in angels, but she now she believes.

A woman came to look at a house for sale with her young daughter and told her child not to touch anything. In the magical ways that children are curious about everything, the child responded that she would not touch things she would just feel them. This stopped my world as I realized that even though there are boundaries, there really aren't any when we know how to go beyond them. In the sense of facing a crisis, a heartbreak, news of the latest shooting, we must go beyond to a place where we have something other than anger and hopelessness to offer. Yes we feel this pain, but we reach past the why of it, to hold onto what good is still alive.

During a time when many people in business were not being honorable, I kept thinking about why I attracted them. I could not work it out until I came to the realization that I needed to go beyond this entire way of thinking and let go of blaming. The message was to focus on what had integrity, even if it was just me. So I decided to stalk love in the face of hatred, to maintain peace in a time of war, and to empower new ideas in the crux of hopelessness. I took my inner child's hand to go beyond what was and to support what has to be.

Abracadabra Rx: Fare Well. We were gifted with a sack full of alchemical gold in the party bag we got for coming here. This gold bestows our energetic ability to fare well no-matter-what. So bang a gong to let the universe know we are here to love life and as such life just has to love us back. On the days that we don't feel loved and the days we feel like we're in a wrong world from the one we envisioned, then like the child told not to touch anything we must still feel the love, beauty and light, even when we can't see it.

A friend slipped off the edge; she spun out and acted insane. I decided to love her anyway even from afar, as love might spin her back around. Either way I could not spinout with her by arguing or talking her out of it. To transform our painful reactions to the insanity in this world bodes us to continually hit the refresh mode. This embodiment of restoring ourselves back to being a being who can thrive is supported by all the powers that be once we even consider thriving, and then our thriving empowers itself.

I showed up for a New Years Day yoga class during a harsh winter with many challenging lessons. My stomach felt queasy and I felt weak. As class began, the teacher asked us to think of one word for the year. I figured my word was *"Hell."* Laying in child's pose my knees bent open wide with my forehead on the ground, I felt like I couldn't breathe. The next word that came to me was "Shit!" and it came with a wave of fear that I was going to puke right there on my mat. Suddenly another word flashed, it was *"Trust."* Bending into the first forward bend, I was already bone-tired and once again I heard *"Trust!"* Then moving into downward dog I wondered if I would make it through, so I started to pull back. Again the word *"Trust!"* resounded. Now moving more quickly through the postures, I find myself asking for help from any higher source I could possibly conjure up. The conversation was going like this . . .

Higher Me: What's the worst that can happen?

Me: I just drop dead—right here in class.

Me: This would be a good place to go—I could surrender to that.

Higher Me: What else could you surrender to?

God: You could also surrender to a breakthrough.

Me: Excuse me who is speaking?

God: Maybe this lifetime is not all about you and your comforts, maybe consider being Ok for the sake of the world and offering that out.

Me: That is a very freeing thought, which would relieve me of caring about every annoying thing, if I am here to be Ok for the world.

God: Try it.

Abruptly, I hear the teacher saying your heart is now having a conversation with the crown of your head. This is priceless, as I'm having a conversation with a Godly voice from another dimension. I start to breathe and feel like I can do this even if I'm exhausted, I will be perfectly Ok. I am moving at my own pace, again into downward dog, when the teacher comes over and pulls my hips back, my stubborn hips. Moving quickly into up dog, I hear *"Surrender and Trust."* I remember my hips, as Rodney Yee is always calling me out, to narrow my hips. It makes me pull up my stomach, as in strengthen what you assimilate and come from your core. Narrowing my hips, releases my lower back, the place from where I carry the weight of my world. I focus on my core and realize I really am one powerful woman. I'm coming back, I feel strong—I'm smiling.

Right foot forward between your hands and boom, I look down at my big toe and all my groovy blue toenail polish has just rubbed off on my mat. Mind you I painted my toes late the night before so my feet would look acceptable for New Year's Day class and now I have a naked toe. I am imperfect. Staring at the blaring bald right toe, the word "Naked!"

keeps coming up. I feel vulnerable and exposed and then I realize this is hilarious, even ironic, as what makes me think I have to present perfection, it's a cover-up. I am then inspired to be defenseless, raw and unveiled, and now I feel a surge as if I just plugged into the truth. My word for the year, "Trust!" is bursting out of my heart and exploding fireworks across my crown chakra. Moments later, coming back to what is going on in the room, I hear the teacher saying, *"Bring your hands to prayer and dedicate your practice."* I go through my list, sending prayers to everyone I love and then a final prayer for the entire world. I open my eyes and realize I forgot to pray for myself and I smile because that spark of a message I heard that said, *"Maybe this lifetime is not all about You and Your Comforts, maybe consider being Ok for the sake of the world and offering that out,"* that message went in deep and I trusted it.

We must reach for the relief we are seeking. Especially when we've walked through the mud, survived a winter, don't have what we want, have forced ourselves to exercise when we're exhausted while we trust that we're Ok. Our relief is our retaliation to thrive anyway. So we're Ok even if our dream fell flat because we have many more. We're strong enough to turn the corner and come back from disasters, traumas, and huge transitions because we have the bounce back gene. I was once like Cinderella waiting for a prince to save me, instead my inner warrior showed up and taught me how to fare well as the princess I am.

Abracadabra Rx: Assist Your Good Karma. Relating to Aikido, you grab the force arriving in your direction and you can do one of two things with it, either fling it elsewhere or gently assist it into a more comfortable posture that changes the dynamic of what exists. Flinging it creates more karma while assisting it will alleviate bad karma. Many people think they've come here only to help themselves at the buffet table, as if this lifetime was a menu of appetizers and entrées. The truth is we're here to serve the goodness of all life, which serves us back. So think before you act and notice before you speak if you are serving goodness or just yourself.

Goodness has a boomerang effect that we have to act on, to get it to move. Someone is being a jerk and we bless him or her. Yes we do! And then we walk away leaving a trail of goodness that is banked in our karmic account. So in a world gone mad we don't react in fear, instead we coax goodness along and sit around with our rose colored glasses on and imagine the best. It's not about being delusional in a Pollyanna way, as it's really about our great expectations and the magnetic charms of attraction they draw. Karma wants to pave our road with gold and as such we must offer it the gold to do so.

Abracadabra Rx: Honor Your Human Experience. How do we live a life in paradise amidst what looks to be one of the most tumultuous dark times in history? Spirit reminds us often that we are pure consciousness residing in a sacred human form and it's through this human form that our consciousness has the ability to touch, taste and feel the essence of this physical experience. I have a sense that we came here because our consciousness wanted this exact experience in view of the fact that it knew this was going to be intense because it also knew we would be strong enough to thrive on it. As a matter of fact, we all have a little saint hanging out in our temple and they're ringing our bells to remind us that they are with us and to connect with them.

How do we thrive while there is so much suffering and pain? We offer ourselves to assist it, we give what we can and we sincerely care. Our caring is the *Thank-You* note we write to the universe from our saint within. So when you feel bad, when you have anxiety, when you're depressed and feeling hopeless, then ask your inner saint to come forth and take the wheel while you rest. During the times we can't handle the grind, it's best to surrender all control, as our human experience needs a break. I had troubled feelings over a disagreement I had with a yoga teacher and quit going to yoga for three months. It was a good break but my body toward the end did not agree and was screaming, *"I Need Yoga!"* I honored my body and even though my mind was leery, I returned to class. While doing the practice, my mind surrendered to my love of yoga and after class I hugged the teacher. She said she'd been waiting three moths for this hug. The most yogic lesson I learned from that experience was that my body had needs that overrode my mind, so I was forced it to stop arguing because the health of my body was more important and needed to be nurtured.

My father was a blackout drunk and on his deathbed he said he loved his life. He suffered greatly as he left this world but interestingly in the end he still blacked-out all the bad things he ever did and only remembered his good times. I stood at his bedside and told him that I forgave him for all the awful things he'd done to me. He looked surprised and said he had never done anything bad to me. Totally not true, but in that moment I decided to let him go with that as my gift to him because his gift to me was to learn to transform my pain and grow out of it to become my own hero.

Our humanness is a story and when we drop our bodies to turn to dust, our spirit becomes the main story. After my father died, I went to an energy healer. She put her hands on me saying, *"Your father just passed and is in a heavenly hospital. He is crying for what he did to you and now he is healing."* I wondered if he remembered that I forgave him and I hoped that was why he was crying. Our relationships continue across dimensions, so we must make peace to keep the peace.

Our human psyche has been conditioned to run around in a one-dimensional reality, while our great spirit is out there dancing in the cosmos. As spiritual beings having a human experience we're in the process of remembering that we are powerful heavenly beings, when we've forgotten. My yoga teacher told a story in class about her cousin who had just passed on. Fearful of his impending death he resisted dying while passing in and out of consciousness. Every time he came to, he was agitated and cried out *"No!"* His father had recently passed a year prior and right at the end of her cousin's journey, a huge grin crossed his face and he said, "Hi Dad," and left smiling.

I believe we are escorted in and out of this existence with love and in the middle of our comings and goings, doing this thing we call life, it's up to us how much love we can hold. When we are sufficiently evolved we will ride beyond the waves of *Samsara*, which is the Sanskrit word for the stories of our world. It is said that liberation is attained through being born in a human form, which is considered rare and revered. Liberation is considered the emancipation of the soul out of bondage, beyond karma, being free from samsara to transpose our suffering. If we understand the suffering that we feel, as only in this dimension, we are open to letting it pass through us. These bodies can bestow us into a state of Nirvana, which in Buddhism is referred to as the highest happiness. So this human experience is worthy of regard because it has cherish-able aspects, as each birthday candle is a flame that honors our existence. By holding our magical consciousness above everything else, we make the ordinary sacred and we thrive.

Abracadabra Rx: Liberate Yourself. Standing in the hub of this crazy reality, free from emotions, fears and anger, is where supreme liberation exists. Many of the masses don't even have the consciousness to want liberation, so they live in bondage. To come into at-one-ment with all that exists, binds the separation between our humanness and spiritual ways. As the winds of change rush by, faith is the hand we hold that walks us through the abyss of crazy thinking and mental war zones to show us the perfect spot to sit and consider our plight. If we consider our emotional tangents as a workout that will lead to our liberation—we are free.

I once had to make the hard decision to put my mother in hospice when the time came. Everyone else involved did not agree and insisted on continuing with measures that I saw as futile and going against a natural course of evolution. I went alone, signed the papers and moved her to rest peacefully in her own home. While barraged with negative opinions, I could have gotten entwined in the disagreement, but instead I focused on what I felt was lovingly best for my mother and went with that. She passed on peacefully shortly thereafter with her caretaker and I holding her closely as she left. I had liberated her from unnecessary procedures to let her to have this kind of loving passing. I had also liberated myself from caring what anyone else thought about it.

Liberating oneself does not mean there will no longer be times when things are downright hard. Things will continue to be hard and we will still show up to do what needs to be done and then we will do what is needed to heal. The difference is we will not be involved with any extra unnecessary, as they say in Yiddish, *Mishegas* meaning craziness. And we will not *Schlep*, another Yiddish word meaning drag around *Schmutz*, the Yiddish word for dirt. As a child when my grandmother spoke Yiddish, I could tell from the tone alone that she was complaining, but her humor always liberated her.

Someone I love and I get into power struggles; it bothers me, though when I consider who she is in her highest state, I love her anyway. People think they can control love, they can't. All we can do is control an abstract version of our own experience that's in lockdown. So I disregard these power struggles because I don't care to poison her or myself with more negativity, as loving anyway is supreme liberation.

Abracadabra Rx: Recover, Revive, & Restore. One moment we're holding on for dear life and the next moment we're rolling down the thriving river. What we do in-between is what holds energetic weight and defines what will happen next. In the way that a flower blooms because it's programed to do so, we too are programed to be magnificent, but we have to believe it. The flower does not try to blossom, it blossoms because it's in the right spot with good soil and light. We too must have essential necessities to grow our lotus. So when my deals fall apart, people act like dirt bags and nothing flows, it's because I'm not in the right space with the right people in the right light. And in the way that we move a houseplant to the window, we have to move ourselves into our blossom zone.

This is a time that calls for us to bounce back. A child can be deep in woe and then run out the door to play. They have full-blown tantrums followed by bliss. We need to be that authentic being who shrieks down the hallways on their way to bliss. Our infant psyche is a most evolved archetype, a bona fide expression of our authenticity. So we cry, we curse out the car window and then we laugh to the hilt as our healings take many forms. In this way, we become a rightful being who does what they need to do. At the same time, it's challenging to do the right thing, which might mean walking away from a pile of money attached to what is toxic, or going on vacation and staying for the rest of the story. The right thing is not usually obvious because we are teased by the mind that loves to feed our ego, while right consciousness fuels our sense of ultimate self. So we must exercise inner satisfaction because it's an energy field enlightened enough to make something out of nothing.

A friend was depressed over what appeared to be hopeless exterior circumstances and described his feelings as a rightful reaction to what was happening. Though when I asked what he was going to do about it and he said, *"Right now I'm going to hang the new blinds that have just arrived."* A Zen saying goes: *"Before enlightenment chop wood carry water, after enlightenment, chop wood carry water."* This was what my friend was doing as he owned his feelings; he was still doing what needed to done in a Zen way so depression didn't own him. Another friend was abruptly fired from a high level position, so she went on an eight-month excursion to the other side of the planet where she kneeled in temples, sat with improvised children in downtrodden countries, prayed on beaches, partied in Greece, flew to Bali, met with shamans, healed herself and came back. We too must journey and can do it right here, right now. So close your eyes, drop perspectives, connect in and take the time to recover, revive, and restore.

Abracadabra Rx to Thrive . . .

Rx: *Don't get lost in being lost.*

Rx: *There is always light in the darkness—find it.*

Rx: *Create your own energy prescriptions.*

Rx: *Release pent up emotions privately when necessary.*

Rx: *Do new things to change habitual patterns.*

Rx: *Place your pain on your inner shrine for healing.*

Rx: *Feel for the light at the end of the tunnel—reach for it.*

Rx: *Honor the story that took you down and grow out of it.*

Rx: *When you have hit bottom keep passing through.*

Rx: *Surround yourself with love—your own.*

Rx: *Be in the moment with your higher vision.*

Rx: *We come from a supreme source—remember that source.*

Rx: *Be in wonder around what could come out of this.*

Rx: *Have faith and keep dreaming.*

Rx: *Release your burdens and see who you are without them.*

Rx: *Ignore your egoist lies and bathe in your truth.*

Rx: *Put your feet on the Earth and pull in vital energy.*

Rx: *Remember this is a hero's journey.*

Rx: *Decide to fare well through your difficulties.*

Rx: *Use everything as a catalyst for liberation.*

Rx: *Tap into the saint in your temple.*

Rx: *Tune into the state you were in before you were born.*

Rx: *Go beyond this existence to where you are free and happy.*

Rx: *Be in touch with your inner child and play.*

Rx: *Bypass conditioning and follow your heart.*

Rx: *Go into the hub of silence and listen to the cosmos.*

Rx: *Remember you have the survival gene—activate it.*

Rx: *When others are selfish, support yourself in lieu of them.*

Rx: *We are healers aligned to the magic we need.*

Rx: *Tap in and activate your magic and your spark.*

Rx: *Activate your imagination and travel with it.*

Rx: *Always hold a magical consciousness above all.*

Rx: *Be your own assistant.*

Rx: *Focus on what revives you and imbibe that.*

Rx: *Go to your good karma bank account and withdraw.*

Rx: *Take a break, drop everything, smell the roses, and smile.*

Rx: *Expect miracles and imagine you are thriving.*

Rx: *Blossom like flowers that grow in dirt when covered in it.*

Rx: *Be hopeful in the face of adversity.*

Rx: *Take a bed day even when you're not sick.*

Rx: *Activate the bounce back gene that wakes up the survival gene to come to the front lines and then bounce for no reason.*

Rx: *When your heart is shattered, don't keep trying to glue the broken pieces back— you are growing a new heart.*

Rx: *If you are fighting for your life, know your life is worth it and ask it to fight alongside you.*

Rx: *Be hopeful even if you have to pretend, this triggers good prospects to arrive and kick the bad ones out.*

Rx: *Tap into the vibration of Hero-ship and be your own hero.*

Rx: *At the end of your rope let the love of others pull you back.*

Rx: *Remember that we are here for the reason being that our survival and revivals support others to do the same.*

Rx: *Be Ok for the sake of the world!*

6) The Magic Of Integrity . . .

"You are in integrity when the life you are living on the outside matches who you are on the inside."–Alan Cohen

It was as if my life stepped around and slapped me upside my head and the searing message was: *You will not get away with one inch of anything that does not resound from a resonance of right action!* This dispatch was a missile that hit my destiny and destroyed all my maneuvers. I was trying to go back to a place I felt good in and it wasn't working. Everything I was visualizing and trying to do also wasn't working. It was because I was doing things for the wrong reasons instead of coming from my soul's integrity. Quickly, from one day to the next, my getting away with anything quota was full. The universe was demanding that every action I take must be done sincerely and with virtue. Since my habitual reactions and patterns created constant distress, it meant I had to stop everything and reconcile my entire way of being.

Living within the means of integrity warrants being under

onstant surveillance; our witness is on guard to scrutinize our every move, every thought, every intention, every activity, and our total way of being. This forthrightness is either all or nothing, as the time has come for us to walk our talk. We all have misplaced our integrity at times, but face it we're now being exposed and so is everyone else. The veils are lifted, so there are no longer cover-ups and everything is obvious. The truth is at the frontlines and it's evident that we can't play with the essence of fake power anymore. The only real power right now is our own hand placed on our hearts in a pledge of allegiance to the highest part of our selves.

I walked with my ego for a decade and when my passion left there was no way to retrieve it in the same ways I had in the past because I had to get real. Getting real is honoring our heart even as it's broken, as by honoring what is broken, we are now mending. While being the do-er, we are the one that is doing and undoing our reality. We're the one holding the bag and the big question is what's in the bag? Consider that it's our heart energy we're holding and imagine that you're carrying your heart around in your briefcase or purse, because that's what we're really doing. Our heart is on the line right now and it's not taking any more garbage and will continue on with us only in the name of love. If there's no love in our experience or the love is only self-serving then integrity is absent, so there will be no magic.

In a conversation with my brother about the many dark discrepancies of our father, it was obvious my brother had the luxury of just loving him. I had always stood in front of my brother so my dad's bad behaviors happened to me. My brother said he saw who our dad was behind his pain and he loved this part of him. This stopped my world as I recognized that to honor another being is to drop the roles and meet them heart to heart—even if this has to be only in spirit.

I have learned from being a mother to trust that all disagreements will always come back around to love when love is involved. Love is the highest form of integrity for it stands true no matter what and waves us through. Integrity like love goes beyond deceit, as it strides past ego, slams the door on unworthiness and holds pure sincerity. Sincerity creates the perfect integral condition that can bear anything because it holds itself to the highest standards. We've all done things that haunt us, things we're ashamed of and wish we'd never done. Though when we learn from these things, we are in our integrity and will be gifted to release guilt.

Welcome to the searing lessons that bear the magic of teaching us to know better. In instances of remorse, we're graded on how we forgive ourselves by acknowledging what weakness took us down. During the times when I was feeding my distorted illusions, my weakness dragged me to the underworld. Blinded by selfishness, something came and shook me so hard that I had no choice but to come back to myself. It was integrity. In the words of Cecil Beaton, "Be daring, be different, be impractical, be anything that will assert integrity of purpose and imaginative vision against the play-it-safers, the creatures of commonplace, the slaves of the ordinary".

The Abracadabra Prescriptions for Integrity:

Abracadabra Rx: Go With Integrity. Once when I was going the wrong way, I experienced a jolt where I was yanked out of my game so fast that it felt like a death. My heart had shattered and nothing meant anything to me anymore. I wallowed there for a while as pain was clearing a path. Then blink, I was transported and delivered back to an original aspect of myself. It felt as if I was dropped into a childlike state where nothing mattered but the experience of say finding your toes and being in awe of how they move. The strangest part was that on the exterior nothing had changed. I was still doing the same things except everything and I mean everything inside me turned an about-face and none of what mattered prior mattered at all anymore. I was in the blink of my truth where all delusions dissolved and all that was left was sincerity and virtue.

As I look back on my past motivations, I can see this transformation had been a process of cracking open my heart and then finding and freeing my conscience from there. I had been acting in ways that were less than congenial, but the scariest part is that we think it's fine to be that way so we don't even care. Wham! Something then happens that spotlights the laws of cause and effect and we're slammed with the consequences. It's transformation time when we've practiced dark ways of being and haven't paid attention to the integrity of our soul's values. We get reminded that our soul is the main art director of our goodness to come and we have to listen. Since the frequencies of virtue have sped up, the laws of karma have also sped up and when we are doing the dance of hard knocks, it's a message to go home and wrap our soul's integrity around us like a blanket.

If you want to meet your soul and understand the integrity it holds, then sit and converse on the intuitive channel and you will know your honorable purpose. Our integral knowing says it doesn't matter what we do, it just matters how we do it. We could be anything from the garbage man to the CEO of a big company and nevertheless our attitudes and ethics define us. So we learn that it's not always about what's best for ourselves, as caring for others opens the flow and frees us from dependence on falsity.

A friend adopted two abandoned teenage sisters that put her through the ringer on every possible level. She was immersed in hellish non-stop difficulties. I asked her if she wished she never adopted them? Without hesitation, she said she had no regrets because prior to adopting them she was not a nice person. She said she was selfish and they cured her. So when things become difficult beyond means, find your integrity and take it to the frontline and fight for it. We all rant at times but when integrity demands that we get on its bus, it's best to drop everything and go—or be dragged.

Abracadabra Rx: Adapt. We are in the process of adapting to an initiation of the highest order—Ours! This initiation is about knowing to the bones that this lifetime is about a sense of union between our spirit, our heart, and our humanness. These adaptations are divined to accommodate all that is heavenly into our element. I asked a wealthy buyer considering purchasing an oceanfront estate, how long it had been since he had stood on a dune and watched a sunset with his wife. He looked at me blankly and said twenty-five years. I told him his money was worthless if he did not take the time to bask in beauty. He then looked at me sternly, I thought I was about to be fired and then he said, *"I will buy this house now."* He heard the truth and adapted.

Believe it, that the universe is on our team by constantly sending us messages and wishing us to converse with it. On a day that I got a driving violation for making a wrong turn, I was not paying attention. This lack of focus sent me to traffic court to go before a judge. There I sat, surrounded by a very downcast group that was also there to plead for leniency. I had to adapt. At first I was appalled to be there and then from witnessing these people's difficulties, my heart started to break for them. I sent them light and realized there are no mistakes. I was going the wrong way and trying to get around things instead of having patience. As a result, I got to sit in the presence of others who were also going the wrong way and wish them well. Wake up calls come in all forms.

Our comfort levels are multi-faceted. I have learned about this from my cat. There are certain areas in my house that are the jungle to her and when she is in the jungle she's on high alert and you can't get near her. It's all about where the boundaries are in this world and we're in the jungle when our minds are actively on the emotional, judgmental, and pirated channel. When we let people, places and things steal our bliss, the solution is to tap into and activate bliss anyway. The mind does what it does and we do what we do and eventually integrity steps in and we must adapt. In this way, when the mind is hollering about all that is wrong, we just have to tap into the symmetry of all that is right.

People do crappy things. My mind screams that I don't deserve it. I want them to stop and keep coming across the same scenarios of unconscious self-centered people who are inconsiderate and out for themselves. I wonder if I am attracting this or if I'm just passing through it on my way to liberation? Sometimes adapting is not about accepting or agreeing, but knowing when something isn't worthy. Don't touch it. Adapt to the highest order that exists and don't resonate with what is less than that. Adapt-a-ca-dab-ra is the first step and the second is the advantage of what's best.

Abracadabra Rx: Groove. Imagine succeeding on your own terms while leaving a sublime trail of peace as opposed to dysfunction. It's always better to prevent than to cure, so if something feels wrong, why waste time trying to fix it when your best time is spent being in your groove. The poet Saint Kabir said, *"I laugh when I hear the fish in the water are thirsty."* This means find your groove where you are, don't travel from place to place looking for happiness, just uncover the gold buried under your house. Notice when things get bleak, notice if you are only seeing a reflection of your mind, then discover what's hiding in plain sight. Now look through the eyes of your soul to see the truth that is never hiding.

A concept of taking pleasure leads us to understand that one can take pleasure even where it does not exist. Suppose we've been kidnapped by woe, we still have options and the lesson is to peruse them. I received a rejection letter on one of my books, saying magic didn't fit into their company's format. My first thought was to write back and tell them my philosophy on living in the box. I thought about my options and doing nothing seemed to be the best one, so I did that and carried on with my passion. They were not the right company for my philosophy. Though ironically they said they would publish a diet book if I would like to write one. Funny that they couldn't see that my Abracadabra books portray a complete misery-reduction plan!

A friend who is always telling me the latest conspiracy theory found her life circumstances were getting more and more confined. Here she was exposing plots and schemes, while feeling hopeless each day because these collusions owned her. One day she called to tell me she still believed in all the covertness that was happening in the world, but she had decided to be happy in spite of these general betrayals. She said that pleasure would be her retaliation against all the fraudulent artifice that was running rampant.

It's a practice to know that when slime is being thrown around outside our front door, that we are going out anyway in our raincoats and stepping over it. The slang of being in our groove is metaphorical as it allows us to dance to the music we enjoy. I read that monkeys don't particularly care for human music but still groove to a certain beat they find in a song. When presented with what's not pleasing, it's best to find a rhythm around these things and groove with it. Then when things aren't going well, we're not enmeshed, but can groove with the integrity of what matters more.

Abracadabra Rx: Take The Grist From The Mill. Our ability to separate the gold from the dirt is a practice. Some years ago, I asked a friend her opinion on promoting an E book I had published and was shocked when she said, *"That book is useless, throw it in the garbage."* I told her that this was a hurtful thing to say and her response was that she needed to be honest. This woman is a powerhouse who teaches yogic philosophy to many students. Her harsh opinion needled me to look at the concept of whether I should dump the book or not. There was some nasty grist in this mill and I was drawn to see if it was right. If you ask someone's opinion you are showing up for the Russian roulette of perhaps not hearing what you want and maybe hearing what you need, or it might be that you have to figure it out for yourself.

I consider it funny that the universe is always talking to us through other people and it's up to us to define if what we are hearing is the truth or not. I had written the book in question seven years prior. Many people still tell me how this book has helped them and how much they love it. Though when I looked at the book again, I realized I had something different to say and decided to rewrite the book. My new version of the book morphed into a current message I could stand with now. So this harsh tongued woman ended up spurring me into doing something I felt was better, as when I sifted through her dirt I found my gold.

Thich Nhat Hanh said, "*There is the mud, and there is the lotus that grows out of the mud. We need the mud in order to make the lotus.*" It's up to us to find our golden seeds and grow a lotus, as either we do that or we sit around covered in mud. My way of being does not give up even if I am slayed because I am coded to find the gold. I am not sure how this coding happened in me, maybe I arrived this way or I innately coded this gold-seeking aspect into myself. Either way the process is a gift, as I always do find the gold, most probably because I am always looking for it.

It's time to understand that when covered in mud, there's a lesson to be learned. I was once standing at a bus stop on my way to work and was suddenly bombarded with pigeon shit. In that moment I went down. My mind affirmed that I must deserve this and then I remembered my mother saying, "*Birds shitting on you or your car means good luck is coming!*" I took the second option and arrived at my job surrounded by people who helped to clean it off. Remember when standing in a pile of dirt, it's time to start planting, but before you plant you must pull out the weeds and sift through the dirt for gold!

Abracadabra Rx: Go Right. On the day I got that traffic violation, there was a new sign that was never there before that said: No Left Turn. The traffic was at a standstill, so I went down a side lane that I always go down and made a quick left not seeing the sign. Suddenly an entire shebang of authority with sirens and flashing lights surrounded me. I sat in my car for too long, as an officer screened my entire legal life. I imagined that he would see my clean slate, and say, *"Be more careful next time."* It didn't go that way, as the officer said, *"I am giving you a ticket for disobeying a sign, you either have to plead guilty or go to court and plead your case."*

The word plead was blaring as he said it twice. I realized I'd been pleading with God for the transformation I was experiencing to be easier and handed to me on a silver platter. At the time, I was maneuvering my way around in circles trying to make right what was wrong. In a transition we tend to get jerky and cling to old ways. I was getting a definite sign from the universe to pay attention and go the right way, even if it wasn't the easy way. "Go right!" I actually heard this loud and clear just before I turned left, but did not listen. Considering that we'd pay a hefty sum to a therapist, an astrologer, or a psychic, I reasoned that the fee for the ticket was payment to a universal guidance counselor for such a definitive sign. Pleading our case is a waste of time—getting the message is all that matters.

Abracadabra Rx: Don't Create More Of What You Don't Want. Opinions are opinions but to use one in a hurtful way creates karma. This karma circles around and is felt as a direct hit by its creator. Suddenly business is not flourishing, no one is investing in our ideas, no one is asking for our hand in partnership or marriage, as our actions are being reflected back to us. Measured by our virtues, we prosper by the magnetism of our actions, which carry over all timelines until they perfect themselves. In this game of life we are often misunderstood or not valued by people who are not satisfied with themselves and blame us. Satisfaction is guaranteed by remembering to serve the highest advocacy. So when disturbing circumstances arise, our integrity whispers: *Make an evolved choice and go the way of least resistance.*

Right now, we're in a revolution of right and wrong and have to choose. Resist is the new banner and really it should be "Disagree." To resist is to be part of a force, in the sense that we are in it, but going the other way. To disagree is not to be part of any force except our own. I have wasted much time resisting when I sincerely disagree and so now my offering is to not hide in my Pollyanna world but to serve all my disagreements with the allurement and charm of what I find more becoming. My mother always used to describe certain women as: *Quite Becoming!* She was always on about what was attractive and looked well on women. She would define what was proper and appropriate, but really she was just parroting her own mother's guidelines.

I always took my mother's keen fashion perception deeper by acknowledging how certain women had this charisma, which pushed their potential into actuality. These women were my role models, as they were not as ladylike as my mother revered. They were wild and edgy and could care less what others thought because they dared to disagree and followed their calling. Being charming is most becoming!

I once had a longing to get a tattoo of the infinity symbol. Upon arriving at the ink parlor something was pulling me back and I asked the beautifully inked tattoo artist, *"What if I don't like it?"* He sincerely said, *"Then you will have to learn to like it."* A gong banged in my head, as an important life message was being delivered and mind you the word tattoo also means drum roll or a strong pulsation. At the time there were many things going on in the world environmentally, politically, energetically, and personally that I was not in agreement with. I needed to hear this message to learn to accept the things I cannot change and still hold peace within myself. This concept that was not in my normal patterning and ta-da there it was talking to me. I didn't actually need the infinity tattoo—just the message it was delivering.

Contemplating the huge amount of energy I invest in adversarial thinking, I found that by releasing my resistance to the things I cannot change, I would stop the counterattack of these things continually coming back around for clearing. To pardon what does not activate our passion excuses us from dealing with it. There will always be bothersome things, though our providence lies in not enmeshing with them. Imagine hearing your higher self tell you: *"You are excused from this experience, now go to your higher state and play."* This does not mean I am going absent—it means that I am doing something about it in a more enamored way.

A crazy woman in my town, with a reputation of having an evil streak, screamed curse words across the street at me.

My first thought was to cleanse my energy field, but then I realized that I would be investing in her energy, so I excused myself. We don't have to protect ourselves from what does not exist and we don't have to keep investing in what we don't want. I decided she was yelling at a person behind me, which was possible since she has many targets. I was not going to look back and see who it was, so I got in my car and drove away. I erased her actions because there was nothing of quality there for me to take from. *Our Inner Sage* hangs out on a luminous level and is the hand that grabs us from walking into the street when a truck is coming. Meanwhile the wizard within whispers: *"Invest in the way you believe it should be to create more of what you want."*

Abracadabra Rx: Turn It Around. I remember my younger days of having a hair pulling fight with a girl at school and the next day ironically becoming best friends for life with her. This irony taught me that things are not what they appear and that animosity can always be turned around. The underlying premise of an argument is that it's an appeal to come to an understanding. If we succeed, the argument then turns into an agreement. Diversity only happens when its contrast is not acceptable, so we can hold a bone of contention about it or we can find accord in what is dissimilar and come into reconciliation with it. We tend to get upset over what we don't agree with, though turning our perception towards understanding changes the vibration. We can still not agree and understand at the same time.

The turn around is usually to pivot our ways of dealing with what is incongruous. For instance when we're upset about world pollution, we stop eating junk food. When we oppose corporate greed and we give money to homeless people or causes that save our planet. We get angry with politicians and authorities for discrimination, but anger is also discriminating. We balance these things out by doing what it takes to turn them around.

I was in an argument with a client who I felt was sending mixed messages and wasting my time. I realized it is a pattern sellers have that's based on what's best for them and not a mutual consideration. This scenario always bothered me and pushed buttons. I decided to go deep and hone in on the source of what annoyed me most about this in order to be done with it. After turning off the cap lock on my responses, I saw that my disparity was about being right and I needed to progress past ego instilled righteousness. We can't change self-serving people, but we can serve ourselves what we need. The strategy is to not spin out, but to define our direction, continue on our way, and see what follows.

Every time there is a disturbance we have gone too far for too long and need to find ways to come back. A friend loves roller coasters as the upside down, out of control feeling, releases his childlike happiness. Another friend loves to go skydiving, as freefalling is the opposite of her very controlled existence in everyday life. Lastly, a stressed out relative with an over-active mind composes music when he gets home from work. I write books on magic to remind myself that when the world turns, I'm having a conversation with what turns me on. When we feel screwed, the real us is never really screwed, it's only our reactions that are screwy. Therefore in the moments in which we look at our actions and choose the most positive facet, we are in the process of coming back into our spotlight. The sage within talks us into neutralizing the mind from believing that we are screwed, because we are all actually unscrewing.

Abracadabra Rx: Be Well Affected. Anxiety is having a party in my nervous system. Hopelessness pulls me into believing I have no power. Anger is feeding me fire-bolt tales that make me feel falsely powerful. Sadness arrives to sweep out my heart. These dispositions remind us to come to terms with what is behind these sentiments. In the truest sense, we must take what affects us and make evolved sense of it and then we must tread on the fact that we're not going along for the ride unless it's going somewhere magical.

During a time when I was stressed out, a deer hit by a car wandered onto my front yard to die. My neighbor, who is a Native American Medicine Man came over and performed a ceremony for the deer. He told me that Deer Medicine is about gentleness and represents an opportunity to express kindness, which brings serenity wherever it goes. At the time I was not being gentle or kind to myself. In response the universe was being harsh. Even my town, refused to come and pick up the deer saying since she was on my lawn and not the road she was my problem. I sat and meditated with the deer and thanked her for the message. I promised her I would be gentle, and then another neighbor showed up with a tractor and took her to families in need that would have venison all winter.

In the ways that we create our realities in reaction to our feelings, being in harmony attracts our magic. When things are off kilter we mustn't freak out, but instead find our progression in the evolution. My niece once posted on social media that she felt like her jeans, which were blue and shredded. One of her friends responded, *"I'm so glad you are feeling divinely holy these days!"* Our relationships are either a reflection of our attitudes or great teachings. If we're well affected during our challenging periods, then these intervals become walkovers on the way to our providence.

Abracadabra Rx: Keep It Clean. We are our own clean up crew, always on the lookout for our own shortcomings. Our cleansings create an opening for one good action to cancel out a hundred bad ones. I think of it as a karmic vacuum cleaner that sucks up the bad stuff and shoots it out into a vortex to be whisked away and disseminated. This is why I'm constantly cleaning, it's not because I am a neurotic compulsive type, it's because I am in the process of undoing negativity. I made up the concept about a vortex vacuum, but make-believe is real to me. So if I believe I am sweeping old garbage into a vortex to be sucked away and things in my life shift because of it then this is my reality. This perspective works for me so I will continue to cleanse my concepts when my reality goes sideways.

We need to understand that we are having an energetic experience as much as a physical one and when the energy goes off kilter, you can bet something in the physical plane is also going to get weird. So we must clean up what messes with us on an energetic plane before it reaches the physical plane where it will seriously affect us. I recently watched some episodes of an old television show called *The Guardian* on Netflix. I watched it because it was about a lawyer who worked in an upscale law firm whose clients were doing bazillion dollar company takeovers and the goings on that happened behind the scenes and in the conference rooms were despicable and reminded me of the real estate business that I was working in.

The star lawyer on the show got arrested for drugs and sentenced to do community service, helping underprivileged people for leniency. I studied this show for nuances to learn how to be better at letting bad things roll off me. The dichotomy this attorney portrayed in working for billionaires to working for people in need was striking. What was most captivating was seeing how this lawyer, being a levelheaded guy on a healing journey, handled all the sleazy interactions that crossed his path. He always gave the perpetrator a very potent look and then turned away. It appeared that not one inch of the sleaze he witnessed had penetrated his being. He just did a mental jujitsu on it and kept moving. What I took from this character is that you show up, you go into the story, you offer your goods and the rest is up to the Gods.

Though most importantly, when you show up, you hold your state, the one you want to live in just for you and as things come up that could disrupt this state, you decide whether these things are worth it or not and then go back to your sacred frame of mind. Tip: We must roll up our sleeves and get down on our knees to scrub underneath the covers of whom we believe we are. We are our own holy maid service, so take out the trash and start polishing.

Abracadabra Rx: Grab Happiness. Consider how a drop of lemon juice spoils milk but a spoonful of honey sweetens it. In the same ways that happiness overrides misery, can we just be happy? As a child, my escape into happiness at school were all about dreaming and doodling. My drawings covered the pages of every book I was forced to read and my dreams took me out the window and satiated me. Always in trouble, I realized that escaping into happiness was where I could never be captured. After school, coming home to watch cartoons and laugh at the hilarity of stupidity was the perfect elixir of delight that released my distress. As children, we so easily turned off the world and turned on happiness and then we grew up and got robbed of these daily ponderings. In truth, we have not been robbed, just blinded by social mediocrity and rules. Everything magical is actually right here waiting to be touched upon and a flash of happiness is our admission in.

I believe I must instill happiness into my psyche to not get infected with seriousness, self-righteousness and fear. I parole my blues by learning the language that commands an *"Open Sesame"* on happiness. In countries where the misery factor is high, like in India where poverty is pervasive, the happiness factor is equally high because family and spiritual community are valued over money. India has a rich spiritual tradition and its history is loaded with tales that revolve around the battle of good over evil. Then there's Iceland, a country in financial drought, but even so this country has a high-happiness factor, maybe because it's far removed from mainstream affectations and even within its periods of darkness, there's so much beauty. In Bhutan, happiness is a priority, as it's all about values and happiness is their most valuable asset. My *Open Sesame* zeroes in on bliss moments, which instills drops of joy into my reality.

The secret is that if you look for happiness you will find it. Artificial flavors of happiness will not do the trick and will just take you away from real happiness, which is organic. So find one little thing to be happy about and blow it up to be the biggest thing you have in the moment. For me, when I'm hit with a slew of disappointments, I still go out the window on a light beam to remember what defines me. My integrity holds a lot of gratitude these days and becomes more alive in the fact that I seek and find happiness. It's not so much an escape from what exists, as it's more about deciding which way to sway. Happiness becomes a powerful force against the paradigm of opposites, as it stands up to resistance, breaks down opposition and delivers the otherwise because it has its own integrity.

Abracadabra Rx: When You Need Help—Ask. Many times when the view looks bleak we have to mentally climb a ladder to see beyond where we are, as when we're singing the blues we've forgotten to expand our vision. Maybe we don't love the situation, but finding appreciation for something in it removes the red tape. We all quell when being understood, as the gift of recognition is like a big hug. The big question is how do we get the Universe to hug us? Since our minds are always describing and defining, it's best to drop expectations and hug ourselves constantly on behalf of the Universe.

I was talking to a healer friend and told her I was caught in the conundrum of living my dream, while being successful at work was robbing my energy, I was exhausted. She asked, *"Have you discussed this situation with the Universe to request specific help?"* She wanted to know if I was honest about telling the Universe that I wanted energetic support in my work. Oddly enough I had never asked for support on being successful with something that was not my passion. Not being sure that I deserved success in this way, I hid the desire. Bingo! There is magic in everything, so I immediately put my cards on the table knowing that my desires should never be not considered or they would never manifest. I looked at myself and appreciated that I am one who reaches for stars. My enchantments unfold the fortune cookie while I'm hanging out in dark tunnels, as storms hover and the energy field has gone blank, it's the perfect time to look at yourself with appreciation, which makes the universe want to hug you. So ask for help, hug yourself, and keep on.

Abracadabra Rx: Talk To Energy Fields. Consider talking to an energy fields as if it was alive and then wait for an incoming response. Something will always arrive because energy is alive. It could be an innuendo or a point blank directive, as all we're doing is having a conversation with the integral force and finding out what it needs. This is not like praying, wishing or begging for help. It's an intuitive hook up where we dial into a dynamic and go to its energy source for information and fuel. Energy has its own story with its own power that is available for us to tap into. As human beings, we vibrate on electrical gridlines that connect and exchange frequencies with the energy around us, while our awareness is what connects us to our like-kind frequencies.

I asked a visionary healer friend if a certain situation looked to her as if it would come to be. She said it had a fifty percent chance and I needed to push it. She said that talking to the energy field of the situation would empower its energy to accelerate. She also said, *"The energy on the other side is way more powerful than the energy here because this is where the helper energy is."* She was referring to the energy fields in alternative dimensions that are more potent because they're not diluted by Earthly rigmarole.

Oftentimes, I talk to energy and it will tell me to leave the situation alone and be okay without it. It's a fine line when dealing with the energy fields, because it's about the bigger picture and being in conjunction with it. A friend demanded a huge fee for an editing job when she was working on her self-worth. She got the job and then lost it because her fee did not fit in with the overall budget for the project. The project had lotus energy with the potential to eventually pay her even bigger dividends than what she asked for. However, she missed that memorandum and did not see the potential because she was focused only on herself and wasn't inline with the overall promise. An assistant I had did the same. We went through a sparse financial period, which freaked her out. As an old-timer I knew the energy would shift, it did shortly thereafter, but she had quit right before it rolled in and missed it. I tried to tell her, but she was listening to fear.

A conglomeration of energy fields will touch everyone and everything in its vicinity. It also likes to play follow the leader, so we have to pay more attention to the energy of things rather than the exact circumstances. If the energy slows down, then slow down to see if where it's going is well founded and if it takes a sharp turn into a bad place then don't follow it. Energy has a push pull that communicates, so speak to the energy of all things and it will surely tell you if you can travel with it or not.

Abracadabra Rx: The Future Is Now. I envision the future reaching through time to pull me into it. The experience is more of a feeling than an actuality. It's about my desire that's telling me I already own it. If this is true then the future is a delivery service of a story that on some level we have already created in the past. Our stories attract more stories, unexpected endings and new beginnings. By turning the now around and throwing some imagined future instances into it, we're pulling the future into the now.

Eternalism is a philosophy of time that takes the view that all points of time are equally real. I consider the future as a direction with a sense of being, so as the past holds our old stories, the present is where we create from and the future is what inspires us to create. Since time has been segmented it affects our timelines and as a result Mondays are always demanding. So if the past, the present and the future are all happening now, then why worry if there's a moment where nothing makes sense? If we can feel our way into the future, not impose on it but just feel it, we will find that the past and the future speak to each other. The future invites the past and the now to be part of it and this is where time obliterates segmentations because it can't be ruled and does what it needs.

In truth, all our affairs are waves of energy that keep giving when they are full. Inspiration is our lotus that is programmed to grab us at certain points; so when things radically shift, the future is totally in on it. Suddenly there are no plans necessary because the future has penetrated the now and we're off to see the wizard When this happens, don't grab onto the door jams, but know that you're needed elsewhere and go. As we get older we stop defining time and feel the sacredness of this lifespan. It's about our standout moments that have an elixir that's imbedded in us as pure possibility, which has blossomed. These blips are our solid gold holdings; embracing them timelessly holds us.

I collect orchids, I am not an expert on them but they always blossom again for me because I communicate with them by asking them if they have more to give. I also ask them to tell me what they need as I trim and water them. I believe they want to keep giving because I don't throw them away after the first bloom but let them do what they do. It's the same with the future in the sense that if we don't worry about it, it will clearly let us know where it's going. So consider that in an organic way the now is not really the now, but a combination of everything coming into the moment to be part of the occasion. So when nothing is happening and we're done blooming, we will bloom again in the future since we always have more to give.

Abracadabra Rx: Be Clear. Show up to where you are cherished even if it's just you and a tree. When others are hurtful, the message is loud and clear: *They don't really care about us!* Do we ignore it and keep going to the empty well at their house for a drink? You know the scenario well; you're talking to someone while they're looking around the room, and not listening. Hello! These instances are telling us we're with the wrong tribe, while possibly thinking there's something wrong with us. Honey, there is nothing wrong with you, you are in clarity. Clarity does not get all involved in reasoning, but sees the truth and once seen, it demands action. When we're not appreciated, the perfection of our integrity is talking to us. It's saying these are not the people you can rest with on this journey—so move on.

An old friend decided I should be a dumping ground for her anger. It's amazing how anger has a life of its own like a rash and when inflamed it travels into places it does not belong. She texted me a rant that had nothing to do with me, crossed a five-lane highway of boundaries and then involved my brother in her bad story. My dear old friend then cursed my brother out saying his company and business partners were greedy, all because a building they owned evicted her yoga studio for not paying rent for almost a year. I told my friend that it was not appropriate for her to go off on me about my brother, to which she replied that I am not a safe friend. I agreed with her because to me a safe friend holds consideration and does not spew anger, as there is room for truth, even when sharp, because integrity has guns.

Clarity turns on the lights, dispels darkness, and attracts our confidence to come along with a big umbrella to escort us out of gloom. Confidence is not a delicate station, it has moxie and holds its own. Spunk demands that we question things and move away from what feels wrong. At a restaurant with my brother and husband, we had to literally scream across the table to converse. I said I wanted to leave and their response was, but we're already here and seated. I asked the waitress how long it would take to be served and she said at least an hour since it was so crowded. I got up, because to stay there would have been an awful experience. Getting up was an act of total self-reliance, since I could not relax in that atmosphere. We ended up at a nice quiet restaurant down the road and had a peaceful dinner.

The question I always ask when things get tough is, "Does this come from love?" My natural tendency is to crack open the walls around my heart to let beauty in. I want to not back away from the darkness, so I can still see the stars in it. I want to accept the things I cannot change and still have hope. I am clear about this desire, so the things that show up in my world have an edge of charm to slide along on. We are responsible for placing our orders, owning our truth, and getting up off the floor when we are slammed.

Our reality is a partnership where integrity delivers the pure truth and when we're not clear, it's because we're not seeing through the fog. Sometimes we must believe in the unbelievable, a truth that does not exist yet, or a dream that percolates inspirations that we can walk into the sunset with. It might be cliché, but when I'm holding onto hope, while all the old ways I've depended on fall away, sometimes a sunset is all I have. So I go along with those inner voices that say: "*Let everything go and wake up to the dream inside.*" The fog will always clears when we get smudge the shadow in our minds eye. As the late Carl Jung said, "*Your vision will become clear only when you can look into your own heart. Who looks outside dreams; who looks inside awakes.*"

Abracadabra Rx: Time Out. A moment's retreat is a remedial life force. We don't need to take forty days in a desert, though that would be amazing. Forty days in Italy would be even more enticing, but four hours of reprieve or even four minutes in a time of chaos will do it. Actually, literally one moment geared as a turn around is our most potent countermeasure. So take a moment, sit out a story, and get holy when you need an upgrade.

Sacred space is the zone we drop into to commune with our spirit and dream. As a child my son always needed time alone, as an adult he still does, we all do. We need this quiet time to play leapfrog with reality and divine ideas. In time-out, we stop putting the pieces back together and working things out, instead we rest. In the meantime, our nervous system calms down and we give ourselves a break, while trusting that the Universe is in on this with us. We are shifting our psyche back into balance. So meditate, lie on the floor, the earth, look at the sky; focus on your breath and just rest. A nervous system gone awry must be chamomile'd out. Time-out is the crock-pot that simmers everything down to its magical potency.

Abracadabra Rx: Hang Out With The Saint In Your Temple. Consider that the moon is in its perfection at night and smiles at the sun when she says she is going down for a while. Stars shoot across the sky and entice the sun to rise once again because the cosmos is so beautiful that the sun just has to be part of it. We do the same during the times we go down, but get called back because love entices us. My brother and his wife lost their daughter recently to an overdose; this was Hell. He will never give up on loving her as long as he lives because his love carries him. His love for his wife is keeping him alive because he can't forget how much his daughter loved her. Is he upset? Damn straight he is. Yet, he gives it over to show up for love, even when his daughter is on the other side because he is connected to the saint in her soul and this connection is his temple across boundaries.

Holiness has its own reasoning in that it explores higher wisdom. I recently watched a video presented by Gregg Braden, author of The Divine Matrix, where three healers cleared a woman's cancer in minutes. The healers were trained to create the feelings in their hearts that this woman was already healed. It was documented on a scan as we literally watched the cancer disappear. It happened as the healers toned out a word with a powerful belief instilled in it. Everyone present was in agreement with this process so it over-rode anything that was not in accord, which in this case was the patient's cancer. Most importantly, the patient completely believed in what was happening energetically. Braden said that in our culture this would be considered a miracle, but in these people's culture this practice was just correct right action. You can watch it on YouTube. (Google Braden healing cancer in three minutes.)

If seeing things in a certain way is that powerful and our beliefs have such strong considerations, then by hanging out in out temple, we're projecting grace. Understand that we've already arrived as complete enlightened beings and we activate this fact by remembering it. By visioning goodness into darkness, greed, and lunacy, we are not doing spells but honoring the goodness that was there before. Granted, it's hard to hold love and light when life's dregs are banging on the door, but it's really a matter of choosing what we believe in. So when we fall into a Hellhole, we flash an SOS for our higher-selves to come and get us. And when others show a lack of integrity, we sit with our own integrity that fulfills our promise. The days of going to the empty well to drink are over as the message is to turn on the love faucet from within. At these intense turning points our real sustenance attracts grace when we don't give up on ourselves.

A woman asked her Guru in a demanding tone, *"Will you bestow grace on me?"* He responded, *"Will you receive Grace?"* We cannot have what we do not already own or are not open to accepting the possibility of. A client used to always ask me if I was a team player when I was not going along with his hijinks. He wasn't a team player himself and dealing with him made me pull my inner team into such a strong huddle that he was no longer important. I wondered why people like him were still in my world and realized even mosquitoes are attracted to the light.

In seeing the ugliness of what others do, we must still hold love and light. Our most important act is to come back again and again to that one sacred place where we put our burdens down and embrace ourselves. Integrity demands a solstice, a turning point where all that is wrong has no power because it is overridden by what is more powerful. The Saint in our temple is more powerful than a mind in chaos or any needy aspect and will not fall victim to our emotions. Our Saint is free to be the Saint and we are free to hang out with our Saintly selves. Integrity is always a choice.

Abracadabra Rx To Instill And Maintain Integrity . . .

Rx: *Keep the peace in your words, actions, and behaviors.*

Rx: *When things fall apart don't fall apart with them.*

Rx: *When things are falling apart, let them.*

Rx: *Refine your circle of being.*

Rx: *Be grateful for the truth, as it's setting you free.*

Rx: *Treat your mistakes as sacred teachers.*

Rx: *Do what's right so what's right is what you can count on.*

Rx: *Don't react, just re-activate.*

Rx: *Insert good ingredients into bad ones.*

Rx: *Use forgiveness and understanding as your arsenal.*

Rx: *Act well when you have to act.*

Rx: *Do what you feel is right or do nothing.*

Rx: *Empower positive action.*

Rx: *Say less and do more of what is in your best interest.*

Rx: *If it feels wrong, it's wrong; don't argue with your gut.*

Rx: *Investigate what attracts a higher resonance.*

Rx: *Use your mistakes to stop making them.*

Rx: *Converse with energy fields, you will get distinct answers.*

Rx: *Believing that integrity is mandatory is mandatory.*

Rx: *Holding integrity over surmise supports our future.*

Rx: *Integrity is groundbreaking.*

Rx: *Question whether what's going on comes from love. If it doesn't then add some, if it's being rejected than let it go.*

Rx: *Knowing better leads to doing better.*

Rx: *Feelings are not facts; keep it high and feel how you say.*

Rx: *When you fall into a mud hole, consider that the mud is* *pulling out impurities and slather in it.*

Rx: *Treat the situation as you wish to be treated.*

Rx: *Good will breeds integrity.*

Rx: *Integrity is guilt free.*

Rx: *Integrity prospers valid likelihoods.*

Rx: *Good merit is just worthiness dancing with itself.*

Rx: *An argument with one's self to reach integrity, is integrity.*

Rx: *Values over personal gain is integrity over selfishness.*

Rx: *Ideas hold integrity when you stand by them.*

Rx: *Instead of thinking about what to do, think of how well you will do it and you will be in your integrity.*

Rx: *Do secret good things for strangers.*

Rx: *Always come back to love.*

Rx: *The saving grace is when our integrity comes forth and says not today on reactions, defense modes, and judgments.*

Rx: *Like a seed, integrity germinates itself into supporting our overall best story, which empowers our magical life.*

Rx: *When others act dishonorable it's a message that they are no longer your tribe members—let them go.*

Rx: *Reach for the highest point of view, since you aren't going anywhere good until you get there in your mind first.*

Rx: *Send your goodness into the future so when you get there it's waiting for you.*

Rx: *Doing the right thing is a decision, so keep making that decision until it becomes a way of life.*

Rx: *We will always be challenged to do the right thing and that's how you will know it's the right thing!*

7) Keep Dreaming . . .

"Dreaming about being an actress . . . is more exciting than being one." –Marilyn Monroe

Beautiful things put me in an elevated state so sometimes shopping is my medicine. I don't need to buy all the things I see; admiring them is more than enough. On one shopping expedition I was perusing a rack of dresses, when I went into an altered state. A particular blue velvet dress grabbed me and suddenly my mind started to swirl out of focus and I saw myself in a different life wearing this dress. The dress made no sense for me now, though it appeared a future version of me, seemed to need this dress. It happens that sometimes our future is shown to us in a vision that feels like it's on a zip line pulling us along with it. This dress was telling me a story that inspired me and really I did not need to buy the dress, as the experience was enough. The message is that if we allow ourselves to delve into visions, they will entice us to dream up something we need into our future story.

Dreams and visions are passports giving us the code to the lock box that holds our bounty. They also have exit portals that defy normal concepts and explore wonders. The great dreamers of this world vision the future, shift reality and divine magic. Dreaming our way is a serious endeavor that offers us possibility. Actually when dreaming, we are making subliminal agreements in virtual realms, by doing what we cannot on the physical circuit. By visioning other actualities, we take our difficulties apart and marry them back together another way. So step into your dreams, see what they say and follow them, you will come back bearing gifts—your own.

Marilyn Monroe, as a young girl was scarred by traumas, which had activated her emotional sadness. She had big dreams of being a star and always wore a lucky red cardigan that she imagined would energize her future. Her dream manifested but unfortunately her past sadness kept creeping back in and if finally engulfed her. In her search for love, she did not take the time to learn to love herself. Self-love asks us to drop our baggage in order to get into the hot air balloon with our inner child to heal their woes. Children constantly dream, it's their sustenance, and it's truly ours too.

Visionary dreams are amusing; each one is its own potent slice of the pie and like vignettes in a movie the images jump around showing us many avenues. When we're dreaming, things stretch so that there is an expansion around the edges and we can easily move beyond where we actually are. We enter time warps where the outcome is now and have a full on beginning to end epoch. All our normal agendas are bland after a visit beyond our concepts, as our psyche has been permeated with the fact that magic has been imposed. While dreaming, a definitive underlying shift is set to ensue and through an open state of mind this new manifestation is modulating its way into being—let it.

In grade school, sometimes a feeling would overtake me and I would start singing. There was no time to control myself because I was in rapture. I would sing from my heart and suddenly the bubble would pop to the sound of other children laughing at my inappropriateness. I was considered an oddball and ignored, which was fine with me as I could get away with more dreaming and not be bothered. During those moments of euphoria, my daydreams took me out of places that I could not stand being in, like school. I found I could leave a bad scene and travel into a substantial reverie that satiated and healed my woes. After visiting this fool's paradise, I was then shamelessly Ok, as I had discovered my own form of natural self-medication.

Understand that we've dreamed our way into every reality we have ever touched upon. Sometimes our dreams call for us to play out new roles, as if an enchantment has tapped us on the shoulder to say: "Tag you're it!" Our dreams may lead us to do battle, to face the bad guys that we can't deal with in reality and to become heroes. In dreams, we run for our lives, leap off cliffs and we fly. We drop our ego; our mental blather and go into reveries that hold bliss. And when we have to we face the monster that tries to slay us, it's to restructure our despair. All realities are temporary, we are not supposed to get lost in them but travel though them. So we must dream our way when things are unfolding, when we have no idea where we're going, and when we cannot count on the usual means of shifting existence and finding magic.

Our dreams are personal when they are empowering us, they are sacred when they are prayers for others, and they are holy when they wrap their arms around the world to heal it. We must honor and hold space for them to do their magic. So when pulled by the needs of the world or others, decide if you are in agreement with their dream and if not continue on in your own dream mode. We will marry the dreams that move our hearts, as they become lovers at hand. We may take what exists in this dimension and transform it or we can travel into a dream state to find a valuable ingredient and simulate it into the mix. Our sentiments around our dreams remind us that the magic exists. So drop your burdens and dream, for you are being far flung by God's ricochet.

The Abracadabra Prescriptions For Dreaming:

Abracadabra Rx: Dream To Your Heart's Content. We must never ignore our hearts pursuit and this means we have to take down the invisible walls that hold us away from our true calling. We've been trained to follow rules and support systems that don't support us and we've been told not to make waves. Well hello in there, this is your heart speaking and here's the message: "*Please pay strong attention to me or I am shutting down and when this happens you are guaranteed to* *have no fun and even die."* Yes, this is a strong message and unfortunately not fooling around. Our hearts are constantly talking to us and when they are not addressed, the neglect of our hearts calling literally takes us home to heal. Our huge hearts are powerful warriors; they can break and heal over and over, but being ignored is fatal to them. When the heart leads, then everything else falls into place as our instinct wakes up and creativity sparks. So make waves—big ones!

Welcome to the only conspiracy to be concerned with; it's our relationship with our higher-self telling us to ignore all the lies and the madness. The truth is that the gold is buried under our house, so click your heels together, get the shovel out and start digging. Meanwhile forget about outcomes or back stories because it's not about what we achieve, but how we feel while playing with it all. Our pumped up love zone never promises us perfect outcomes, due to the fact that there's a treasure in everything and it's pushing us find them. The secret of the heart is to awaken our passion even where none exists, because as we look for it—it awakens.

Abracadabra Rx: Dream Your Way. We get into a panic over the anomaly of things not working out and we think the solution is to do things another way, when the real way is in our state of mind not an actual destination. Not being in our natural way feels like an allergic reaction to life and we can't fix that on the physical plane. So when things are not right, it's a message to dream our way to where they are right. If you think about it, our ethereal pondering has a natural inner compass that goes right to auto-find on where we thrive. Thinking about it takes us there, so think about it.

In reality we are bombarded with other people's energy and the ways of this world. I have a hard time acclimating these days and while out to dinner with my husband at a restaurant where the tables were so close, it felt like we were having dinner with strangers. I felt crowded in, enmeshed and wanted to leave. My husband was fine and said I should just focus on him, which I did. It worked. I remembered that I always dreamed my way out of discomfort as a child and now when necessary, we must be holy where we are and see the rest as the dream that we're not part of. This way we don't keep gyrating but hone down to the bones the fact that the right place is in our light filled state of mind. And know, if we have to leave dark situations—it's to shine elsewhere.

Abracadabra Rx: Dream Bravely. A young friend, who is a talented photographer and artist, was captured by low self-esteem. Feeling trapped by this abduction, she turned to heroin to distract her pain. Heroin is aligned with a crew of dark people who promised they loved her, which was a lie. Addiction to substances geared for escape doesn't work, as you still have to escape the addictions. This dear girl had to dream bravely into her wounds and journey with them to face her pain. When we are being hurt by the world, our inner world is the hero. We must go there and pull out our sword to cut the cords on darkness so we can pierce the veils and let the light in. In a healing crisis, we will be asked to surrender the things that have power over us, including our pain, to be truly empowered.

I was working on selling a house for a man who was a bully. It was all about his ego and having the power to make people kowtow to him. He threatened to destroy my reputation if I did not lose a potential deal that I worked hard for because he wanted someone else to have it. The bully stigma is a big one these days. A part of me wanted to just give in and let him have his way so I could be done with him. Though I quietly dreamed on it and saw that it was not about winning, but about standing up for me. In doing so, I was also standing against and exposing the bully dynamic. I thought about my reputation and realized that if I believe in my goodness, it will shine through lies. Even an attorney in my company said, "Stand by what is right!" To dream bravely is to know that our dreams are the standard to live by. In the beginning it might seem that they're not able to carry us, but what really matters is that we are able to carry them!

Abracadabra Rx: Reflect. Our play of consciousness is a multi-dimensional production starring us in the leading role as the one who is playing us. We're also playing our co-star that is also us along with all the stand-ins. Imagine that! In reality, all that goes on is like an allegory of one story with many stories in it. The surface story is not really the main story; it's just the story we are focusing on now. Most stories are surrounded by supportive stories with other stories that are trying to take the main story apart. Stay with me, because the assignment is to quit playing all the roles out and just be ourselves in every story we step into. What to focus on is to find out who we really are behind the one that thinks it is someone. It's about being the witness behind the witness, being awake in our dreams and taking the time to fearlessly reflect on the core of us and who that is.

It's time to peel away the stigmas, to stop kneeling to false Gods and playing bad roles. Once we zero into our soul identity, we get humble. We stop searching for the other to complete us, as we're already complete. So step out of the grey zone and measure yourself by the authentic truth that defines your spark. It's divine liberation to not be ruled by any collective and tap into our inner warrior who follows dreams. To reflect on our highest state delivers us there.

I read a fairy tale where a young boy was searching for gold that he heard existed on the other side of the mountain from where he lived. He went on a journey to find it and got lost in the deep woods, which represented his mind. He was weighed down from carrying a heavy sack of belongings and was terribly thirsty. He then stumbled upon an old well and as he leaned over to fetch some water his heavy sack fell down into it. The boy cried because he had lost everything, though after great lament, he found he was much lighter without the heavy sack of belongings, aka all his old stories, and could travel easier. He effortlessly found the mountain path and reached the top to find that the treasure he was seeking was in the fact that he traveled. Once his burdens were released, the message was that his riches were found when he journeyed alone reflecting on what is meaningful.

The metaphors and allegories of this life are symbols that have strong meanings. For instance, the well where the boy lost his sack mirrored his reflection of hope. This well also represented his wellness, so it took away from him what was unwell, being his heavy burden. Our dreams and visions do the same, as when we have a nightmare we are being shown an underlying feeling or situation that runs along our stress lines. This exposure of what creates our unease is being brought to light to be cleared. There's a quote that goes: *Spiritual death happens one compromise at a time.* Like the boy in the story, we are all on the journey of remembering we have the gift that reflects our light. In order to claim this gift, we must first give up the beliefs and lies that cannot own a treasure and then reflect on what can.

Abracadabra Rx: Be Wild By Nature. Many of our stories come with rules. It's not a matter of good or bad, just a matter of if we are free or not. I was always called an unruly child and unruly children must be tamed. You cannot tame nature, you can manicure it, but it will always come back to being wild. In captivity animals are trained but the moment they are set free they go back to their wild attributes. In the same sense, if we are held captive by even our minds, our wild trademark features are still resonating in us and are constantly pushing to set us free. The point is we don't have to act wild, we can just sit and tap into our wilderness and play with our wildness and that's good enough.

The nature of the beast does not question if it's okay to have its way. A lion doesn't question its roar. A hawk does not question capturing its prey. In the same sense, we should never question love. As a child in school, I saw things in abstract ways and could travel into a crack in the plaster wall and rebuild the room. Little did I know back then that I was in a training course that went way beyond the schoolroom. I was teaching myself to travel beyond a humdrum routine and be in magic. The great visionaries are doing what others don't believe is possible; menial interruptions don't deter them. Maybe a young Steve Jobs got his first spark to create Apple in the midst of a boring classroom. So when things get banal, consider we're being squeezed to go into the wild unknown. It is our nature to question things, to fall through cracks, and to leave our minds in the dust when love calls, because we're wild by nature.

Careful people don't believe in the unbelievable, they only invest in what is proven. I gave my chiropractor a copy of my first book and told her I was in the process of changing my life again and she said it was amazing at my age. She didn't get the memo that we live in a timeless reality called eternity. Sometimes in eternity we're older or younger or not even here at all. I believe that I'm exempt from all reasoning as to why I can't change my reality at any age. So be careful not to be too careful, lest you be trapped by being a grown up when real growth is in our youthful explorations.

I was reminded of the fact that we never grow up, when my adult son's response to the "*Grow Up*" statement was:

"You know I have seriously looked for a grown up inside me and I can surely tell you, there isn't one." I was relieved to hear it because magic lives in the fact that we're growing in all directions and even into other dimensions. By going out there, we're matching up the bliss we get from dreaming that follows us back to be part of this reality. The philosopher Samuel Taylor Coleridge said, *"If a man could pass through Paradise in a dream, and have a flower presented to him as a pledge that his soul had really been there, and if he found that flower in his hand when he awoke - Aye! And what then?"*

Abracadabra Rx: Be In Bliss. Our dreams no longer belong on the back burner while we're out in the world busy surviving. Surviving to live a mundane existence is a spiritual death. Supporting someone else's dream while not holding our own shuts down our charisma. We can still be part of a communal dream when we must, but the trick is to find bliss in it and if it doesn't exist, create it. It takes great moxie to not buy into imprisoned concepts, to be the rebel who plants their own seeds in the mud to grow a lotus they can sit on. So when things become difficult, I always ask: *"Will this bring me bliss in the future?"* I ask this question because not all positive change feels blissful in the beginning.

A young friend coming of age in a very materialistic culture in downtown Manhattan was figuring out how to not be affected by what she didn't have. She described her generation as being under harsh pressure to be successful and found that every time she achieved a goal, she always then needed something more to be OK. She then realized that if she kept this up, she was never going to be OK. Her apartment was excruciatingly small, but she was focusing on an inner space where she was free to explore her creativity. I asked what triggered this inspiration; she said she decided she was finding her bliss now and owning it so she could walk out from there with it and not always be chasing it.

I got in a New York City taxi and oddly the driver had no safeguard partition between him and the passenger and it felt as if I had gotten into a car with a friend. The driver said he owned the cab and that he felt totally safe because in twenty years of driving his cab, he'd never had a bad experience or felt in danger. He said he loved driving his taxi, which to me is one of the most stressful jobs I could imagine. He also said he loved it not because he was a people person but because it gave him the freedom to dream as he drove. His cab was immaculate and as soon as I got into it I could not help but relax because his essence was so peaceful that it gave me the space to dream along with him.

I once knew a garbage man who sang gorgeous opera sonnets while collecting refuse. People waited for him to come by because his joy was infectious. Whatever robs our bliss is a thief of the heart so we must take our bliss back. What we are battling is the aspect of ourselves that is over-ruled by our misgiving mind and allows us to give up. Bliss never gives up on itself, as it always comes back around to entice us back into its domain. So don't waste time in warfare when you can just be in bliss.

I recently dreamt that I was trying to maneuver a stick shift automobile that was stuck in park. The shift had become disconnected, so I had no control of my vehicle. Hello? How perfect for a dream to deliver me an analogy that was telling me I was stuck in a place where I was cut off from my creativity. I woke up knowing that like in the dream I was not going to move my human vehicle out of park until I got out of the car and called a cab, aka my magic carpet. In reality I needed to get out of the situation I was stuck in to become in awe as a tourist. So I daydreamed of paradise and saw things through rose lenses until I was infused with bliss, and then I put myself into drive from there.

Inspirations happen in the most ordinary instances when we go into a wondrous state. Amazement stirs up bliss when the odds are against us; like when we're taking out the garbage, calling the phone company, or waiting on lines. We must remember that we have this power to shape-shift reality in any instance. Recognize that we come from what we allow, what we create, and what we manifest, so it's up to us to be in the state we want to live in. The outer circumstances then don't matter when we're percolating bliss. Take Nelson Mandela who managed to walk eight miles a day in his tiny jail cell while his dreams and messages went further still to affect the world from there. In a sacred state we are all that powerful as visionaries and mystics and it matters not from where we are broadcasting, but simply that we are. Joseph Campbell said, *"Follow your bliss and doors will open where there were only walls."*

Abracadabra Rx: Vision Miracles. By energizing a formless notion we are signaling a matching energetic to come and meet us in form. This miracle is the essence of the seed that grows the best options. Entry into a miracle zone is about changing our consciousness and getting into the state of mind where the exterior does not matter, only wonder matters. A focused thought form is sparked with energy that will begin to manifest on a physical plane. In the sense of visioning miracles, as we play with ideas we're subliminally empowering them to come to be. The best outcome is not so much in wishing for things to happen, but in the realization that there is something miraculous always happening and we must be in a treasure trove mindset to find it.

In a transition that asked me to rely only on my faith in miracles, I agreed. The Universe told me to finish this book and not worry about the fact that I had to let go of my real estate business for the time being. Oddly, at this time, I was constantly receiving gifts, even from strangers. One morning, stepping into the elevator in my building in Manhattan there was a woman carrying a four-stem orchid. I love orchids and commented on its beauty, she handed it to me, smiled, and walked away. The Universe was saying, "*See, gifts are constantly arriving and you will be fine.*" Every time I began to worry, it was an alert to instead vision miracles. Our magic exists in knowing that miracles when focused upon create more of themselves and also knowing that we are part of one is the greatest miracle.

Abracadabra Rx: Empower A Manifesting Mode. One powerful thought, realization, heart expansion, and swell of gratitude opens the floodgates of manifestation. Even when the conditions are not complimentary, we must dream of what gives rise to abundance, which creates it. A panorama of energetic phenomenon is a corroboration of our worldly and spiritual agreements. So dis-believe all the commentary around what isn't possible and play with inspiration. When I first started in real estate, I loved going to open houses and driving around buyers, my bliss flag was flying even though I was broke. Within weeks I was flourishing, as energetically our real allowance is in the conceptual target practice that validates two words: I Deserve.

I was once advised that if I wanted to be rich, I should sit in luxurious hotel lobbies, have tea in five-star restaurants, and test drive luxury cars to imbibe wealth. All we are doing is telling the energy field of abundance that we are now here to be part of it. In the belief that we deserve our bounty, the vibrational core of worthiness is stimulated. So think rich! A friend who created a musical production company was questioning if what he was doing was worth anything and if he could make a living from it. His friends constantly asked him to do freebie music for their projects, web sites, videos, and short films. He did and then realized his work was worthy of a new bank account. Once he banked on his own worthiness, his music shifted from being a hobby to a trade. He manifested supporting himself by doing what he loved.

I constantly thank the Universe for my manifestations, as if they have already come to be. I also ask the energy field for permission to be part of its affluence and to prosper with it. I was once offered a listing of a friend who had passed on and I wanted to do a good job for her son. In the beginning there were complications and many low offers. So I asked my deceased friend to help me sell her house for her son. The energy immediately shifted and the perfect buyer showed up who paid the right price and was easy to work with. The point is we don't always manifest alone!

Our energy goes out on a daily shopping spree and if we don't give it the shopping list, then the energy has no idea of what we want or need. The highest form of manifestation goes beyond things into enlightenment. As such, the practice of manifestation shows us that beyond getting the goods that the real goods are miracles. I once posted a photo of a luxury vehicle on my fridge. My brother came to visit and had just hit a jackpot in his business and the next day he overnighted me a copy of the car brochure. I opened it to find a check for the car inside. It was not a special occasion, but to me it was very special, as what excited me more than the actual check for the car was that the manifestation came to me with such great love. The directive is that when giving the energy field our shopping list; always add that all overnight deliveries are to be left at the door with love.

Abracadabra Rx: Dream Magically. My business was at a crossroad and I was unraveling because I could no longer continue on in the same way, as I was exhausted. Without my mojo I felt like I was losing it and could not thrive, when in truth the Universe had stepped in and said, *"You! Go sit on the bench in Time-Out."* In actuality it was perfectly right that I step away because my mind was listening to distorted lies and believing them and this had shut down my mojo. We think our party is over when things are being rearranged and in truth we're still manifesting but in a more magical way. So when things get complicated and don't work well or stop flowing, it's time to sit on the fence and dream magically.

I was a hair and makeup artist in my twenties and while I was in transition on my third life shift, I had a dream where I was surrounded by a group of women telling me to go back to being a makeup artist again. I told them I had no clients and they said they would send me all the clients I needed if I just showed up as a makeup artist. I told them I no longer owned a make-up kit, so they handed me a suitcase full of new cosmetics. They told me again to just show up as a make-up artist and everything would work out. I woke up thinking about this profound dream and at first I thought the dream was telling me to go back to doing something I had already done. Suddenly a light bulb ignited and I realized it was telling me to make things up—to be a makeup artist. The dream was telling me that if I focused on making things up, the Universe would send me everything I need!

Our dreams hold our aspirations that are delivered with directional forces that pierce through all realities to remind us what direction to go in. Dreaming bring us back to what we need to remember and then slams it home. Dreaming has a cosmic push that pierces our destiny, as dreaming will slap down lies, distill what is necessary and remove what's beside the point from where it has no right being. Like a swirl of smoke that rises out of our Genie lamp, our enticing dreams go around waking things up and sparking our magic. Anais Nin said, *"Dreams pass into the reality of action. From the actions stems the dream again; and the interdependence produces the highest form of living."* This means that we are tapping into our relationship with an astral macrocosm that is impressive and brings out what's culminating. Our dreams bestow magic; they heal misgivings and put us smack in the right place at the right time to receive.

Our highest state includes bliss and folly, so be like the Fool in the Tarot deck who is mesmerized by the dream of his life. When dreams take us to the edge of one reality, it's only to step into another. As we dream, we are also part of a bigger dream, like the dream of the world. That dream might appear to be going crazy, but we still get to dream our own dream within the dream. Thereby we instill magic as we dream for the world, play with our potential, invest in our worthiness and focus on goodness, grace and miracles. The highest form of living is always magically instilled, therefore it does not matter where we're going, it just matters that we dream to our hearts content so the dream will takeover and spark the magic we can really thrive on. Dream of the future you wish to be part of, honor the dream and Pass Go!

Abracadabra Rx: To Dream Magically . . .

Rx: *Dream magically.*

Rx: *Dream your way around your mind.*

Rx: *Dream into the wisdom that sees the truth.*

Rx: *Let your dreams lead.*

Rx: *Find your heart in the dream and delve into it.*

Rx: *When fear arises dream up its antidote.*

Rx: *Navigate towards the whereabouts that feel right.*

Rx: *Our limited energy becomes expansive as we dream.*

Rx: *Offer your burdens to the dream to be dispelled.*

Rx: *Dance with yourself in the dream of your life.*

Rx: *Reflect on dreams, write them down, explore them.*

Rx: *When dreams deliver bliss, know its time to be in bliss.*

Rx: *At a crossroad connect to your essence and dream with it.*

Rx: *Vision miracles.*

Rx: *Don't hold yourself in place—set yourself free to dream.*

Rx: *Be your wild self in your dreams.*

Rx: *Let the dream do what it needs to bring amnesty.*

Rx: *Reach for the hand of grace in a dream and don't let go.*

Rx: *Offer your pain forth to be healed in a dream.*

Rx: *Speak well to yourself, to your spirit, to your dream.*

Rx: *When in doubt—dream.*

Rx: *Dream daily.*

Rx: *Visit your ancestors and ask them to dream with you.*

Rx: *Dream of light-filled things and pull them in.*

Rx: *When lost in the dark, vision the darkness bearing light.*

Rx: *Find your power in your dreams and pull it into reality.*

Rx: *Dream daringly.*

Rx: *Daydreams are necessary journeys that alleviate reality.*

Rx: *Marry your dreams.*

Rx: *Program your dreams to define your Ok-ness.*

Rx: *Show up to experience the abundance you dream of.*

Rx: *Dalliances are also dreams.*

Rx: *Take your dreams seriously.*

Rx: *While dreaming there are no boundaries.*

Rx: *The winds of bliss will direct the journey of our dream.*

Rx: *If you hold space and wait for the dream to arrive, it will.*

Rx: *When pushed beyond limitations, it's for us to know we have none and it's time to believe in the unbelievable.*

Rx: *Be brave enough to face the monsters, courageous enough to wake up your inner hero, so you will be fearless in reality.*

Rx: *In a struggling dream, know you are just un-struggling.*

Rx: *Dreamtime is grace in action.*

Rx: *Grace loves to hang out in our dreams and surprise us.*

Rx: *While dreaming you are free.*

Rx: *Dream so all that matters can come to life in you.*

Rx: *We are vessels attracting our goodness and when dreaming we are taking the lid off to receive it.*

Rx: *Dream so high that you have to reach for it.*

Rx: *Dream wildly.*

Rx: *Once upon a dream there was a spark that you decided to become and now here you are.*

Rx: *Dream for the World, Dream for Love, Dream Magically!*

8) Align With Magic . . .

"One can stand on their tiptoes to see farther, or drag out the ladder to see higher, or kindly ask the person standing in front of them that is blocking their vision to please move over. Or, one can simply close their eyes; see everything and align magically!"

Part One — Change Your Energy To Magical!

A woman on the shopping line, who was bothered by the slow cashier, was causing a ruckus. Her turn came up, the cashier went on a break and another showed up who had to recount all the money before helping her. This woman began cursing out loud and made the new cashier so nervous she repeatedly had to count again. Finally the angry woman checked out and it was like a storm moved on. When Ms. Nasty Pants arrived to the parking lot, she found a big fresh dent in the driver-side of her car door. Cursing to the Heavens, she then sped through a red light to receive a ticket. This woman was attracting the bad energy she was giving out. The Universe was crashing into her driver side to warn her to slow down and then gave her a ticket to stop her. What could come next would be worse if she didn't pay attention. We all know this woman because we have all once been like her, which is why we must consciously choose what energy field we are resonating within and why.

A pattern can be contagious and in the world of energy there is no separation between all living things, including the natural elements and the cosmos. *The Hundredth Monkey* effect proved this when the number of monkeys on one small island took to washing their sweet potatoes prior to eating them. When this activity reached critical mass, then monkeys all over the world began washing their sweet potatoes before eating them. There were no monkey cell phones back then saying, *"Hey fellow monkeys, we're doing it this way now."* It was telecommunication in the energy fields that broadcasted the memo that a pattern had changed. The monkey world picked up on the new pattern and matched it. It's the same with humanity, as when critical mass accepts a new pattern, it becomes a new precedent and the rest of the world then accepts it.

Crazy chaotic energy affects the general consensus that tunes into it; by aligning with what's harmonious we become the countermeasure. In order to convert the energetic opposition: Stop everything and pinpoint where your focus is. We are energetic hitchhikers who watch the waves of energy roll by in order to see which waves to catch the best ride on. A rough wave will roll in and toss us around until we learn to respect the ways of waves, then we surf.

We are actually learning how to learn and how to take these lessons to the next level and step into the magic with them. Magic can be demanding and sometimes asks us to toss everything to the wind. Like the Fool in the Tarot Card, lets make things up as we go and believe that the universe is an ally. The Fool never knows what to expect, but believes he is in the right place at the right time. The Tarot depicts the Fool standing on one foot on the edge of a cliff. He carries a satchel and is leaning as if to jump off while looking towards the Heavens. A small dog is barking to warn him or call him back, but the Fool is gone. Leaving his worries behind, the Fool leaps into his or her own freedom with no regrets. Leaping into new beginnings with beginner's luck, the Fool is playing with the magic of the world. So let's be the Fool!

Abracadabra Prescriptions To Align Magically:

Abracadabra Rx: Think Magically. Our prior beliefs were always questioning was the world round or flat? Is there life on other planets? Did Atlantis exist and could humans actually build pyramids? Could we fly through the air from one continent to another in a long metal object with wings? Once we couldn't and now we can. How about the concept that we can be in more than one place at the same time, the concept that when we die, we don't really ever die and all the beings we have ever loved will love us back through eternity? Considering the tides of change, many times things get churned up before they settle, which pulls us into the mire.

The mire is a sign that energy is moving and it tests us to see if we have what it takes to move through it.

During the times when our minds or the world is in chaos, remove yourself. Yes, it sounds crazy because we have to basically step out of the world and forget. An example is we might be in a relationship that suddenly ends and it might feel like it never happened because we've moved so far beyond it that it hardly exists. So to be in the world but not of it, means go to your job, vote for the least dangerous candidate, do what you have to do but think magically. By thinking magically, we go beyond the old ways of believing things are a certain way and tread past what's not pertinent anymore because these things are no longer magical. Once we realize that our storylines portray segments that happen so we can breakthrough them, we get clear on our memoir entries. I thought I was doing one thing but the truth was that my life could be filed in fragments of time where:

A) I broke away from my family.

B) Money was my God.

C) I have to prove I can take care of myself.

D) I was in love.

E) I was betrayed.

F) I felt like a failure.

G) I lived in my ego.

H) I was angry for a decade . . . these are all themes!

A theme is the overall topic that controls a paradigm with a unifying idea. So if we're feeling desperation then that will be the overriding keynote on the matter at hand. When addressed, these themes magically shift into revealing higher motives. So the time I felt like I was betrayed was really about me finding my power. When I lived in my ego, I got so beat up that I was angry for a decade until my underlying essence came into focus and kidnapped me. When money was my God, I was cruising around in a Range Rover looking for treasures, which did not fulfill me until I flipped the hunt towards finding the gold within. The theme of being in love became a recurrent verse in the chorus of my life and carried me until I was angry for a decade. The love was there but I couldn't see it until I stopped being angry and focused on it.

A friend had a nervous breakdown and kept repeating the story that took him there. Every time I brought up releasing the story, he said he was trying. On his drive home from our dinner, the police stopped him and accused him of crossing a double line. The officer then realized my friend was sober and told him to stay in the right lane. My friend was appalled, but this was really a direct message from the Universe that said, *"You've crossed the line and this is a warning to stop going into a lane that could cause you to crash. We are now letting you go, so do the same on your stories that cross the line into nowhere good."* Magical thinking is an extraordinary overtone with the motive that catches our fortune in the wind and engraves our future with it.

Abracadabra Rx: Know The Unknown. Talking to a tree would be going out of a known dimension of reality for many of us, though some of us may feel the tree breathing oxygen into the yard. We know living realities exist when we see a flower, look into its blossoming cluster, take a whiff of its elixir and become lost in its world. By delving into a flower, breathing with a tree, dancing with an energy field, or tuning into the divine cosmos, we're going out of bounds to experience beauty in the unknown. If you want to experience the unknown, have a conversation with it.

I've been known to converse with a ball of white light dancing around someone. I see their auric fields, hear things people are not saying and play with idioms that appear out of nowhere to show me magic. Idioms are peculiar, their language and meaning make no sense, like, *"It's raining cats and dogs."* True sense is made by playing around with what we don't understand until it begins to speak to us. So we can be under the weather or over the top or simply kicking the bucket, as our perception defines what we conceive of and makes up its own story around it. Theses ball of light I see around people could be their spirit essence that is following them around or their deceased mother. I am not imagining these things, I see them and you can too if you look.

Other worldly things bring messages because there is something important to know about what exists beyond what appears to exist. These experiences bring me to know there's always more than meets the eye. My open mind converses with what it does not understand and in a most uncanny way, I find I am in conversation with a floating orb circling someone. When we incorporate such pertinent evolved information into our psyche, we are then using our intuition as a directional force. As things that are beyond our imagination come to the forefront, it's just the unknown becoming known. In reality we're doing one thing and in dreams we travel far and wide, we go into the dark and face our monsters, shoot it out with criminals, and experience our pain and rage in other dimensions to workout what we can't in this reality.

In the unknown, entire other worlds exist where we have allies. We might be at a party in summer, standing on lush green lawn having a cocktail when right beneath our feet an entire ant colony is building a new home. Meanwhile, a dog is chasing a squirrel, a child is crying because they see meanness in someone's aura, and all the while the grass is growing. Our deceased mother might be standing right behind us trying to show us something, as our child is tugging on our skirt to go home. Suddenly the dog is barking because he is seeing our mother in spirit. There's a lot going on in the unknown and in the middle of it all, we're having a cocktail while surrounded by other worlds. Look around, open a dialogue, create a conversation, and then hone into the concept of seeing all things through a magical perspective. This expansive range of view lets us see what else is in the party bag, so always look to see what more exists that you can dialogue with to get to know the unknown.

Abracadabra Rx: Be Sagacious. Beyond going into the unknown, elaborate ideas have sagacity, which tap into possibility over misconception. If the world appears flat, we must decide if we agree with such viewpoints. For instance, the concept of life on other planets could be a possibility, while being productive at ninety is our likelihood, if we believe it's possible. Discerning the messages in the things we see is one thing, while deciding what to align with brings forth attainable circumstances. For instance I might get in a panic over a portrayed direction my reality is going in, but instead I lasso my beliefs towards the magnetic attraction I ascribe to. Panic is another fear-based story and the stories we believe are the ones we live. There is no separation between what we think and what we do, so when I need to spend weeks alone, I don't think of my weirdness as a disability, instead I honor that I am elaborating my sagacity.

At a company cocktail party, I met an art director who was elevating the corporate enterprise we worked in. She even created a magazine called Elevate. We were toasting elevation when I suddenly said, *"This is not your real life."* She looked at me in shock, like I was crazy as she loved her job and asked, *"What do you mean?"* I had no idea what I meant. Though within six months she abruptly left the company. Oddly enough what I heard that day was true because this woman was a treasure of elevated offerings and even though I had no idea where she was going, I saw her going. One moment we could be rolling along and suddenly an elaborate idea arrives; reality shifts so our real life can grab us. It happens this way because life is sagacious in a wise but discerning way. A magical dynamic does not conform but perceives what's best—it shifts our vision to shift our world.

Abracadabra Rx: Be The Revolution. It is said in the chaos theory that as a butterfly is flapping its wings on one continent the environment around the world shifts. In the same way that one raindrop raises the level of the ocean, what we do matters. Therefore our thoughts, our actions, and all our visions count. We are altogether responsible for the conditions of our time, so we must stay balanced when caught in rampant low-level realities because we are all like butterflies flapping our wings as an offering to this world.

It's easy to be in a good mood when things are going well, but pulling positivity out of our hat when we're in Hell is heroism. No one and nothing can kill a revolution of love, so consider the powerful words of Martin Luther King, who said, "*I have a dream.*" And Gandhi, who said, "*Be the change you wish to see in the world!*" And, John Lennon's, "*All you need is Love.*" These statements continue to radiate their powerful vibrations because influential words create a revolution. A radical change progresses when a spark of magic inside us enhances itself to become a lightening bolt.

In the way that a declaration laced with pure wisdom turns what's ordinary into a straight shot of sacred, magic, take what's ordinary and transform it. Successful people get knocked down often, but keep picking themselves up. I'm more interested in how they got there over their success. It's interesting to me how some people can sit in a circle of lousy facts and elevate the odds. To see the magic in what people do beyond their actual doing is the real gift being offered.

Mother Theresa, who was not ordained a Saint in her lifetime, was busy being at the forefront of her revolution of love. Saints do not look for a return; a title or an award, as offering goodness is their reward. The great heroes of this time may not be known or famous but they are the ones quietly igniting change. They are all of us who wake up and consciously affect reality as an offering to this world. Our tour de force is a flash of faith, the drive of integrity, a turn-around on hatred and a return to love. We don't accept less than what's sacred and while craziness rocks the boat, we just continue to paddle and this is how we change the world!

Abracadabra Rx: Shake It Loose. We often get stuck and feed the pool of useless remembrances while historic details lodge inside us. I always remembered a mean girl in high school who tormented me; she became a mascot of my ill will. Years later when I saw her profile on social media, I noticed fear behind her imposed perfection. I realized she had made me a stronger person at a turning point where I was deciding who I was. Her meanness did me an actual favor by pushing me to go another way. Though it took me years to shake loose my reaction to her and have compassion for what it takes to grow ourselves up.

This planet, like the woman whose side door was dented by the Universe is quaking, blowing volcanoes and flooding shorelines—she's shaking loose. We too must shake loose all the evil and hatred that gets churned up in this world and lodges inside us. Compassion is the energy field that says:

"Forgive them for they know not what they do". In doing so, we are shaking loose our reactions in deference to healing. We have to shake loose all that does not bode well, all our self-talk that does not honor self-love and all the fear that the biggest safety net in the world can't hold. The biggest shake down is to release the dark mode that pollutes us.

During the time that I decided to shake loose my control issues, after I released control I had a hard time making decisions. So I deferred all decisions to my husband and experienced that most of the ones he made were perfectly in line with what was best. Our roles flipped and I noticed from taking on this new aspect, my husband had shaken loose a historic issue of not making decisions. It was a miracle because he started to focus on what he wanted and started getting it. While I had dislodged the need to control, I saw things in a different light. My attitude went from, no way to *Ok!* The domino effect was effervescent, as one person in the act of uplifting themselves will uplift everyone around them. The ability to shake loose is our inner thunder that moves energy and shifts stories. A storm will always clear the air, but so will a smile.

Abracadabra Rx: Take Yourself Out. On one of those days where nothing was working out, I shut everything off and went on a date with my higher self. We went for lunch, shopped in a bookstore and then went to the beach where I turned off my phone, read my book and took a nap. My higher self and I had a quiet time, we didn't talk, but just communed. When I got back to my phone everything that was crazy was still there, but I was so calm it didn't affect me.

I realized that if I were acting as my own Mother, I would stand up for myself and tell myself who is not allowed to play in my sandbox and I would know whom I can't speak to anymore. I would know what food was good for me and what I need to do for my own good future. We all have the mother gene inside us telling us how to consciously take care of ourselves, so take your hand and walk yourself across the street away from what does not serve you. As we take ourselves out of bad relationships, loser mindsets and hurtful reactions, we are shifting towards being the magic. We might not know it right away, as at first there will just be space, but quickly the magic arrives and we can step into it and be it.

Abracadabra Rx: Be Selective. On a day when I was questioning the quality of my life, I realized I had left a door open for things to get in that were not invited. Low-level inferences are always circling around us and sometimes we must have a touch of their experience to know we don't want them. It's like a tasting a new flavor or touching all the fruit in the market to feel which are rotten. We also must notice when we are not paying attention and not checking but just grabbing fruit and a rotten apple gets in our bag. Ever notice how one rotten apple spoils the entire bag of apples? Similarly we must pay attention to the energy around us and not let rotten energy in on a cellular level.

As a magical being holding integrity, I sometimes curse

out the car window and then catch myself, as I don't want to revolve with curses. We must be discriminating around the underlying sense of goodness we carry and choose the quality of life we aspire to. The ability to choose what supports our good life force is the guideline for receiving abundance. So step away from the false wizards, stop trying to pull back the curtains on what's wrong and just wait for your heart to say follow me. In the meantime be selective, be choicy with your feelings—choose the ones that have lift off.

Abracadabra Rx: Pay It Forward. An Astrologer friend told me that they couldn't answer questions for friends for free, after I asked one that had a simple yes or no answer. In the amount of time it took for him to defend his principals around giving, a quick answer could have been a gold coin in his good Karma bank account. Our Universal bank accounts will always pay out higher dividends to the givers, as every time we go against the giving grain, we shut down our flow. Even in scarcity where we have little to pay forward, we can always offer love, kindness and consideration.

Rosie, a saintly woman who took care of my Mother as she was passing on was an example of unconditional love in action. Rosie lives with people who are dying; she holds their hands, washes their faces and loves them from the depths of her being until the end. In the beginning, most departing folks are mean to her; they call her names, accuse her of stealing things and refuse her love. My Mom was angry that she'd lost control and in her duress she was like a child having a tantrum. Rosie never flinched like I did when my Mother turned into a demon from Hell. Rosie treated my Mom as if she were her baby. After a while all my Mother's defenses came down, as pure love pummels what is in its way until it meets more love.

During a period when my brother had moved states, had a new baby and was not financially abundant, he set our Grandmother up in the most lavish assisted living home he could find. When my Grandmother would ask him how much money she had left, my brother would tell her she had millions. Our grandmother never knew that she didn't have a penny to her name because she had love, which covered her for life. When we were growing up our Grandmother was like *Auntie Mame,* a total giver. She was a wealthy woman who never said no, she gave everything she had to others during her lifetime and in the end she was covered. Many times we do things and there is not a return from that particular source, I think of it as our investing into the greater pool where the returns are miraculous and come from the great unknown.

Abracadabra Rx: Love Yourself. I read a quote by Scott Stabile that said, *"Don't worry if you're making waves simply by being yourself. The moon does it all the time."* Even as we make mistakes and fail, when we love ourselves there's no sorry beyond the first blip of sorry because we are learning as we go. So never be sorry for being sorry, we have to let that sorry-ness go, because sorry is another wave and all waves merge into the bigger ocean. Loving ourselves is about living in the wave that gives us permission to shine. We accept ourselves when others don't and we forgive ourselves and appreciate ourselves when others don't. So do the inner work of facing yourself, see what needs to go and what needs to be uplifted. Loving ourselves is honoring what's holy in the holiness of our container and so we fill it with love.

Abracadabra Rx: Play With Your Consciousness. In this game of life, we are playing with variations of reasoning and sometimes we become immersed in the performance. Swami Muktananda states in his book, *The Play Of Consciousness*, that we use theatrical drama to try to get to the source of truth. So there we are caught up in a scene and suddenly something shifts, the game is dropped and out of the blue we are the real version of us who sees the real other. In these sublime moments we drop who we are and start playing around with our consciousness, then our entire existence dissolves and only our essence exists. If we play everything out with an overriding plan of always coming back to what is pure, then the stories trigger truth.

Imagine walking down a crowded street in Manhattan and getting jostled, it's noisy, people not paying attention, traffic, blasting horns and all the while we're trying to hold our peace. The way to peace is the exact opposite of our reactions while stressed and the trick to achieve it is to play with the consciousness of being calm in the hub of discord. Whatever we play with becomes the reality of the moment.

In the movie, *Life Is Beautiful,* a father held captive in a concentration camp made up tales of being on an adventure so his young son would not know the danger of where they really were. I too make up tales when things are not going well, like the delay is really protection and how lucky I am. I thread my dark insights into light-filled narrations because they empower me. Playing with enlightenment passes go on reality because consciousness is like a cosmic traveler that transverses all realities. So weave threads around the light-filled stories inside all stories to make your magic carpet fly. Think about the story you want to be part of and step into it. In truth we can't control what goes on around us or to us, but we can always create a good story to get through it. Maybe we go into hiding where we find our soul who is playing hide and seek with us. How's that for a story?

As human beings, we are all living in different realities on the same planet and the common thread is that we all want to feel love, have success, and be secure. The desire to flourish is our intrinsic bond, so in the times that we're not flourishing, we're not in flourishing consciousness. Can we stalk what is sacred and pull it to the forefront of our reality? Can we bypass what is not important or valid enough to not be true for us? Can we get down to the nitty-gritty on what fuels our existence and drop what doesn't? We must.

These kinds of questions don't beat around the bush, but spotlight divine thinking. The answers are game changers on the reality spectrum and define the plot on where our truth is and how to get there. Ask yourself these questions . . .

What pulls me into union with love?

What can I bring that is sacred to my reality?

What are the reflections I experience and what can I add to them to make them divine?

What can I change inside myself to change the reflections?

What is my life dream? Do I trust that my dream is manifesting? If not why and can I play with believing otherwise?

What are the boundaries I encounter? And can I transpose these boundaries into learning experiences?

At what level am I connected into the Bigger Picture?

Do I uplift the reality I encounter?

Do I feel the awesomeness of life and if not where can I find this awesomeness?

What inspires my heart?

What do I wish to leave behind when I go?

Part Two – Be The Magic!

"Love does not exist in gazing at each other, but in looking outward together in the same direction." –Antoine de Saint-Exupery

Growing up in New York City, every time I went to the country, it was as if my soul would unravel out of my body and begin to dance. As a young adult urban dweller in a circle of creative friends, my husband and I bought a car and would constantly drag our friends into the wilderness to sit on beaches and wander through forests. These escapes always reminded me that there were other worlds out there and to be in balance I needed to explore them. I didn't realize it at the time but my magic was in my ability to run interference on everything that did not hold my happiness.

I was creating an opening for the future to come towards me bearing gifts and as my periphery expanded beyond my reality I could easily see where I needed to go. All I had to do was follow my bliss. We often think we don't have time for this sort of nonsense, though the in-between time is exactly from where we advance. Our little inner devil is a robber of time that sits on one shoulder saying, *"You suck! So forget about dreams and let's go to Hell"* Meanwhile our magic is flashing its razzle-dazzle and one blink in its direction runs interference on the self-curse that has been imposed.

Recently, I had a dream where I was trying to move into

the exact town that I already live in. The dream showed me how time will slip around to go back and forth over old issues when it has something to say. In that dream I was lost and arguing with myself, I thought I was already here but the dream was showing me that just because I'm physically here, I wasn't really here at all. In real life my passion had run off so I was not all there. Back in the dream I was thinking about settling for less, but saw that complacency was lifeless. I woke up to realize that being lost and feeling cursed is an energetic push to advance. I followed the message.

We came here to play with wonder and be in service to the best parts of reality. Though since chaos and enmity also exist we must hold a state of equanimity. Still, we can't sit around with a big smile when all hell is breaking loose. We have to do something about it and this means validate what's important and live within its means. So we advance off the dried up mushroom we're sitting on, as the muscle of life wants to work us out of being stuck. A man who had lost his wife in a Paris terrorist attack, made a statement to the world that he and his newborn son would miss this woman terribly and grieve her loss, but they would not let terrorists win their hate. Instead they would continue on in the name of love for the woman they lost and in time they would come back to being happy. We must do the same, over and over, as the constant coming back to love is the highest advancement.

Where are we going? We're snapping out of always doing the same old thing. We stop fitting a piece of ourselves into an unchanging puzzle and advance our consciousness into what's new. We introspect our patterns and suddenly an old dynamic breaks down because we have advanced beyond it, just by seeing it. Lillian Hellman, the writer, said, *"People change and forget to tell each other."* Our advancements begin on the inside when we decide where we are magically going and then everyone and everything else will either catch up or fall away. The future is the advanced version of the now, so when the now is full of versatility, the future will be the enhanced magical version. When we let go of what no longer supports us, it lets go of us. In the same sense, when we hold onto what holds us, we become the magic.

Abracadabra Prescriptions For Being The Magic:

Abracadabra Rx: Be Magic. What if all the prerequisites for our goals dissipated and we could suddenly arrive in the exalted state of where we were striving to go now? We would be living the magic. So what if we tried a new concept on for size and when it perfectly fit, we then owned it? This is how it is to be the magic. At first we claim it, then we step into it, and then we are it. We actually really are it and all we are doing around here is finding that out. So what if in a blink we decided to acknowledge this spark of a fact? Then our world would change and we'd be surrounded by magic.

It's weird that we are part of the human race, a term that classifies humans into groups that are all rushing in many directions. In Hindi humankind means mankind, I wonder who made up these explanations? And since someone or a group of someone's decided on these explanations, then as far as making things up, anything goes. So as spirits who've manifested and created these great bodies, I say we are here as magic beings. I think we should change the title of human beings to magic beings. When you think of it and realize that you are a pure magical being then no matter what you do— you are that.

A magical being turns stories around, they don't have to make things happen, as they always just find the best in what's happening and expand on it. Imagine being anything you feel a need to experience, just to try it on for size. I cherished my nursery school playtime where I was a doctor, a nurse, the mommy, the daddy, or whatever I wanted to play with being at the time. Reality is like this too, as we are playing out certain roles to have a taste of them. Sadly, my husband told me that when he was in nursery school he wanted to be the mommy, but the teachers were always telling him he couldn't be a mommy. It really affected him because he needed to be in touch with mothering. To this day my husband is always in the kitchen in his apron, cooking meals with such love. Little did those short-sighted teachers know back then that we would come to a day of male mommies and same-sex marriages because we have passed the bar on small-minded realities.

Possibility is unregulated and there are no rules, so if I want I can marry my cat and live happily ever after. Maybe I can't get our photo into the *New York Times* but I can still publish it on my blog. Therefore when coming face to face with an obstruction there are always two options: 1) Be miserable until the grossness moves away or 2) Immediately create a magical story around the grossness and behold it as a chapter in the adventure. Magical beings don't get stuck in small-minded issues, as we are busy with grander things. So anchor into the full spectrum of what's magical, as just a blink in this direction pulls us into it.

Abracadabra Rx: Since You Are Magic—Use it. I recently had a dream where a very big man in a business suit was laying on top of me. He had very dark energy that was hurting me. I was trying to push him off and couldn't as he was too heavy. I then remembered that I could remove him energetically. So with one finger I sent an otherworldly force into his being, he flew in the air and basically disappeared. I realized the business-attired man in the dream represented the corporate edge of the real estate business I was working in that had changed and was not supporting me. The other message I comprehended was not to push, fight, or even run away. The best option was to use magical energy to remove the aspect that bothered me by bringing light into it.

A therapist friend coined an analogy around bad thoughts as being like a gang that grows in numbers while the mind keeps picking up new aspects to support the bad thoughts. He also said that one good thought dissipated the gang. In the process of instilling our magic, after we remember we have it, we have to use it. Our everyday thinking is usually influenced by emotions that run on stimulated streams of reactions, while our normal attention is busy balancing o◄ what's unreasonable. Meanwhile our spritely spirit wants to explore and be astonished by what we find and the question is: What aspect do we follow? The answer is: Follow the magic and request for it to admonish a good outcome.

Stepping beyond knowing what's going on is like stopping for a layover in the magical mystery zone where we're open to options. There are now huge chunks of time where we are in the wild unknown and at these turning points we can only affect the moment were in. It's happening more so because we're accustomed to using our magic in the now. So consider that when life goes wonky, we need to let go of the future for the time being and in a step-by-step manner, we inspire our magic into the here and now for it to travel. So as things in the world are flashing the insanity warning, we do the opposite, which means putting both oars in the water and paddling towards the reality that holds our certainty. Mind you, our paddling works out all the insanity.

The cortex section of our brain, which scientists have found stays awake as the witness analyzes what it sees and recites it back. The messages are then transcribed into visions and feelings that either take us across or take us down. We then choose which way to go and like Alice we can shrink or grow to get through the keyholes. By owning our magic, we empower good dynamics and disempower what is dark and disorderly. We do this by being active in the energy field of our choice. So wave your wand, our magic is alive in the Abracadabra realm—to be in it simply use it.

Abracadabra Rx: Pay Focused Attention. During the times we trip and stumble, we were not paying attention. We heard a message and didn't listen because our awareness was traveling on the Ferris wheel of crazy patterned thinking. Enabling our attention to focus is the ability to navigate on impressions that regenerate artistry. Our focus is a scanner that sees everything and then zooms in on what's important. There are times where we want to believe what we believe, instead of focusing on what actually exists, but the trick is to see what else is possible. Our moods are either anchored in the intelligence or the unintelligence that sway us, so check your mood and don't follow the bad ones.

We've all heard the statement, *"It is what it is."* It's actually just the way we see it, I got glasses as a child and was shocked at how clearly I could see. It was painful, as I noticed things I did not want to see and then realized what we see with our eyes is one story and what we see in our mind is another. To see through the eyes of a magical being doesn't remove the harshness, but has compassion for it. Our heart has its own perception that revolves around love and not our minds.

A person who is at the top of their game mentioned that when they looked at fear, they realized they were always trying to keep up with the Joneses. Sitting there, I always considered them the actual Jones, as the one that others wanted to keep up with. Funny where the focus goes when it goes off and then it's the inner vision that must bring it back to a more clear actuality. We can be blinded by adoration, by overbearing people, by our fears—and it's all distortion.

Some friends didn't do the right thing by me. Th[e] actually did the opposite of the right thing, as after taking months of my time looking at houses, they went and bought a house from another broker on a whim. It is said the truth sets us free, but that's usually after it slaughters us. As the pain subsides, we must not blame, but instead zoom into the signals we missed to see where we were blindsided. I didn't notice how it was all about what was best for them and not me, because a fuzzy line between friendship and business blinded me. So when we're not paying attention, we will wake up through painful experiences to pay better attention.

The truth is always a wake up call and in the ways that we wake up from intense night dreams; we must also snap out of playing the peek-a-boo game. We no longer need to play guess who, as we zero in on the why and whereabouts of how we've lost ourselves. What part of us ran off to see a false wizard? The magic is in the fact that even though we dipped into duplicity, it empowered us. So maybe at first it took us apart, but when we put ourselves back together we found our focus, used the truth to our advantage, and shifted.

Consider taking the now and imagining an attractive future into it, by paying focused attention to its most magnanimous aspects. The now then becomes enhanced, accepts the new idea and runs off with it. If we consider the now as complete and full to the brim with magic, then we don't need to do anything further except be in it. Another way to step into magic is to assimilate the energy fields of great beings, like the Dalai Lama and others who live in alted states. Go in and soak up their demeanors, try their characters on for size and get lost in their substance. Wander around in their actuality as if you are on a shopping spree for inspiration and genius. Imagine being lost in the persona of a Holy Being and coming up for air to find you are not who you were before, but have shifted to who you wish to be now.

Abracadabra Rx: Be Enlightened. I constantly ask myself if I'm in an enlightened state and what an enlightened being would do in this situation. This concept alone turns on my lights and helps me to come around to where my real gold stars are. As a child in school we got gold stars on tests. Since I failed tests, I went to the store and bought my own package of gold stars and put them where I felt they deserved to be. I even arrived at school with them pasted on my forehead, the teacher did not think it was funny and I didn't care. My enlightenment back then was in knowing that goodness can't really be measured by other people's standards, it must be owned and celebrated by our own.

My brother loves Gandhi and always uses him as an example in his actions. His daughter as a child would tell him that he was not even acting ten percent Gandhi when she got mad at him. We use this analogy often and laugh, as we constantly fall off our spirited high horse and get into low-level crap. The Gandhi affinity is the joke in my family that sparks enlightenment when none exists. By pinpointing that we've lost it, our enlightened state immediately begins to flash its location and it's best to drop everything to get there.

Our moments of enlightenment reveal that the whole shebang of *Bodhi* realization already exists and is just waiting to be activated. So welcome to the understanding that we've all arrived here previously enlightened and have to lighten up to know it. The secret is to constantly shift into an enriched state and illuminate from there. So swipe the mental screen, drop the ego, erase who did what to whom and dive into that luminous state to see what it wants us to know. The trick is not to get lost in any of, but consider that if we were acting in a movie and playing the part of a holy being, in order to play the part well we'd have to become that. It's the same in reality; we now must become the enlightenment we are seeking. So be the enlightened one and then drop that too because real enlightenment is not anything in particular—it just is.

Abracadabra Rx: Escape Time. Due time is magically doing things behind the scenes, which is why we mostly have no idea what's going on until the unveiling. The energy fields around our existence are now so accelerated that every thought has precedence. Everything has sped up and rotated our entire *shebang* in a blink, because our shift has become timely. It's been said that timing is everything, though it becomes so when we let go of the constraints of time. We must stop measuring ourselves and all that time imposes, so that things become about the experience not the limitations.

In the ways that things are finished, as their energy field goes void something new arrives to envelop and expand us.

Our energy field moves beyond timeframes and when left to its resources it attracts magic. So take a Buddha squat and let go of the parameters of tick-tock reality, it's time to escape into that which is eternally timeless. Drop all beliefs that force you into a limited time consensus, don't get lost in the belief that there's not enough time, and don't measure your vitality by the aging clock. As an elder, once we let go of time we are more alive than ever. William Faulkner the writer said, "*Only when the clock stops does time come to life.*"

Abstract time has overlaid normal time and as a result we can't tell what's going on anymore. We can't predict the economy, the future or what's rational, because everything is unpredictable. Since nothing is normal, forget about trying to be normal—normal is over. It's time to understand the workings and to stop thinking things are wrong when time is restricting reality. We often feel ill, as strange symptoms arise in our physical beings, but what's going on is energetic and not physical. It's a restructuring of our frequency and an initiation into transformation. This is the new normal and we're in the right place with it if we believe it as so—that's the Magic

Abracadabra Rx: Discerning A Magical Mistake. It's not a mistake that we're uncomfortable, it just a mistake that we let discomfort own us. By considering what's happening as accidently on purpose we no longer let mistakes take us down, but use them as the bridge for our next leap. The concept is that nothing is by accident or on purpose, it is by

magic. In this way, whether we fail or succeed we're still c
our way. How we handle mistakes, is about how we handle
life and if we find the perfection in it. While fierce honesty
changes a mistake into an accomplishment, we're breaking
down all that's false to get past it. A mistake is a showstopper
that makes one forget their lines, drop their acts, and have a
heart to heart with the truth.

We have all sat on the ego throne, stubbornly not seeing
our mistakes as bearing truths. These slip-slides are rides on
the wake-up wheel that enliven us to snap out of ego stupors
and look for the absolute truth that wants to be found.
Realizations spark when we shift our perspective to see where
a mistake might happen not for us to fix it, but to let it fix
us. We don't need to be perfect, we also don't need to go sit
in a cave, stand on our head, go into spiritual rehab, or try to
be holy. We already have the holy gene, though we may have
forgotten this fact, but nevertheless our heart remembers. So
grab the whiteout, not to cover things up, but to create the
space to rewrite your new story on. A magical being owns
their mistakes and becomes holy with them, but we can only
be holy once we activate our holiness.

Abracadabra Rx: Return To Your True Form. Each
time we turn our minds around, turn off the chaos, turn our
frequency up to channel bliss, our physical being releases old
scars and heals. The ability to take what feels imperfect and
find where it evolves activates our healing. Most healing
happens first in our psyche when something is resolved and

.en in reality. When we decide to un-believe the things that imprison us and cause us pain our physical being does the same. So smell the roses and open your mind to light-filled thoughts that oppose what doesn't serve you. To question if something serves us or not goes beyond all discomfort into the resolution, as a wake-up question quakes truth.

Perspective around what matters most is like a zapper that removes what's not important and advances what is. All things will coincide with what we are now energetically in possession of. So when we consider that there's beauty in imperfection, we find it. Our pain is often considered an imperfection, but when it's a worthy pain there's beauty in it. To find something right in what's wrong is about us leaving wrong in the dust. Can it be this easy to consider healing and heal? Healing does not mean the experience did not happen and that we were not dis-eased and in pain. It means that we have come to terms with what happened and have return to our true form as the perfect outcome around it.

Abracadabra Rx: The Magic Of Anxiety. Can there be magic in anxiety? To trust that there is an energy bank of goodness in everything brings us to meet it. Rumi the great poet Saint said, *"There is a field between right doing and wrong doing, I'll meet you there."* This is where we must go to meet ourselves, to commune with our hearts, and call forth the spirit that helps us. There is a spirit in anxiety, a sprite that wants to open all the drawers in our inner room and make a huge mess. I used to think of this nervousness as a robber of my tranquility, but I now consider this unease as an inner strength coordinator. Anxiety is like an annoying friend who while visiting, stays just long enough to make her mark, which is her only intention as she does not want to take us down, she just wants push us across.

My Ode to Anxiety . . . *She scratched her glass nails across my blank slate and I felt her piercing screams creep up my spine. She always comes out in the in-betweens of where I've been and where I'm going. I know all her tricks so well by now and she knows mine. She taught me not to try to wrestle her away or even interact with her motions, as they will only gain more velocity from my every encounter. I must let her be as she passes through my fields and if I can do this, she will pass more quickly and not break anything or slam the doors on her way out. Her temperance is not like sloth, which renders all things meaningless; it's like an alarm that wakes you up to ignite your flight. She lies and tries to steal my dreams away, but here is a secret: anxiety really doesn't want my dreams to die; she is just a messenger who wants to restore my footing. She is as lost in the moment as I am. And like a rash that inflames my soul, she touches upon my skin, which is the first place she goes, as she tries to get under it.*

I realized that after so many years of her visits, it was now time to let her roam the halls unattended and just watch. She once beckoned me to check attics and basements with her and I told her "No you go on and I will wait here till you are done." I knew she would pass like a storm, scaring all the animals in the yard, causing one to stay inside, as I hid in my bed. She doesn't mean such harm, it's just her nature and when I can detach from her ranting, she is ny teacher. I now see her as another zestful spirit who likes to play childish games by sliding sticks in my wheel spokes as I ride by. So I just sit on the curb with her and wait until she is ready to move on. The other secret is she only comes to visit when I am very close to the gold and that is how I know, just how close I am.

Since everything is a form of energy, anxiety has a kinetic energy field with a flight or fight progression that alerts our nervous system to possible danger. To consider there's magic in anxiety, transforms it and shines light on it. We always try to control anxiety when it arrives and it's not controllable only we are. I have tried to talk myself out of it and disbelieve its lies as it slithers through my nervous system. I've found that anxiety thinks it has visiting rights and if I control myself and not entertain it, it will get bored and leave. A magical maneuver is to sit in meditation with it to see if what it's freaking out about is valid. Meanwhile keep sending calming energy through your nervous system and decide that anxiety is not attacking you, it's come for healing and heal it.

Abracadabra Rx: Go Out On A Magical Limb. Think about going beyond what's happening and holding hands with a higher force. It's time to stop seeking help from only earthly sources and tap into an essential power place of spirit. Going beyond is like shopping for coconuts, as when one store runs out, we go to the next. When we can't get what we need on this plane of existence we must reach into anther element for it. Maybe we're playing with imagination and the mystical, but this is what reality is built on.

In the sense that we must stop seeing things as only one way, it's time to get expansive. As we see in 3-D at the movies when we put the 3-D glasses on each eye is seeing a different picture, our brain then compiles the pictures for us to see a combined vision. What's interesting is that we have two eyes set apart, each one is seeing from a slightly different aspect, while our mind is like the third eye that sees beyond seeing. This is huge stuff because since we have learned to multi-task, we are on track to learn how to multi-live. It's like watching one screen and having another preset that is keeping track of other channels. Our expansiveness is the magical limb that connects us to the other channels.

A woman I worked with thought I was a pothead because my far-out escapades and intuitive edge created a magical reality that did not fit her format. She was the kind of person that ignored what she didn't understand because it was not pertinent. Small-minded thinkers are not interested in what is beyond their noses, but the universe threw her into my corner to expand her horizons. When her horizons did not expand then mine had to. Dealing with someone who was on such a different frequency taught me that we don't need to know why certain people show up in our arena, as just by continuing to go out on our magical limb, eventually they'll fall off. This co-worker was exposed to what she called, "My Weirdness," as I sat in open houses and called on the Universe to send a customer that could help me move a heavy table and a big strapping fellow would show up and help move the furniture around for me. I would ask the

Universe to send the perfect buyers and to clear karma in order to make a sale happen. This assistant thought I was nuts for talking to the cosmos. Since alternative ways of using energy are now acceptable, such as Reiki, we get that the planets are not fooling around when they go retrograde, because things break and nothing works. Once Yoga was considered bohemian, women who used herbal medicine were witches, meditation was for spiritual eccentrics, and psychics who spoke to the dead were considered gypsies. Now we rely on all of it because we are tapped into advanced evolved frequencies and the ones who think we're nuts will not be accompanying us farther than the next corner.

The late author of *The Hidden Messages In Water*, Mr. Masaru Emoto, proved that the energy of words affects matter. He photographed the molecules before and after he taped certain words onto glasses of water and proved that the water was distinctly changed by the word. If the power of the written word can transform energy and the spoken work creates frequency, then thought is a directive. The power of us is an ingredient in the power of now when we instill our magic in it. It's time to go out on a limb and explore the outer edges of this reality so we may see what exists beyond what exists. It's now the time to put our minds on the cosmic channel, for as the Zen saying goes: *Knock on the sky and listen to the sound.* This means a farfetched reality is the new wave of the future and to groove with it—takes us out on the limb.

Abracadabra Rx: Begin Again As Magic In Action. Our experiences move us to reach mastery and we repeat them until we get the spark of enlightenment they offer. If we consider what we're going through as the perfect vehicle that unhinges things, we know newness is being ushered in. Our life force is always flowing in constant motion to endow our evolvement, so we have to constantly step off from where we are. I go to advanced yoga classes even though I am not a physically advanced yogi. I go to be part of a practice that's beyond my capacity. Often I just sit out the poses I have not mastered, as the teacher calls me out to stay with the class and do the postures in my mind. This concept fits into my belief that the mind is creating reality, so if I can do very advanced yoga in my mind, then I am still part of the experience and have tasted the fruit of it.

My yoga teacher, Rodney Yee, instructs us to receive the pose, as in the act of receiving we are no longer doing. To receive the breath instead of taking a breath is about being in our natural rhythm; so consider receiving your abundance, your passion, and the magic. When we receive, we let go of the lasso we have on our ideas and relationships because none of it is free to expand when it's all tied up. The truth is there are no lasting conclusions, just adjustments into the act of beginning again. So keep going, get lost, get found, get down, then get up and get through and begin again.

I met a well-known advertising producer in her sixties who was paring down. She explained that her industry was no longer hiring people her age. I imagined her becoming even more edgy, more exceptional and not buying into those role models. She pooh-poohed my ideas and would not budge on believing in the precedence of forced retirement because in her heart she was done. She was using this story to advance past completed accomplishments, as in her mind it was perfect because she was done there and was going to come to light elsewhere.

The thing about magic is that it has an energy field and to be in it you have to follow it, so when it dissipates in one place, we must follow it to the next. Magic loves to play hide and seek, as it wants us to play with it. If you can't find it, go back to the beginning of your child's mind and look again. Considering that every thought is a new beginning, by following our magic, we are waving our wands and changing the energy fields around us as we go.

A Magical Mediation To Be The Magic: Mentally go back in time to the beginning of the essence of you. It's a magical trek past all the stories created, back to the core of your spiritual spark that brought you to life. This is a place of pure magic, a space that pulsates with cosmic consciousness and is the essence of what sparks our creation. Now sit in this essence and thank the magic for being what created your ability to traverse in all realms and play in this Earth field. Thank this magic for accompanying you here and being your gift to use. Sit in gratitude with it and see what your magic has to tell you about this life. We might have to sit quietly with nothing going on and wait for it. The thing of magic is that when we converse with it, it converses back and has a lot to say if we listen. The best way to listen to magic is to try to hear what you normally can't, like your heart beat.

In the ways that we explore the realms of exquisiteness even in the worst places, we are adding our symmetry to the mix. Magic is a supreme consideration that accompanies all that exists. We once sent this exact consideration of magic to our future selves before we were even born and this is the identical magic that has been hanging around waiting for us to remember it. Think about how far out that is, that you've had this magic all along. Of course we have it, as it created us in a way that enamors us to continue to create with it. Our magic is our never-ending alliance to a source that functions from being used to bring more of itself into actuality. In the way that infinity denotes an unbounded limit, our magic is literally the infinity call.

Meditate on becoming one with the infinity of magic that exists. Promise to serve the magic that assists you in the highest way for the highest good. This promise is the magnet that invites more magic to arrive. Remember in the sense that everything has a consciousness; we must be in the consciousness of magic to call it in. Once you feel it around you, then instill it fully into our being, into your future, and become one with it. You are now sitting with your magic, it's scintillating inside you and is now manifesting as you. Magic is your new partner, your old acquaintance, your spark, your imagination, your antidote, your defense, and your essence. It's you!

Abracadabra Rx To Be The Magic . . .

Rx: *Never take things seriously always take them magically.*

Rx: *Always wave your wand for the highest good.*

Rx: *Pretend you are enlightened at least ten times a day.*

Rx: *Knowing we are magic is magic.*

Rx: *Live in magic time not real time.*

Rx: *Imbibe the energy of enlightened beings.*

Rx: *Look for the magic in the moment.*

Rx: *Tap into your magic and go from there.*

Rx: *Step into new beginnings and bring magic.*

Rx: *Meditate with magic.*

Rx: *Use Magic.*

Rx: *Go out on a magical limb when you need to be magic.*

Rx: *Magic is our inheritance that is everlasting.*

Rx: *Take things apart to find the magic and digest it.*

Rx: *Be the magic you wish existed.*

Rx: *Magically move energy and once it gets going—jump on.*

Rx: *If it's not working you are not in magic with it.*

Rx: *Listen to the pulsation of alchemy running through you.*

Rx: *If you look for the magic, it exists.*

Rx *We are the magic we are looking for.*

Rx: *Sometimes the magic hides, so we have to find it within ourselves and become it.*

Rx: *When you don't know what's going on, know that magic is going on, it comes in all forms.*

Rx: *Trust the Universe and Add Magic!*

9) Vibrate Higher . . .

"Raising our vibration into a light filled resonance of divine consonance obliterates darkness."

All the nature deities were dancing in the forest, the monkeys were swinging from trees and the hummingbirds were drinking nectar. The huge green palm leaves were swaying in the wind and a fine warm mist was rolling in off the sea. The sun went behind a cloud, the light changed, and my mind came back online to worry about when I was going to have to leave this beautiful place. I caught my sneaky trickster mind trying to steal my bliss and immediately focused back to the absoluteness of being in Costa Rica in a jungle by the sea. To stay in a nourishing vibration satiates us and yet it's our mental patterns that pull us away.

I once worked with an energy healer regarding releasing an issue around my mother that was toxic. The pattern was not moving and the healer was asking me all these questions to dislodge it. I asked him to ask me if I wanted to actually release the pattern and the answer was surprisingly no. There was a revelation to be had. My next question was: Is this pattern helpful to me? The answer was also no, but I did not want to let the pattern go, because I was worried that I would be throwing my mother's love out with the bathwater. I then questioned if I could I keep the love for my mother and let go of the rest? My mother was already on the other side, but this unhelpful pattern I inherited from her was damaged goods. These questions I asked myself made me realize that many times our low-level imprints are really shift bombs because if we don't use them to shift on—they blow us up.

We are high-level vibratory beings in an environment bombarded with too many opinions and low-level realities. We get caught in the undercurrents of things, which takes us way off our paths. It's said that when caught in a riptide, to relax and don't fight it, as if we let it pull us it will eventually release us. It's the same with the mind, we catch it doing its tricks and we start arguing and then become lost in its game. I am constantly questioning my mind and have found that if the questions have a strong resonance and meaning they cut through to the core of reasoning because they are influential enough to shift our thinking and naturally change patterns. A good question must be persuasive enough to oscillate in a way that changes our foundation. These kinds of question are like a needle when used to remove a splinter. They don't need answers because the reverberations that arise from the questionable truth are the answer.

<u>Vibrational Questions That Shift Us:</u>

Is what I am doing bringing me up or holding me down?

Is there something in this situation that I can learn from?

Where is the Higher Perspective?

Did I attract this situation?

If I did attract this situation, how do I clear it?

Do I need to cut this dynamic off?

Am I stuck or just processing something old out?

Do I need to be doing this?

Where might it go if I let this situation continue?

Is it best to do nothing?

Do I need this experience to evolve?

Am I evolving or rotating in a stuck pattern?

Where can I shift?

An important aspect of questioning is that we must not ask others to know the answers to our questions. When we ask these questions it's best to direct them to our higher selves. Here, we are bypassing our ego to get to the place of truth, as it's only from here that we will have the ability to vibrate higher. After I had worked with that healer, I realized we must never give our power over to someone else to heal us. In order to heal, our energy must be an equivalent part of the healing process. This agreement creates the shift, for if our vibration is not in accord with the co-creation of empowering our own healings, they will not hold.

The late author and famed neurologist Oliver Sacks, when dealing with terminal cancer decided what the quality of his remaining time on Earth would be. He said he would no longer pay attention to politics, continue to watch global news, or participate in arguments. He also reported that he was now able to see his life from a great altitude and felt a deepened sense of connection. He was actually more alive than ever, which was the vibration he would shift out of this existence with. Oliver Sacks also expressed that he planned to live his time out in the richest, deepest, most productive way he could. A passage like this is an example of coming to terms with your true power, as even on the brink of his death this man was living his life to the hilt.

Nicola Tesla, another game-changer, was the scientist who introduced the concept that high frequency oscillation existed in nature and if we could adapt technology into this limitless source of energy, we would be able to move beyond dependency, while not continuing to destroy the Earth and inevitably humanity. Tesla spoke about frequency and was devising ways to use vibration and natural power instead of fossil fuels. In the 1900's, he came up with an invention that was the basis for computers and cell phones. He also used laser power beams, which connected buildings to a cosmic generator to purify water systems along with the air and pollution. Tesla's concept was to use the natural caliber of waterfalls, along with wind and light to create suitable forms of power for practical ways of life. Tesla said, *"Of all the frictional resistance, the one that most retards human movement is ignorance, what Buddha called 'the greatest evil in the world.' The friction, which results from ignorance, can be reduced only by the spread of knowledge and the unification of the heterogeneous elements of humanity. No effort could be better spent."*

Tesla's approach around energy, frequency, and vibration came from his elevated state of being. He saw everything not as beneficial for now, but for how it would affect the future. A mind this empowered could have been self-serving though he was not a slave to the machine, just a wizard. He was alternatively creating a new machine that would enhance our quality of life, not destroy it. Appreciating and getting involved in this kind of consciousness that supports the planet gives one the ability to serve humankind kindly. It's about seeing what is in distress and then visioning what is needed to relieve it. There are people on this planet who are balancers, as they hold integral vibrations that uplift this world.

Vibrating at higher frequencies, we may become invisible because our story has nothing to do with the story we were in prior, so we are no longer seen. Being invisible happens when our vibrations don't match with others. I was once sitting on a bench and a stranger sat on my lap. It wasn't because they weren't paying attention, but it was that I did not exist in their reality. It happens to me in restaurants, as the waiter will inevitably ignore me until I make myself shown. It's because I often go into my own world and travel so far away into a dream that my body becomes transparent because so much of me is no longer there. This kind of vacantness also happens when I'm on the phone, someone is talking and I drift away, I still hear him or her, but I've gone into another dimension. They always sense I'm gone and ask: *"Are you still there?"* Usually this happens when I am getting information from higher realms and am figuring it in.

I am also known to say odd things to others that make no sense to me but are consequential to them. Many times my descriptions of what I see around people will lighten a burden they carry, as when we see someone's brilliance and tell them about it their burden becomes less important. The Native American Indians used a burden basket as a symbol to be self-reliant. They made these baskets to be left at their front doors so that one could leave their troubles in them and not bring anguish into the sacred Hearth. Still we must have compassion for those amongst us who carry burdens and for ourselves when we are carrying ours. At the same time, we must know when to put theses burdens down and raise our vibration. The deciding factor is to question if the vibrations running are worthy of our energy fields?

My dearest late mother was a powerful teacher who lied constantly. She never owned up to her mistakes and loved to antagonize me. Not long ago I manifested an assistant who had the same traits; she was just like my mother. I knew she was not right, but continued to work with her for years because I was still in a conversation with my mother's energy field. This co-worker's vibration was irritating to me and I was constantly yelling at her. She lied and had the entire gamut of addictive behaviors my mother had. I put up with it because it was familiar, though as soon as I realized I was entertaining my mother the pattern resolved. The woman abruptly quit and of course lied her way out the door. A big part of changing the vibration was my wishing her well. As I moved off the old frequency of feeling victim to my mother's energy, my vibration changed, I no longer attracted a match for this dynamic, as there was nothing further to workout.

Energetically we are like magnets that attract exactly what we're in conversation with. So if we're affected by aggression, anxiety or fear, we're actually working that out. Everyone has hidden monsters under their bed, as our bogeyman still live in dark caves in our minds, so we must go find a fairy like Tinker Bell to shed some light on them. As children, our monsters empowered us with the courage to create an even bigger boogieman to beat-up the one under the bed that scared us. Nothings really changed because we are still all basically children playing in the sandbox. Some kids get really bossy and think they are in charge, others are playing war games; I'm masquerading as the White Witch waving my wand around. It's all a play of consciousness.

The vibrations of our words will seal our fate, so when we make derogatory jokes on our behalf, we are ordaining our future. The Universe is not a Joker and delivers on what is said. We say things and make statements all the time that come from a place of doubt that will affect everything from where we're going to how we receive. Our inner verbal lingo is a light language that we must learn to use in a way that enhances our actuality. When we were little we had to find our words, now we have all our words and have to find a more powerful way to use them. Since the relationships we have out there are reflection of the ones we have inside, it's time to be clear. Our words are literal *mantras* that hold a pulse, which materialize creations from their vibrations.

Speaking vibrationally is about the practice of using our words as wands. The word Spanda in the Sanskrit language represents the underlying pulse of the Universe, which is the vibrational movement of pure consciousness. All energy fields have an underlying foundation that emanates activity from the center outwards. This is why our authentic potency is the spark in our center, known as the *inner being*. As we move energy, we are constantly moving from a state of being, to becoming part of the creation our being manifests. Our Spanda is a vibratory pulse of energy that sparks into action; it manifests from our state of consciousness into form. By guiding it, it will shift our reality and manifest our magic.

A Vibrational Spanda Exercise

Answer these five simple questions and be completely forthright without editing the honest expression of what you think and believe is possible or real. Answer the questions as if your life depended on the truth of them. Know that the deeper you go to access your truth is equivalent to the level of change you can make. This following exercise is your diagnosis that will reflect the outcome of how much positive life force you can expect to flow through your frequency. I am asking you to believe as you answer these questions that all the sanctified energy of the Universe is aligning to exalt the transformation of your being.

Five Honest Questions:
1) What is your life's dream at this time?
2) What are your inner feelings that make you believe that you cannot, should not, or will not be able to have this dream?
3) What are the outer life circumstances that seem to make your dream difficult?
4) If you had the power to change something either in yourself or pertaining to your circumstances what would that be?
5) If in a pretend mode where anything is possible and reality doesn't count, how would you define yourself in the highest possible way?

Please take a moment to understand the depth of the answers you've written and how these answers resonate within you to create your life circumstances. Then fill in the blanks on the statements below, as you are now defining and replacing your words inspired by the pure Spanda coming from the center of your being. These statements are now your **Mantras,** as they are the vibrational sparks you are resonating with that hold your new frequency.

Five Vibrational New Affirmations:

1) With the highest of all possible consciousness, I offer out my dream of _____, which now attracts all that is needed to manifest in real time by Divine Grace.

2) I now believe that my feelings of_____ are not authentic and don't have any valid power or authority to hold me back or away from creating my dream.

3) The life obstacles of _____ are now absolved. My path is absolutely clear and open to an omnipotent and sacred flow.

4) The situation of _____ is now targeted to shift itself as I now stand freely in the light surrounded by my highest good.

5) I Create As I Speak that_____ spontaneously manifests from a divine partnership with my Highest Self.

Now say out loud: "I ordain these words to be the only reality allowed to be sparked in benevolence for my greatest good!" Repeat these statements often including before sleep and always on an empty mind. These statements redefine old belief systems and shift actuality. Our words when used this way as wands of *Spanda* are a powerful force, so use your spanda to recondition your psyche from imposed conditions that don't support your desired attainments. At this stage, in order liberate ourselves, we must first do it vibrationally and then doing it physically becomes a piece of cake.

Since all things hold a vibration, from the food we eat, the thoughts we think, and the people we hang out with, be mindful. We must be aware and on alert of what reality we empower by using our words as wands. I was shopping in a second hand shop with a girlfriend and she found a very outlandish outfit. My friend described where she would wear this outfit and what kind of an experience she would have in it. She decided what she thought it was worth and then went to the proprietor to make the pitch and said to the shop owner, *"I guess you would not consider taking thirty percent off this outfit as that's all I can spend."* The owner promptly said, *"No absolutely not."* I knew right away from the words my friend chose that she would not get the discount and asked why she chose her opening with the: *"I guess you would not consider"* statement. These words sealed her fate, as they imbibed the vibration of no way is this happening.

My friend was not in her right light beam that day. We talked about it after and she recommitted back to her desired vibration. It's a relief to see the truth around how we're not manifesting what we want with our words. A realization creates an automatic shift and since we are light beings in physical form, we're magically empowered to substantially raise vibrations inside and around us. We can impose light into cells, lift energy fields, and change realities by vibrating higher. Having this kind of intelligence is our birthright and our legacy. So embrace the vibration you wish to resonate on and start vibrating from there.

Abracadabra Rx to Vibrate Higher . . .

Rx: *Be aware of what you are vibrating with.*

Rx: *Vibrate with the things you love.*

Rx; *Be conscious of the way you speak and what you say.*

Rx: *Choose the words that resonate with your purpose.*

Rx: *Saying less and vibrating more holds potency.*

Rx: *Instill higher vibrations into lesser emotions.*

Rx: *Notice your state and vibrate accordingly to uplift it.*

Rx: *Go into your original essence to recalibrate.*

Rx: *Vibrate with the beauty around you.*

Rx: *Divine your vibration to match your desires.*

Rx: *Vibrate love around yourself.*

Rx: *Be in the vibration that moves around obstacles.*

Rx: *Trust the vibration you sense—vibration doesn't lie.*

Rx: *Be in the vibration of abundance to attract it.*

Rx: *Let go of the things that you no longer vibrate with.*

Rx: *Maintain compassion, which is a very high vibration.*

Rx: *Constantly forgive and bless others.*

Rx: *Vibrate healing when needed.*

Rx: *Accept what is and vibrate higher around it.*

Rx: *Vibrate with miracles.*

Rx: *Drop your negative agendas and raise your vibration.*

Rx: *Be around and do what raises your vibration.*

Rx: *When the mind dips into darkness, vibrate lightness.*

Rx: *Question if you are in the highest reasoning possible.*

Rx: *Commune with the vibration of your higher self.*

Rx: *Request for the Universe to vibrate goodness with you.*

Rx: *Use your frequency as an offering for what is best.*

Rx: *Always vibrate a clearing to change the channel.*

Rx: *Remember that your frequency contributes to your reality.*

Rx: *You are never helpless; your frequency is a power force.*

Rx: *Vibrate your best wishes for others.*

Rx: *When others go low energetically surround them with love.*

Rx: *Don't match bad energy.*

Rx: *Clear patterns that you are not thriving on.*

Rx: *Bring much love and goodness into your consciousness.*

Rx: *Think of the bigger picture and what it needs.*

Rx: *Be the vibration you wish to revolve with.*

Rx: *Think before you speak.*

Rx: *Speak less vibrate more.*

Rx: *Arrive in your highest vibration and leave with it.*

Rx: *Love is the highest vibration.*

Rx: *Vibrate with love.*

Rx: *Let your dreams vibrate your substance.*

Rx: *Vibrate with the magic of this world.*

10) Our Alchemy . . .

"Imagination is the true magic carpet." —Norman Vincent Peale

I had a dream where I was floating around in a space of literally nothing. There was no sound, no movement, just pitch-blackness. I did notice that my mind was still active as it checked in to begin a dialogue and document what was going on. I had no idea where the heck I was and had no identification with the actual me that I think I am. All that existed was what appeared to be a state of consciousness and even that was fuzzy. It was an experience that terrified me as I questioned if I would be stuck here forever. I wondered if I was in Hell and then totally freaked out. My next thought was, Get Me Out Of Here! In a nanosecond, I awoke in my bed with a start very shook up.

Calming myself down, I began to research empty space and found that I had encountered a void. I learned that a void is the space where alchemy is created, as it's the womb of all manifestation. It is in this empty space that everything coming from nothing is beginning to come into something. Unfortunately, I was not prepared for this experience and since I had never consciously traveled into a void before, I learned after the fact that a void is waiting for our command. So the first thought I had, which was Get Me Out Of Here, was charged with my intention and made manifest at light speed and poof I was out of there. After the fact, I wished I had asked for divine love or to experience seeing all my loved ones who are on the other side. Instead I saw the expanse of nothing as Hell, got scared, and lost it.

I then realized that this is how I live when I believe the ramblings of my mind. I learned from this experience that a void is potent and alive with every possibility. While in it, I thought that maybe I had died but I still had a mind so that was not possible. I then realized that death was also not possible, as I remembered I had once died and was also still consciously here at that time. This experience was telling me to go beyond my mind and to expand my consciousness until the great spirit of all things was incorporated into the mix. The key was to be as attached to the wanderings of my soul as I am to the wanderings of my mind. Granted I did not go to sleep that night with a plan of jumping into a void and creating my reality from there, it was actually my soul that brought me there. And honestly it didn't matter what I did in there, it only mattered that I have the experience to learn from it.

Considering that the energy field in a vortex is a complete reflection, I came out of it seeing that I can be terrified when pushed beyond my comfort zone. If I would have had more faith I would've recognized where I was and known this space was a stepping-stone into something magical and not an eternal fall into nothing. I saw that I was processing the experience from an old wounded paradigm of, thinking, "I am surely going to be screwed!" I quickly saw that since I had come to the fork where I was being shown this ill-fated belief I carried; it was therefore time to clear it. If we think we are going to be screwed, we are totally screwed.

While in that void, I would have surely liked to visit heaven and talked to the gods. I would have loved to revel in bliss and divine new realities, but my mind was not on-board. I had the experience with zero training and then understood clearly that in this new world we're our own teachers and we're learning as we go. So we delve into the unknown to find what's holy in the hole only to find that our alchemy exists in our actual delving. A consciousness that thrives on holiness can easily see when what's not important has kidnapped us. Meanwhile our spirit has a good hold on our puppet strings, so it's no wonder that we constantly get yanked out of our useless games and put in time-out in order to come back to our magic.

During the Middle Ages, alchemy was known as the transformation of baser metals into gold. In the modern world we can consider it as using our creativity to transmute a lower situation or what's of a lesser value into something more worthy. This magical process of transmuting one thing into another is actually happening when an objective is being enchanted to alter itself. The trick is to entice good energy to come and dance with our objectives. Since we can make art out of garbage, great meals out of leftovers, and transmute thought patterns to manifest for us, we therefore have the ability to shift things up and we must.

Consider the energetic force of nature that unfolds to create living beauty. The alchemy in nature inspires us to understand that we are part and parcel to this beauty. I get upset when a hawk flies off with a small bird in my yard or an animal is hurt, though it's a lesson to come to terms with nature. I must consider that the animal was released from this incarnation because it fulfilled its existence. Similarly we fulfill our existence when we are in divine communion with all that is sacred.

An uplifted state of consciousness alone has the pure alchemy that satiates our spirit enough to create our cause to come into matter. The nature of things always embodies a spirit essence and breathes life into these things, so we have a choice of where we plug into. Consider plugging into the highest ethereal magical state you can dream of and pull energy from there to empower yourself right here. Our intimate rapport with the essence of the spirit of things has power, so converse with the sublime magical influences around things and you will be tapped into your real power.

Our spiritual considerations raise the vibrations of bad moods, adversity, blockages, and crisis. Instead of falling in the hole, sit and commune spiritually, which pulls the entire flux of our vibration up. Remember we are only passing through, so instead of getting lost in a vortex of need, make the decision to choose gratitude along with bliss and love. And during the times that we have to traipse through lower vibratory fields, focus on your kinship is with what's divine and sacred. What we give cause to is the pure alchemy that creates righteous manifestations that esteem our prize. Welcome to this blessed actuality, it's time to pull our sword from the stone and get going.

Abracadabra Prescriptions For Alchemy:

Abracadabra Rx: Be The Alchemist. When we were born the alchemist manual wasn't in our diaper bags and our parents did not know we were alchemists because they didn't know the possibility existed. Very few people get it that we've arrived here with an array of evolutionary energetic dynamics geared to create a magical revolution. The admission into this magical consciousness is an awakened heart, which sparks a charge that says, *"I now need magic to live fully!"* In other words we cannot thrive on human-ness alone, we need that spark and that connection to our inner magic in order to fulfill our destiny. As fate will have it, it's as if there's a great director out there saying, *"Here is your magic—now step into it, for if you don't, we will hide your magic around a corner to pop out when you least expect it and grab you."*

Fate will always show up when it's time to get real, it demands that when our heart steps into our storyline and says, "Wanna play?" that we respond. When fate and passion begin to groove, magic happens. I watched a video of Eileen Kramer, a hundred year old dancer. She had partially lost her sight and compensated by performing as an expressionist who danced while standing still. It was her spirit that was dancing with her soul's perspective. She said she feeds her spiritual spark by constantly doing new things and that's how she stays connected. It's profound that by even doing the same thing with a new perspective, we are doing the same thing differently. So spark a new outlook on an old routine.

Alchemy draws us into its realm to teach us that anything is possible. If we believe in reasoning alone, then we're stuck waiting for rational proof. The difference between alchemy and reasoning is that the alchemist takes things apart to see what is useable, while reasoning makes excuses. In a heated discussion with a woman over a mistake made on a printing job for one of my books, we went over the logistics of whose fault the mistake was and I realized we were going in circles. I got my inner alchemist on the line and suddenly I was telling this corporate person who was trained to divert issues, all about my dreams and ideas for the future. We talked about the messages in that Abracadabra book and she told me how grateful she was for the call. We hung up as soul sisters because the printing issue did not really matter, as I knew that the book's magic would override it.

Our inner alchemist spins things to turn them into gold. Our transformation is in the process of turning us into gold. So when magic taps us on the shoulder to says: "Tag you're it," then begin spinning things into gold and be It!

Abracadabra Rx: Spend Time In The Void. It's a natural expression to be in avoidance of what doesn't feel good. We don't want to validate continued difficulties so we try to keep people and things that are not of the highest accord out of our way. Sorry to say it's basically impossible because we're surrounded. Instead of pushing things away, consider being powerful enough to transpose negative influences, as this is alchemy. Avoiding suffering doesn't work for the long haul, as the opposite of avoidance is to invite. Wait, hello, invite suffering? Well yes, but only to transpose it.

I am an energetic twin with my son as we often we feel the same things about each other in a crazy way. We are both very expressive and have found that when in disagreement, arguing things out does not work, but just brings forth useless patterns. Many of the things I feel about him when upset, are the things I have to face in myself and change. If I don't I am in pain, so instead of avoiding, blaming, or being victim to our pain, take it into the void. The resolution is usually more abstract than the actual suffering itself. For instance, feeling cheated is really about dealing with self worth and faith. To become an ally with our pain and juxtapose our difficulties, we must have the perspective that can find gold in the dirt pile.

I will consciously go into a void with a difficulty and go around the block with it until it becomes a cohort. As we sit in a void, at first we're sitting with ourselves and reacting to the conditions we brought in with us. Though as we calm down, we will feel a subtle shift. This is the time to ask to see the storylines we have encapsulated into our belief systems. A friend said the Universe was out to get her; it was sabotaging everything she was trying to do. She kept saying, *"They are making everything not work."* I then asked if she could change her belief and she said: "The Universe has to go first and prove it." I asked her to ask the Universe to reveal if there was any beneficial purpose in her belief around this and to experiment with believing it differently and see what transpires. We are all in bed with ourselves and sometimes we sleep with the enemy, as the aspect that thrives on drama and havoc. This delving into darkness is a workout where we work ourselves out of it. So we carry on with our dark side until the process demands a turnaround and then we wakeup from our bad dream and do our good dream.

The reflections of our beliefs can get very weird and uncomfortable in our transitions, as they get bigger and blown out of proportion so we have no choice but to deal with them. I am constantly working things out, facing the mirror, looking to see if what I attract and create is coming from my spark or my fear. Coming to terms with the reflection of being screwed and cheated took apart that concept until all I was left with was the reflection of where I had done this to myself. We must not get flooded by distress, but instead create a void and program our most potent and virtuous desires into it and then offer it gratitude and see what comes.

Abracadabra Rx: Follow Your Calling. The obsessive mind is always looking to fuel its objectives. Everyone desires to do well and as a person who has stood on a stage as the top producer of my company many times, I sometimes wondered if it would be better to be the second best and be left alone. I wanted to get out of the line of jealously fire, as my ego no longer needed to be number one. To me, the most favorable success is to step off the edge like The Fool and fall in love with what makes my world spin. I found that once you hit the top of your game, you either have to keep doing it or create a new game. Our calling will tell us if that game is over. It will say, "*Ok we did it, we won. So now lets play with our heart where there's no winning, just truth.*"

We've all read life-changing books and uplifted our ways and it's not because we followed its wisdom to a tee, it's that the wisdom inspired us to create our magic. Some people try to share their formulas, but we all have a different karmic chemistry and therefore general formulas don't work for the long haul. In the ways that our storylines run in segments, our karma has an addendum that it needs to play out to release itself. Maybe at a certain point success is not on the agenda, but compassion is, so we're called to be a caretaker. Or maybe we become financially successful for a period of time to learn generosity from this. Our calling will move in all directions and we have to go with it or we're following someone else's calling. Our calling is our unique vocation, so it's right that we don't follow the leader, just the calling. Like players in a football game, if only quarterbacks were on the team, there'd be no receivers available to catch the pass. Our calling is about catching the pass thrown by our heart.

A person in the process of finding their calling, made music, became a fashion designer, opened a store, turned it into an art gallery, became an interior designer, created a recording studio, went to school to learn the technology of electrical wiring to take apart synthesizers and rebuild them, built furniture and is now back to making music. Each thing he does is a calling that leads to another calling. Someone might judge that he was all over the place, but alchemy is like that, it's not a straight line. Alchemy goes where it needs to go to gather up ingredients for the endeavor it's building up to. Immersed in his calling this person was alive, though in between the callings he would plummet, which would drive him onto the next calling, as this was part of his process. The truth is that our human design is based on the fact that we're passionate beings that thrive on many levels. So we can do the nine to five gigs and still have an affair with our calling on the side, which saves us. If we don't, we're cheating on ourselves. **Tip:** Book an Alchemy Date with the Universe!

Abracadabra Rx: Fail Well. We've all boarded sinking ships, given our all and lost, or taken a false step and fell flat. These are not mistakes but useful stalemates escorting us to a state of surrender as the guiding momentum pushing us to master frustration. By considering failure as a step towards success, we're changing our strategy from win and lose, to finding wisdom as we go. Our failures might tell us to quit going in a certain direction, but they're never telling us to quit and give up on trying again. General MacArthur said, *"Age wrinkles the body, quitting wrinkles the soul."* So we get down, we slip, we slide, and we get up and try again.

Michael Jordan missed an insane amount of basketball shots, he lost hundreds of games and many times he was counted on to take the winning shot and missed. He said, *"I've failed over and over and over in my life and that is why I succeed."* Our washouts bring benefits that cleanse the wimp out of us. Discomfort doesn't mean we have to accept it, it means we have to adjust something inside ourselves to work with it. When we see discomfort as the enemy, it prods us to go to the fridge, the bar, or into our worst weakness. Instead, commune with it. It will tell us truths that are painful and always life-changing while asking us to honor our mistakes, forgive ourselves and don't blame others. When we inspect every aspect of our failure, we find that the courage it takes for us to do this is not for losers—only for Alchemists.

Abracadabra Rx: Reflect On The Mystical. Science explains many things, but it cannot explain the mystical reasoning for what exists and why. It's mystical to ponder the magic of the planets and how we resonate with them. So when it's said to read between the lines, it's because there's potent information between what we see and what we think. Reflecting on the mystical has a pull that grabs us out of the clutch of reality to open a panorama of *Wow-isms*. The stretch between the moment of one thing and the pause before th next thing is a magical realm. Alchemy is hanging out in that, *"Something's going to happen"* moment of who knows what. Our mystical endeavors are where we divine huge leaps in our consciousness. We actually don't even have to leap; we just show up and are taken.

Abracadabra Rx: Transition Into The Magic. My yoga teachers speak about where we place our attention in the transitions during practice. In transitions, we're feeling our way, which holds an active awareness over knowing our way. To experience even what is known as unfamiliar is where the magic hangs out. If we consider what's transpiring as sacred, we'll have no desire to rush through it like The Mad Hatter who is late. We are never late, that concept is for people who don't get that they've already arrived. Our transition into magic announces our arrival.

In a yoga posture if our hip hurts as we go into a stretch, then we pull back and breathe into it. The pain lets go and we then can stretch further. Yoga is not about the arrival, but about being in the state that takes you there. It's a mystical affair, a vacation from the mind, which is busy listening to instructions while we become deeply connected to the spirit of yoga. In transition we let go of all that's not coming along with us. Our transition into magic is like welcoming a guest, so we buy flowers, set the table and make the bed. We are actually welcoming the patron saint of magic when we welcome the mystery, so forget about where you're going and be immersed in magic, which is the destination.

Abracadabra Rx: Empower Your Alchemy. Imagine that while being in everyday reality, we are also in the school of higher intelligence. This school exists on an evolved realm where our spirit is the teacher. Some people have so much going on that their higher-selves are like garbage collectors just going nonstop back and forth to the dump. Alchemy exists in the bigger picture and we have to clear what our little minds are full of before we can master it. Our spirit teacher is instructing us on solidifying our intentions that set precedence for how we roll. Our magical rites of passage are bestowed once we have committed to leaving conventionality behind, so practice observing what can't be seen with an ordinary mind and regard things as marvels. In the ways that we practice to become the experts of what we intend, as alchemists we practice being in the magic. This blink in the direction of alchemy takes us around the corner into our higher intelligence with it.

<u>Alchemy Practices:</u>

Set Sacred Intentions: As editors we must define what is sacred. Our intentions are alive; they have wings that expand out into the Universe so we can fly. Hold your intention in a ball of light, see it illuminated and release it to go where it needs, to do what's best. Consider your sacred intentions often—always keep charging them up.

Welcome The New: Constantly let go of what does not serve you energetically; be it thoughts, emotions, or actual situations and put them all into an energetic dumpster. Then invite your sacred intentions in and live as if they matter most—because they do. As we welcome the new, it falls into place.

Find The Extraordinary In What Is Ordinary: Wear imaginary rose-colored glasses everyday and never see things as just the way they are. Instead always look for the magic that hides in the ordinary. If you can't find the magic, imagine it. What we vision will change a dynamic from ordinary to extraordinary. So keep sight of possibility and always request the extraordinary!

Aspire Higher: Write what aspires all that exists higher. Write it often, on napkins, on your mirror, and on your hand to remind you. And in times of distress remember that the power of your aspirations will uplift everything.

Hold Magic On Your Transitions: Request a smooth ride and ask the Universe to instill peace within you during your transitions. Ask to understand the bigger picture. Ask for guidance to be in the best mind-set around all turbulence. See transition as dropping everything that isn't remarkable enough in order to be your most stupendous self. Don't strive for the outcomes, just strive to be in the magic and the outcomes will be magical.

Create Abundance: We must be rich in our minds to be wealthy. Then again we must also be rich in spirit to be well off. Write your riches out and carry these notes in your wallet, paste them on your laptop, on your fridge, everywhere. "I am a Money Magnet!" works. I always say: *"Good thing I'm Rich,"* every time I spend money. Cashiers always look at me sideways, as I then explain I'm affirming abundance. Affirm your prosperity and believe it.

Bless All Things: Light a white candle and write out the blessings you are sending. Offer magic to enlighten and enhance what needs to blossom and always request miracles. Bless your difficulties, your arguments, your lack, and your inner turmoil to shift. The blessings we send enhance the blessings we receive.

Instill Light Into Every Story: Instilling light into stories uplifts them. The more light you send out the more light will come back around. To be light-filled, we must constantly pull in light, so sit and breathe it in and then breathe it out. Swirl it through your entire body.

Always Remember You Have The Power of Alchemy: You have the alchemy compass, ask it for directions, ask what it needs to be empowered and for it to guide you. Always honor your alchemy and use it for the high good. You are the weaver of your world!

Abracadabra Rx To Be In Our Alchemy . . .

Rx: *Always remember that magic is resonating and use it.*

Rx: *Alchemy happens when we get out of the way of it.*

Rx: *Create a void; go inside and dream of magic.*

Rx: *Our transitions are alchemy in action.*

Rx: *If you can't find the gold, it's because it's being created.*

Rx: *Follow your callings; alchemy is on the line directing you.*

Rx: *Mishaps are callings for alchemy.*

Rx: *Consciousness is awakened alchemy—stay awake.*

Rx: *Consider your mistakes as alchemy acorns on your path.*

Rx: *Commune with your inner alchemist—be them.*

Rx: *Never take things for granted, always see things as sacred.*

Rx: *In a moment of peace an entire new world exists.*

Rx: *You are so powerful that one thought can change your life.*

Rx: *When it's time for alchemy, stop everything and call it in.*

Rx: *Be creative, imagine your way and then chase it.*

Rx: *Know the thoughts coming from fear do not spin gold.*

Rx: *To spin gold we have to think in a golden way.*

Rx: *Magic is always happening; it's up to us to tap into it.*

Rx: *If you can't find the alchemy create it.*

Rx: *Alchemy creates transitions—trust it.*

Rx: *Blessings are alchemy in action.*

Rx: *The light attracts alchemy, so surround yourself in it.*

Rx: *Alchemy is the spark in our blessings—so keep blessing.*

Rx: *To empower our alchemy we must step off the edge with it and let it catch us.*

Rx: *Alchemy is our spirit making magic with the universe.*

11) Remedies for Life

"Our time here is magic! It's the only space you have to realize whatever it is that is beautiful, whatever is true, whatever is great, whatever is potential, whatever is rare, whatever is unique, in. It's the only space." —Ben Okri

There is softness inside seeds that hold a potent velocity and when the time is right a momentous dynamic forces the hard shell of the seed to break open and blossom. Similarly there's a potent life force inside us that's been activated. There's no way around it, this spark exists in us and it's flashing to attract what it needs. We might be stuck in odd stories, but it doesn't matter what the story is, only that we use our magic while in them. So while covert activities are rampant, the diagnosis came in and needs attention, people are having breakdowns all around us, the remedies we need come to us when we flip our consciousness on to see them. Our shells have cracked open and it's time to bloom—the remedies are the fertilizer and we are the lotus seed of our own magic.

Abracadabra Prescriptions—Remedies for Life

Abracadabra Rx: Prescribe Soul Medicine. We can't hit the targets when we are *the* targets. We become the targets when we react to the reality around us by getting lost in the difficulties. The turnaround is that since we attract the field of energy we are vibrating on, the most compelling magic is to recreate ourselves as we want to be. On a day I was feeling fear and attracting dismay, I picked up my deck of Sacred Symbols Tarot cards and asked how do I get back into balance. The Meditate card came up, it said: *Your current situation needs more time and less attachment!*

A few passing moons can do wonders, as our soul is our pharmacist and the prescriptions needed are being made. Going to my inner medicine cabinet for a cure, a Genie popped out and said: *"Hello my dear, what are we healing today? Please define it."* My inner witch doctor wanted an exact list of the symptoms leading to the problem. As I went over the list, I realized my wounds were mostly lies. My list was: No one listens to me, I have to do everything, and I'm too good for this world. All wrong perspectives! Thankfully my feeling that I'm not good enough was not on the list that day. These lesions are forgeries that lodge inside us, while our witch doctor goes into dialogue with them to dispel them.

I followed their path to my inner child who was swinging ᴑm a tire on a tree, watching clouds and singing. My inner ʰ doctor had now turned into a Shaman and went into conversation with this little being of me to dispel what was affecting me now in my adult self. The conversation went like this . . .

Shaman Me: *May I push your swing and ask you a few secrets?*

Child Me: *Sure.*

Shaman Me: *Who does not listen to you?*

Child Me: *My husband, parents, teachers, friends, and all the mean people who are not very nice.*

Shaman Me: *Who does listen to you?*

Child Me: *My brother and my dog.*

Shaman Me: *Does this really hurt you or is it just an annoying bother?*

Child Me: *It's just a bother because I am happy in my real world that is always listening to me.*

Shaman Me: *Well can we let go of the hurt and go back to playing in our real worlds and not be bothered?*

Child Me: *Sure.*

Shaman Me: *Do you really think you have to do everything?*

Child Me: *All my imaginary friends are always helping me.*

Shaman Me: *And do you think you are too good for this world?*

Child Me: *No, I just made that up because I was mad.*

Shaman Me: *So can we let go of all these hurts so we can play?*

Child Me: *Sure, lets.*

The remedy can be a simple conversation with our inner healer or a soul journey into many past lives that connect the dots. Soul medicine might tell us to take a walk, read certain book, adopt a cat, call someone, or it may deliver remedy we need in a dream. Even our wounds have an intention to heal—open a dialogue for the soul prescription.

Abracadabra Rx: Instill A God Force. Sometimes we feel totally disconnected, as our God force is suddenly missing in action. I am praying my heart out and there's no response, just radio silence. What the Hell? I'm screaming dear God, can you please do something, send a sign, post a miracle, and zilch. Nothings happening. This message in itself is to stop asking out there, command patience and hold faith. In the same way that we have to walk our feet to the throne and place our own crown upon our heads, our God force is molding us to be empowered by our own accord.

Out there on the limb, while shrieking, I'm too emotional to communicate well. God does not read Emoji lingo, just truth. If we're speaking Latin to a French person they won't know what we're saying. It's the same with God; we can't treat God like one of the girls, or think we can put in a take-out order. God is Holy and so we have to become Holy when speaking to God. A blink into the God zone sanctifies us and tells our mind to be quiet when speaking to God. So we can't jive, shoot the breeze, or talk sh*t with God and expect an answer. We also can't sit on our throne if we haven't mastered worthiness. So put down what's not important, get real, speak your deepest truth and honor yourself.

I was working on selling a man's home; he was playing ▪mes. Every time I brought him an offer he would change mind about selling. Fine, I quit, but every time I quit he would say that he really wanted to sell. This happened many times and the message was: Step Away! In the interim my crazy inner talk started shouting at me that the man was a liar. It was true, but what was truer was the fact that I had enough self worth to walk away with my holiness intact. Though was I mad? Yes and that was toxic. I asked myself what would God feel and the answer was compassion, so I tried it on and it fit perfectly. Empowered by my God Force, I walked away blessed to be onto the next endeavor with a compassionate heart.

Abracadabra Rx: Speak To Injustice. At this time, inequality and greed are demanding attention. Injustice is a running commentary these days and granted many things are not right, but injustice has a huge energy field that clears itself by blaring truths and exposing abuse. As we stand on the precipice of darkness and light, we must also speak to the injustice inside ourselves. There is injustice in the voices that tell us what we don't deserve, that this world is too dark to thrive on and that things are hopeless. Even when things look bleak, we must look injustice in the eye and tell it: *"You are not welcome here; I will not support you, go away!"*

An unresolved disagreement leaves us as the lone clean up crew who has to resolve the mess with themselves. A friend was offered a job recording a soundtrack for a well-known company. He needed the money, but the budget they offered him was so low it was not worth it. He felt tortur by this and then decided not to do it. The next day canceled and he was relieved. Being true to ourselves is the foundation we build on that holds us in asylum. To draw the line creates an opening for what we deserve to come to us because we are inline with it. When we stand for justice, we act fairly, hold tolerance, offer kindness, and perform good deeds. Some of us will shout in the streets and others will shout to the Gods in prayer. It does not matter how we do it, it only matters that we care. So in these challenging times while some of us have invested energy into opposing outrage, whatever our calling is, by speaking from the heart we will make our energetic mark. This is not a quiet time, but one where the heart speaks on behalf of the heavens. Let it rip!

Abracadabra Rx: Reset Your Password. On the day I gave the finger to a man acting like a droid behind the counter at Staples when he would not return a wrong item he sold me, I totally failed myself. I acknowledged in the parking lot that my behavior was insane and needed amends. It was even laughable that as the woman who wrote a book on virtue, here I am giving the finger to a young effectual worker for doing what he was trained to do. I hoped I was not filmed at the register and imagined my unveiling as, "*The Abracadabra Writer Is One Big Phony.*" I acknowledged my humanness and went back into the store and apologized. The fellow apologized back and offered me a free pen for my troubles. I used it to write thank you notes to the Universe, which reset my password.

Not doing the right thing is expansive, so when we've

been hacked by our own craziness, each time we come back around we're affirming a new version of entry. When we react, act heartless, and are selfish and uncaring, we've been abducted by bad virtues. It happens. So we must constantly return to being the person we wish to hang out with and stay out of our emotional way. Our password is the magical link into our best actuality and since life is constantly changing, so must our password.

Abracadabra Rx: Be The Teacher You Seek. Imagine that you and your higher self are out there swinging on a cloud, looking at the state of the world and you both decided that one of you would come down to Earth and play while the other would stay on the cloud and watch your back. It's literally like this, as our best friend, higher self, and cosmic guide is out there and has us covered, even when we've forgotten about them. In this school of life, we must reach beyond and learn from the best teacher we have, the one within. The truth is that they're not only teaching us how to be, but are teaching us to remember they are us.

I have sat at the feet of many holy teachers and one such Guru's message was: *"Your God lives in you as you!"* These were just words to me, as I had not acknowledged a God force as being inside me. This Guru also told me to: Be Nice! I wondered if I could ask nature to be nice when a hurricane was flooding the shore, because that's what I felt was going inside me at the time. Kind would have been a better word because I needed to learn to be kind to myself when things were not that nice. The guidance is not the teaching, the translation is and this is when I knew that I was my own teacher. I gratefully did come to feel a God force inside myself and being nice was not it. It was about letting my inner teacher teach. My God force is not always cordial, especially when it has to be fierce enough to yank me out of Hell zones. The teacher within does not tell us how to be, but instead shows us what is possible. My God force takes me out of the game when I'm playing it wrong and it pushes me to my knees when I need to get humble. It was especially humbling when I realized that there is a God force in everything and to be in touch with it is the epitome of nice.

My higher self has a distinct sense of humor and many times I'm offered the exact opposite of what I am requesting. The message in this is that it's first about acceptance and then about finding my empowerment, instead of having my way. The inner teacher says: *"Create your way along the way."* They are speaking of mastery, a humble ball of fire that holds our intentions. I read a quote that said: *"There's no pain when there's faith."* I gathered that I was not there yet and realized that since the quote resounded, it was the direction to go in. I question who am I in relation to what is going on and this puts everything into perspective, as when we see how we fit in or not, we know the next step. Our inner teachers are navigators, soothsayers, and activists that will only show us the way when we're available to follow it. The real lesson is to learn how to learn.

Abracadabra Rx: Connect To Your Medicine Ally. In the way that the Native American Indians honor the Spirit of this world, it is with sensitivity that honor is instilled. By being sensitive to the great spirit of all things they become our allies. So by honoring the four corners of the Earth, we are standing at the pivotal point where the spirit force of the world will assist us. To stand in the center of our heart is to be one with the spirit of our soul. To honor the forces of the moon and pull in the energy of the planets, acknowledges that we exist together with all of the cosmos. This wisdom is our real power and real power is our medicine ally.

A friend told me they believed they were cursed. Granted it did not appear this way, as they had a loving relationship and even though they were struggling to find their way, they were succeeding. I could see my friend was not cursed by dark energy but by his belief. We curse ourselves and must remove our own curses to be empowered by what we honor and stand in faith with. To bring about a healing, focus on the spirit of a story and not the actual story, as this releases the healing agents needed to change the story. When we ask the spirit of a story, a person, a business deal, a book we're writing, or a situation what it needs, we will get a response. I often ask houses what they need in order to be sold and when the spirit of a house is amicable, it tells me and a sale happens easily.

Native American Spirit Medicine holds the dream for an honorable and good future for all beings and so must we. Tap into the medicine wheel of this world and it will speak to you. My inner medicine woman is not soft spoken and at times she yells out commands like, *"Turn Left!"* There is no way I can ignore her when she comes to the forefront to bark into my psyche. She is like a shouting mountain that can make the Earth rumble, so no wonder I am always asking others, *"Did you feel that small earthquake?"* I've named her Shouting Mountain, as she's always hollering for me to take it higher while dancing like a crazy woman around me. I do feel rumblings in the Earth and it used to scare me, though now I honor the rumblings because I know they are healings.

A Native American dance ceremony involves shaking and leaping to loosen sins and open the doors to a healing spirit. When the Earth around me is shaking, I know that Shouting Mountain is dancing and leaping with the Earth to shake off darkness and heal the World. Therefore our bad luck, stress, and illnesses will be removed once symmetry is restored. In a healing mode, we honor what exists as a vehicle and must restore ourselves on the spirit plane first. Once this happens our physical being then catches up.

Native American medicine men come together and pray with their entire tribe to request help from the spirit world for an individual or their community. A medicine person will then go into a dream state to visit the Great Spirit of the World to bring back the medicine needed to balance and heal someone or the area in question. In this modern world, it must be understood that the illness of one person, either emotionally or physically, will affect their entire family and their community. No one thinks of this as we have become so individualized, but we're affected by everything around us. Considering the death of someone we hardly knew, suddenly we're grieving because the circle of life includes everyone connected and we feel everything on some level.

In the elephant community, when a baby elephant is born the entire herd takes care of the baby as if it were their own. And when an elephant dies, even as herds pass from far away they will sit in respect of the bones of a fellow elephant because the connection to the soul of the elephant clan is strong and in every elephant. As such, we must also have respect for humanity and nature and protect it. We must remember to honor what came before and hold light on all things. A medicine being knows that when a person or place is not in balance, it's their job to bring it back.

We all have a medicine spirit inside us and it's time to allow them to pass us the medicine bag. This medicine spirit holds our remedies for life, along with the wisdom that knows when a cold is not always a cold, but is a disturbance of the spirit or a need to cry and feel grief. Someone I know has a hard time incorporating that the dysfunction in the world isn't inside him, it's out there. He's extremely sensitive and constantly tries to fix things on the outside, while inside he feels a great deal of sadness. Sitting with our inner healer rearranges our considerations, as sadness can exist but our wellbeing alongside it must be activated. This is balance.

My medicine being loves to move the furniture around and get rid of old things. Other times I am told to use my power to not let negative forces affect me and transform the energy around me. Our medicine spirit calms disturbance, brings inner peace and heals disharmony. When we think of what is owed, who did not come through, who disappoints us and has betrayed us, we must look to the source of where we receive our sustenance. Our true abundance doesn't come from our successful endeavors, but from the great way, which is the spirit of life that sustains us.

Abracadabra Rx: Find Perfection In Imperfections. In my real estate career the lessons learned about prosperity are often harsh. How we receive is aligned with who we see ourselves to be in the bigger picture. Time and again I would work tirelessly for someone and nothing would happen, then suddenly a buyer would show up out of the blue and I would make the easiest deal ever. If I got upset over the deals that did not work, I would disrupt the balance of the easy deals that would follow. The job was about showing up and doing what it takes, though a career coach would say: *"It's all about the sale!"* Wrong! It's really all about the energy.

Often what I do goes way beyond just selling a house. It's actually more about helping to balance and shift the personal situations of clients and buyers, as I am the gift they need. I've considered myself a *Shaman of Real Estate*, who tracks perfection in the imperfections and goes to the core of what matters most. I had hired a new assistant, we worked on a listing that we couldn't sell and finally lost the listing. As an old timer in the business I felt liberated as the energy was off. My new assistant got very upset because she felt loss. I knew something great was coming; she didn't believe it and bailed. The next day, I got a new listing down the street that I sold in a week at the same price. What looks like lack could be the movement of prosperity. A loss might be making room for a gain, so when that assistant quit, I again felt liberated.

I see the bigger picture of who needs what and during the times when things are not working, I realize it's not me, but the energy of the people I am working with that's not in balance. When I get a message that it's not going to work, it doesn't mean failure; it means my energy is better served elsewhere. A fellow told me his secret dream that revolved around living close to the sea, but his budget did not agree with this dream. It took me four years but I finally found him a beachside cottage he could afford. He went out on a limb and scrambled to get the money and he did. Years later, I asked him for a favor and he forgot that I helped him and said no. I realized there is also perfection in being done, which means really being done. Imperfections are illusions that appear wrong when they're really magic. Sometimes things have to break to come back together in a better way.

A Japanese art form called *Kintsugi* is a technique where a cracked broken cup or bowl is mended with gold. The broken bits are veneered and illuminated to become works of art. In the same way, our scars tell a story that marks our survival, so we must also veneer them. The poet saint Rumi, said: *"The wound is the place where the light enters you."* To consider our wounds as openings for light changes the paradigm of pain. I get appalled over hideous situations a could spend weeks swirling in outrage questioning the Gods. People disappoint us, life becomes hard, and we struggle and feel pain. Can there still be light? If we accept that we're in a learning experience and going through all its modalities in order to come into perfection with it, then there's light. The perfection is about finding our magic in the imperfections, so they still perfectly deliver our goods.

Abracadabra Rx: Let The Great Spirit Bless You. On days that I'm overly sensitive, I know I'm open to picking up negative energies. At the end of the day I fill a bowl with salt, pour in some olive oil and rub myself down in the shower with this salt-glow to clear negative emotions. I smoke out my house with sage and Paolo Santo wood. I bless my car with feathers found in the driveway and I Google the energy medicine of animals that visit my house to understand the wisdom they bring. I program crystals, I program vortexes, I chant mantras, write affirmations, and visualize blessings. I bless people and myself. I create rituals that charm the light and goodness to surround everything around me.

The Great Spirit is my light beam that turns on my magic. When I first started in real estate, I secretly I put a bowl of money on top of the file cabinet in the *Feng Shui* good fortune corner of the office to bring good luck to everyone that worked there. One broker whose desk was next to the cabinet, found the bowl and instead of taking the blessings, he decided I was a witch and started complaining about all my antidotes. Nevertheless, his business went from zero to booming and he realized there was something to it. I left that office thereafter and was told that a cleaning crew went to remove the good luck bowl and this fellow demanded it not be moved. The bowl was just a belief of blessings in action.

In the old world, Elders passed down their great wisdom, though in this modern world many Elders are not respected, therefore society is out of balance. As a result, many of the great ways have become obsolete and now have to be earned to have knowledge of. The native people believe that for the survival of future generations, if there is not respect for the great way, then this way of healing will only become more powerful when practiced in secret and not diluted. My inner medicine woman Shouting Mountain teaches me that the basic premise of a remedy is a pure God Force. Because I respect her as an intermediary of God, she constantly comes through to offer wisdom. One morning during a relaxation pose in yoga class, she yelled into my ear, "CHAGA!" I had no idea what it was but went home and looked it up to find it was a medicinal mushroom that I needed. I got it right away and did a ritual of thanks to the spirit of Chaga for coming to me. I also left Shouting Mountain some on my altar to show her that the blessing was received.

As assistants of the God force, we must make offerings to the spirit of the things we wish to empower. In the words of the American Indian Mourning Dove Salish, *"Everything on the earth has a purpose, every disease an herb to cure it, and every person a mission. This is the Indian theory of existence."* In the Lakota language, *Waken Tanan Kici Un* is a prayer th means: May The Great Spirit Bless You. We've all been blessed to come here, even in the midst of all the craziness around us. When we live our life as an offering for goodness, we are in service to the evolved rites on the tolls of our passage. Believe me, the most blessed consciousness is when we show up and say to the Universe: *"Use Me."*

Abracadabra Rx: Go The Abracadabra Way! The Abracadabra Way has no paths, as it's an energy field that transforms everything. Even just the word Abracadabra is charged with a high vibrational frequency. Try it as a ritual mantra technique to charge an idea or receive the magic needed. Ab–Ra–Ca–Dab–Ra is a highly charged word. So focus on an intention and then with both my hands in a fist say the syllables. On the syllable Ab, release the thumb. On the Ra, release the index finger. On the Ca, release the middle finger, on the Dab, the ring finger, and on the Ra the pinky finger. So your hands are then open to receive, then imagine pulling in your desire.

Many years ago when I first decided to write Abracadabra books, it was because this word kept popping up everywhere. The first time it happened, I was in a hotel in Mexico that had a bookshelf. I borrowed a book and that night opened it to a page where the word popped out and it seemed alive as if it were talking to me. It's a powerful word with a mystical history of manifestation. I realized that as we speak, hear, ·nd meditate on words with alchemy, we come into union ·h the power of them. Our intention around an issue expands its force field to offer us its fruits, so when I want to enhance the magic around my desires, issues, or situations that need a spark, I always say: *Abracadabra That!*

In yoga, we practice locking things in by pulling in life force; we then fasten it in by sealing off its outlets. Once it's instilled, we let it go to do what's needed. *Unddiyana Bhanda,* known as the abdominal lock pulls *Pranic* energy, known as life giving breath upwards. While *Mula Bhanda,* a root lock known as the root of all action, grounds and seals in the energy. You can Google the *Bhandas* and practice them, even on the subway. I constantly pull abracadabra energy, light, and blessings in. I bond with them, they instill, and I release them around me.

The alchemist understands that a magical way resounds foremost in a cosmic realm and that they must come into the infinite-ness of their being to hook up with the unlimited field to create a manifestation. An alchemist will take a proposed or actual circumstance and spark it into a golden resonance by holding light on it. They know we cannot make things happen from desperation or thinking it has to be a certain way. Magic has many ways, but most importantly, our faith spurs it into action. Impressions have a life of their own, so be careful to be in a state of benevolence around your mode of manifestation. An aggressor that pushes their way into the party never really arrives, at least to the *real* party. We are all actually invited to be part of this celebratio when we show up in our party outfit aka goodness. It's same with alchemy, as once we connect to the mag don't have to push it—we just have to trust it.

The Abracadabra Way is a humble path that demands the courage to look when we almost can't, to touch when we want to run, to forgive when our hearts are closed, and to see ourselves as heroes for being here. We are humble when we have to shrink and grow, especially when we must get through keyholes or leap over mountains. The alchemist will get really small, especially when they are about to jump into the bigger picture and once in it, they expand again. We do this over and over as we step away, come back, grieve, heal, hold on, and finally let go. The Abracadabra Way makes us aware that there's no such thing as backwards or forwards, as in a magical echelon things transform from any aspect. We can stand in the same place, go back to where we were, or go around the bend. All that really matters is that we are in the magic with all that we do.

My twenty three year old niece spent months in a drug rehab center and was working on progressing past her addictive patterns in order to solidify her healing. Things came up that pushed every button she had and threatened her sobriety because the outside world doesn't change until we change first. The people closest to her were on alert and wanted to know her whereabouts, as they were terrified that she would fall backwards. People who are recovering are delicate, their wounds sometimes control them and like all f us who have them, they are our teachers. My beautiful ce left this world as many would say too soon. Sometimes nnot heal our wounds here in this time frame and have to leave because we have completed our work. To others it might look incomplete, but the ways of heaven have their own reasoning. My family is heartbroken over her passing and now we also have to heal from the pain of her loss. My brother says there are no words only Love.

The broad view is always in the process of coming into focus and in the interim we must check our energy fields and restore ourselves constantly while we're here. As a practice when every crutch is gone, when our friends are out drinking when we want to be sober, our laptop dies as we're in the passion of writing the last chapter, we've woken up to an empty cupboard, there's no coffee in the house so we have to drink tea, or worse someone we love passes on, can we thrive anyway? What if we can see these things not as oppositions, but as a journey into a new wilderness where we have to redefine ourselves in relation to what life offers? Our transitions might be telling us to breakthrough, get new friends, and stop drinking coffee if necessary. Maybe we have to move or spend a few years grieving, so we can return and thrive on some new magic. And as far as the book goes and finishing the last chapter, we can always finish it tomorrow when we're the new versions of ourselves.

The Abracadabra Way is a state of consciousness that plays leapfrog with the paradigms of this world to go higher. Even our emptiness is the opening for fullness, so if we see everything as an opportunity, we take a quantum leap. At the same time, it's mandatory not to let the rules of this world make us feel small, but we must decide for ourselves when get small enough to pass though the cracks into cosmic consciousness. We might have to get modest in order to go within and commune with our expansive self who teaches us to stand tall enough to see over the hubris, in order to find we are not really victims of anything, but our own minds. So we blink into our higher consciousness and go from there.

The Abracadabra Way is the world within our world. So become a lotus-eater who is indifferent to craziness because we're busy digesting our dreams. After we've feasted upon them and are satiated, we're back in this reality empowered with impressions from our reveries. We might wonder how such genius, such courage and such vitality sparked us, and then we remember it was ours to begin with.

I read a story of a woman driving down the road, when a car came out of nowhere and was careening towards her. She quickly veered off the road, but was now heading straight into a pole. An impending crash was happening quickly, but time slowed down and seemed to morph. The next thing she knew was that another reality appeared. The car careening towards her passed, the people inside it waved and she was still on her way. This woman said she'd always had a death wish and could not wait to be out of here. She said that when this experience happened, she was pulled into another dimension where her karma was cleared and now she was grateful to *fully* be alive. This almost crash changed her commitment to life and when I read it, it changed mine too. felt like I went and came back with her and yes it makes no se, but really most things of value are mystical gifts from the Universe and will never make sense.

In a mystical reality, we are energetically like a lotus flower opening and closing as we take in life to transform our realities. Someone hurt my feelings, I was brooding, and then I looked around at what was still good and laughed. Even as we float down the muddy river of this life we might go under a few times and come up to know we are still here and have been baptized in the art of thriving on mud. Once we realize that we are natural bloomers, we must empower ourselves to live as if this world is our oyster, which means we are tapped into the advantage no matter what. And while discomfort exists, it's because we are feeling the changing of the frequencies and have to recalibrate to be part of them.

Our magical divinity is at the forefront of our existence, so be curious, explore, push your mind out of its comfort zone, be daring and be on the beam like Sherlock Holmes and discover the magic that's sparking. We're in our magic when we're in this state of being. Once in it, magic chauffeurs us around so our pumpkin becomes a carriage and the wicked stepsisters fade into the dust. We've arrived! Our arrival is immediate when we offer blessings on all that exists. So bless the goodness not yet found, bless the question, the discovery, and the magical ways of this world. By being in the energy field of blessings, we are part of the blessings. Our beliefs are the keys that open our way, so if we believe that even a curse is a blessing, so it is.

As we surrender into the I Am That consciousness, we hold the highest attributes and are the most deserving c grace and this is how we show up with our crown to our throne. Our throne is waiting, so bless yourself and then take your seat on the Thousand Petal Lotus. Here the veils are lifted and alchemy is bestowed. Now ask yourself: *Am I committed to being part of my own essential magic by creating it?*

The question alone is the blink that pulls you in. Once in, immediately start waving your wand, wake up your vitality and take yourself higher. You are in the hub of your victory, so feel it and own it. This is how we tap into the most potent frequencies that exist, how we align our physical bodies with natural vital forces, and how we are rocking our emotional bodies back into harmony. We are doing it with our turbo charged ethereal power. Even in the heart of this matter, we still must come to terms over and over. We will do a hundred about faces, we will constantly clear our energy fields, and we will repeatedly break down our perspectives when they go to Hell, We will do it because we are the alchemists who are transforming, shape shifting ourselves and being the light we wish to see in the world. Our magic exists with us wherever we go and when it whispers innuendos we listen. When it pauses, we pause with it, and when it moves again we move with it because we're going The Abracadabra Way.

Abracadabra Rx Remedies For Life . . .

Rx: *Carry this book with you and read it often!*

My Acknowledgements . . .

In Memory of Kenza Lee Schnur my beautiful niece —you are a shining star in my life now and forever.
10/11/93 – 07/08/17

Thank you to my cherished husband Joe Barbaria for coming to this crazy world to be my escort and to always remind me that love rules. Thank you to my visionary son Max Barbaria, for your cutting edge truth—your heart is connected to my soul. Thank you Suzanne Diaz for being my daughter in spirit, you have supported my belief that pure goodness exists— I feel so blessed for you. Thank you to my brother, Robert Schnur and his beautiful wife Soumaya—my heart is broken with yours, I pray we heal together.

Thank you to Darlene Barbaria for your great eye and your kindness. Thank you to Erma, Lisa, and all my literary helpers. My punctuation might be off but I am not.

Thank you to all the Gods, Saints, Angels, Holy beings and Magical Helpers, Gurumayi and all the Yoga Teachers in this world. Thank you to all the animals, spiritual guides, and medicine beings that love us all so much to hang around us in our times of need.

Thank you Polgarus Studio for laying out this book and to Ashley Byland of Redbird Design for such a magical book cover. Thank you Scott Bluedorn for the beautiful hand drawing of the **Caduceus** on the cover. Blessings to all my friends and pets that have loved and supported me.

*Thank you to the Magic for showing me the Way!

Abracadabra Rx Disclaimer:

I am not a certified doctor and these magical prescriptions are my personal exploration of what has worked for me, so by law I must say:

You must not rely on the information in this book as an alternative to medical advice from your doctor or other professional healthcare provider.

If you have any specific questions about any medical matter you should consult your doctor or other professional healthcare provider.

If you think you may be suffering from any medical condition you should seek immediate medical attention.

You should never delay seeking medical advice, disregard medical advice, or discontinue medical treatment because of information in this book.